Dianne Feinstein

Dianne Feinstein
NEVER LET THEM SEE YOU CRY

Jerry Roberts

HarperCollins*West*

A Division of HarperCollins*Publishers*

To Linda, loving soul mate

———

FIRST EDITION

Library of Congress Cataloging-in-Publication Data
Roberts, Jerry.
    Dianne Feinstein: never let them see you cry / Jerry Roberts.—1st ed.
        p.   cm.
    Includes index.
    ISBN 0-06-258508-8 (cloth: alk. paper).
    ISBN 0-06-258602-5 (pbk.: alk. paper).
    1. Feinstein, Dianne, 1933– . 2. Legislators—United States—
Biography. 3. Women legislators—United States—
Biography. 4. United States. Congress. Senate—Biography. 5. Mayors—
California—San Francisco—Biography. I. Title.
E840.8.F45R63   1994   94-1522
979.4'6105'092—dc20   CIP
[B]

94 95 96 97 98 ❖ RRD(H) 10 9 8 7 6 5 4 3 2 1

This edition is printed on acid-free paper that meets the American National Standards Institute Z39.48 Standard.

Contents

LIST OF ILLUSTRATIONS

Betty Goldman with her three daughters. Courtesy of Senator Dianne Feinstein.

The Goldman sisters at home in San Francisco. Courtesy of Senator Dianne Feinstein.

Dr. Leon Goldman in 1956. Courtesy of Senator Dianne Feinstein.

Queen of the Junior Grand National Exposition. Courtesy of Senator Dianne Feinstein.

With husband Bert Feinstein, announcing her candidacy for San Francisco Board of Supervisors. *San Francisco Examiner.*

Dianne and Bert Feinstein. *San Francisco Examiner.*

With new supervisor Quentin Kopp. *San Francisco Chronicle.*

With Bert, at their home after a terrorist bomb was planted outside their daughter's bedroom window. *San Francisco Examiner.*

Dianne pledged to appear in a bikini if the Pier 39 tourist complex opened on time. She wore a vintage suit from the old Sutro Baths to fulfill her promise. *San Francisco Chronicle.*

Acting Mayor Feinstein just after the assassinations of Mayor George Moscone and Supervisor Harvey Milk. *San Francisco Chronicle.*

Outside City Hall an outraged mob protested the verdict in the Dan White assassination case. *San Francisco Chronicle.*

Mayor Feinstein brought a management style to City Hall that matched the dignity of the mayor's formal office. *San Francisco Examiner.*

A rare moment of public emotion before the press at the announcement of a vote to recall Mayor Feinstein from office. *San Francisco Examiner.*

Mayor Feinstein kept a firefighter's coat in the trunk of her car and often appeared at the scenes of major blazes. *San Francisco Examiner.*

With presidential candidate Walter Mondale at her interview for the vice-presidential spot on the 1984 ticket. Associated Press.

Mayor Feinstein and financier Richard Blum set a regal tone for her administration at their City Hall wedding. *San Francisco Chronicle.*

As candidate for governor of California. Associated Press.

With daughter Katherine. Courtesy of Senator Dianne Feinstein.

With Barbara Boxer the day after both women won their nominations to run for the U.S. Senate. *San Francisco Chronicle.*

Senator Feinstein leads a group of women senators and feminist leaders down the steps of the Capitol. Associated Press.

Backed by Senators Metzenbaum (D-OH) and DeConcini (D-AZ) at a press conference after the Senate passed the measure she authored. Associated Press.

ACKNOWLEDGMENTS

More than anyone else, my wife, Linda Kiefer, and my darling daughters, Anna, Maggie, and Rebecca Roberts, deserve thanks for the love, support, and understanding they gave to me at every point in the writing of this book.

I sincerely thank Clayton Carlson, publisher of HarperCollinsWest, for his early belief and continued confidence in the project, and my agent, Brad Bunnin, whose quick wits and business savvy got it off the ground. I am extremely grateful to my editor, Joann Moschella, and to Jo Beaton, Shirley Christine, Mimi Kusch, and Beth Weber for their guidance, commitment, and hard work. Thanks also to Nan Hohenstein for her spirit and enthusiasm. My editors at the *San Francisco Chronicle,* especially Jim Brewer, Dan Rosenheim, and Mike Yamamoto, offered personal and professional encouragement and provided me the time needed to finish, amid my countless cries of "one more week."

No writer could have a better research assistant than Wes Haley, whose indefatigable energy, sharp instincts, unfailing good humor, and major talent for reporting were indispensable assets.

I am indebted to Richard Geiger and the outstanding staff of the *Chronicle* library, particularly Joan Annsfire, Scott Kerrihard, John Miller, Chris Orr, and Kathleen E. Rhodes; to Nancy Wong, for photographic assistance, and to Mike Keiser and Joan Fabian, for invaluable technical support. Judy Canter, head librarian, and Pamela Brunger Scott, managing editor of operations, of the *San Francisco Examiner,* were gracious and helpful in providing information and expertise. Anne Turner Gunnison provided key research support in Sacramento as did Julia Rodrigues in Washington.

Among my colleagues, special tribute is due to Carol Pogash for her insights and exceptional reporting; to Russ Cone, for his lifetime body of work and kindness in making his files available to me; and to the late Jerry Burns, my mentor and best friend, for inspiration and pointing the way. I deeply appreciate the encouragement and constructive suggestions of Susan Yoachum, Stephen S. Hall, Mark Z. Barabak, and Scott Blakey, who took the time to read the book in draft form and made it better. My friend Louise Atcheson offered constant counsel and perspective.

The work of the *Chronicle*'s Herb Caen, Bill Carlsen, Ralph Craib, Diane Curtis, David Dietz, Rob Gunnison, Rob Haeseler, Vlae Kershner, Marshall Kilduff, Carolyn Lochhead, Phil Matier, Carl Nolte, Andy Ross, Steve Rubenstein, the late Randy Shilts, the late Reggie Smith, Susan Sward, Michael Taylor, Bill Wallace, and Maitland Zane informed this book, as did that of Gerald Adams, Jim Balderston, Gerry Braun, Bruce Brugmann, Cathleen Decker, Cynthia Gorney, Mary Jean Haley, Kristin Huckshorn, Evelyn Hsu, John Jacobs, Connie Kang, Syd Kossen, Larry Liebert, Tim Redmond, Bill Stall, and Phil Trounstine.

I also wish to honor the memory of my parents and to thank my brother, David, who taught me to love writing, and my sister, Beverly, who taught me how to read.

I am indebted to the more than one hundred people who took considerable time to offer me their personal and political recollections and reflections in the interviews that form the foundation of this book. I am especially grateful for the contributions of Dianne Feinstein's family, including the openness of her daughter, Katherine Feinstein, and her sister, Yvonne Banks, and the candor and courage of her sister, Lynn Kennedy.

Finally, I wish to thank Senator Feinstein, who was more than generous with her time and patience.

INTRODUCTION

On June 22, 1993, California senator Dianne Feinstein

celebrated her sixtieth birthday at the White House.

THE PRESIDENT OF THE UNITED STATES presented her with a cake, its butter-brickle frosting decorated with three candles and the words *Happy Birthday Dianne,* as Feinstein beamed from a seat of honor beside first lady Hillary Rodham Clinton. In a capital where culture is defined by perquisites of power and social mores are shaped by seniority and status, such flattering attention from the nation's first couple might seem unlikely for a member of Congress just a few months into her first term. But for Dianne Feinstein it was one more demonstration of the political distinction that she attained when she took the oath as the first female senator in history from the nation's most populous state.

The most visible symbol of what has been called the "Decade of the Woman" in American electoral politics, Feinstein went to Washington as a celebrity senator whose style and media image have kept her on the political talk-show circuit, while her legislative skill and grasp of public policy have earned her early respect on Capitol Hill. Despite her apparently sudden success, however, her journey to the highest levels of government has been anything but swift or easy. The life and times of Dianne Feinstein are at once a remarkable personal story and a case history of how a pioneering woman politician achieved national influence and importance only through decades of patience, industry, and practice of her craft in local government.

Feinstein's life has been of operatic proportion, a human drama marked by extraordinary tragedies and triumphs. Her career has been shaped both by an enduring ability to accept and overcome private anguishes, political humiliations, and recurrent defeats and by a driving ambition to prevail against the

1

odds, prove herself, and wield power in a professional field long dominated by men. Behind the public figure, with her practiced smile and scripted sound bites, she is an extremely private woman of great psychological complexity and contradiction.

Despite her material wealth, Feinstein's character and career have been shaped by struggle, personal and political. The oldest of three daughters of a brilliant father who set extremely high standards and an abusive, mentally ill mother who tore her down emotionally, she had a childhood of secret torment, hidden beneath a public veneer of affluence and appearance. The psychological survival skills she learned at home would later help her in her personal life to cope with divorce, single motherhood, and the agonizing death of her beloved second husband.

In her public life, they helped her to endure setbacks and to surmount countless obstacles, as she accomplished a series of historic achievements in San Francisco politics. The first woman to be elected president of the Board of Supervisors, the city's legislative body, she was at the center of every major debate during a time of intense economic, political, and social transition. As a supervisor, she ran twice for mayor but lost both times. On November 27, 1978, moments after telling reporters she would not run for the office again, she was thrust into it when an assassin shot Mayor George Moscone dead and, within two minutes, killed her colleague Supervisor Harvey Milk, whose bullet-ridden body she discovered.

In the days and weeks that followed, Feinstein was a soothing civic presence as she played an unsought role in the tragedy and helped to heal the wounds of grief inflicted on the city. Within a year after assuming office, she was elected mayor on her own after a bitter campaign that proved the political power of San Francisco's homosexual community. After leading her city out of a dark period of horror, terrorism, and mob violence, she was reelected four years later, but only after beating back a bizarre campaign to recall her from office, launched by a left-wing commune that was angry about her efforts to institute handgun control.

In Feinstein's wake, many other female politicians prospered in the city. At one point in her tenure, San Francisco had not only a woman mayor but also a majority of women on its board of supervisors, plus women filling both its congressional seats. By 1984 her national reputation had grown so much that she was nearly chosen as the running mate of Democratic presidential candidate Walter Mondale. In 1990 Feinstein became the first woman to win a major party nomination to be governor of California. Two years later she became the first woman sworn in to represent her state in the U.S. Senate.

Repeating a pattern established when she first went to City Hall more than two decades before, Feinstein in Washington quickly established herself as a forceful advocate for her state, and became a high-profile national voice on issues from the budget to crime, from the environment to immigration. Setting forth an ambitious agenda on a host of timely issues, she became the first Californian to serve on the Appropriations Committee in twenty-four years and one of the first two women, along with Illinois senator Carol Moseley-Braun, ever to be appointed to the Judiciary Committee. In another pattern familiar to those who watched in San Francisco, Feinstein also gained a reputation as a Capitol Hill autocrat, as more than a dozen staff members quit or were fired after briefly confronting the demands of working for a woman who boasts that she doesn't "get ulcers, but gives them."

In 1994 Feinstein will again be a prominent figure on the national political scene, as she seeks reelection in what is expected to be the most costly Senate race in American history. Her opponent is Michael Huffington, a millionaire Republican congressman from Santa Barbara, who has vowed to spend as much of his own money as is needed to be competitive with Democrat Feinstein.

As California voters reexamine her record, they will find Feinstein has been an energetic and hardworking public official whose politics are moderate, opportunistic, pragmatic, sometimes paradoxical and, over thirty years, marked by shifts and reversals of position on important policy matters. Once liberal on issues from capital punishment to taxes and urban environmentalism, she developed more conservative stances as she moved up the political ladder. Beginning her career as a maverick outsider, she became a consummate inside player in San Francisco's political establishment. A trailblazer for women, she feuded bitterly with feminists and their agenda for social change.

Such points and counterpoints reflect her personality—earnest but calculating, ambitious but insecure, compassionate but peremptory, honest but manipulative, resolutely independent but preoccupied with control and order.

Political analyst Rollin Post, who has covered Feinstein for twenty-five years for San Francisco television stations, said that her "career is built around herself, not any cause. This gives her the ability to project herself as an independent force in an authoritative way." Said Duane Garrett, her campaign chairman and senior adviser, "Dianne is the way society used to be. If there's enough goodwill, decency, and good faith, there are no insoluble problems. Diplomacy will carry us through."

Despite her genteel appearance, Feinstein the politician is tough and steely, forged and scarred by years of combat in San Francisco street politics, a cauldron of polarizations and conflicting passions.

Her first defining moment in the Senate came on November 11, 1993, during a debate of Feinstein's controversial proposal to ban sales of semiautomatic assault weapons, offered as an amendment to an omnibus crime bill. Senator Larry Craig, a Republican from Idaho, rose to dispute Feinstein's description of a weapon used by a crazed gunman who killed twenty-one people and wounded nineteen at a fast-food restaurant in San Diego. "So," Craig lectured her, "the gentlelady from California needs to become a little bit more familiar with firearms and their deadly characteristics."

The "gentlelady from California," after duly receiving permission from the presiding officer to make a point of personal privilege, stood to offer a quiet response that transfixed the Senate. "I am quite familiar with firearms," Feinstein coolly told Craig. "I became mayor as a product of assassination. . . . I proposed gun control legislation in San Francisco. I went through a recall on the basis of it. I was trained in the shooting of a firearm when I had terrorist attacks, with a bomb at my house, when my husband was dying, when I had windows shot out. Senator, I know something about what firearms can do."

The drama, which ended when both houses of Congress narrowly approved an assault weapons ban, illustrated the extent to which personal experience shapes her political views. For a woman to whom the political seems so much the personal, however, Feinstein has always tried to keep her private and public lives very separate. While few politicians revel in self-reflection, Feinstein more than most seems to cloak her own emotions, both for personal and professional reasons.

In an interview with the San Francisco writer Carol Pogash in 1986, Feinstein set forth a list of twelve "rules for getting ahead" for women seeking to advance in professions that had been closed to them. Part of her advice, published in *Working Woman* magazine, was this admonition: "Do not cry. Ever. If you've got to bite off your tongue or close your eyes so tight that nobody can see what's in them, do it. Because a man can cry and somehow it doesn't bother anybody. If a woman cries, it's an immediate, destructive thing that goes out and that everybody seems to remember . . . "

As I began work on this book, one of Feinstein's close friends observed that, "For a very public person who's been in the limelight for decades, Dianne personally has always been an enigma." Another longtime friend, recalling that Feinstein worked for several years on an autobiography, which went through many drafts but remains unpublished, said, "Dianne failed in writing autobiography because she couldn't talk about the intimate things. She won't let go of those feelings."

When I told Senator Feinstein in early 1993 that I was writing a biography of her, her first reaction was to put her arms around her sides and moan. Although I had covered her for twenty years and was familiar with her political record, I was surprised to learn over the next months what an extremely private person she is. Almost every time our interviews turned to family history or painful matters, she would seek to change the subject, plead failed recollection, or offer cursory or no comment.

"I don't spend a long time on things past," she said at one point. "I don't really dwell on it."

Asked in an early interview to talk about her troubled childhood, she walked from the second-floor sitting room in her elegant San Francisco home, returning with an old photograph of herself and her two sisters with their mother. As a polished antique clock ticked the seconds in near silence, Feinstein spoke quietly and haltingly about her mother's aberrant behavior. Then, she suddenly shut the emotional window. Standing up to return the photograph from where she had gotten it, she said in a firm voice, "Well, that's in the past."

Part One

BEHIND THE SMILE

1

PRETTY PICTURES AND PRIVATE PAIN

Do not cry. No matter what.

—Dianne Feinstein's Rules for Getting Ahead

DIANNE WAS STILL IN GRADE SCHOOL when her mother tried to drown her little sister in the bath.

No one now recalls what trifle triggered Betty Goldman's rage at her helpless five-year-old child that day. There rarely was a rational explanation for her frequent explosive anger, which filled her rose-trellised San Francisco mansion with screaming curses and secret dread. "We lived on tenterhooks," her oldest daughter, Dianne, would recall decades later. "But you didn't talk about it, because there's nothing you can do."

To outsiders, the picture-perfect family of Leon and Betty Goldman lived an exclusive and privileged life in the picturesque urban village of San Francisco during the Depression, World War II, and Eisenhower years. The three Goldman girls—Dianne, Yvonne, and Lynn—attended private school, wore expensive clothes, were indulged with riding, tennis, and piano lessons, and were treated to white-gloved teas and luncheons at fine hotels and restaurants in fashionable Union Square.

Leon Goldman, a skilled surgeon of national reputation, was dedicated and successful, a Jew who broke down barriers of discrimination to achieve a full professorship at the University of California San Francisco medical school. Tall, scholarly, and diligent, he was esteemed by patients for his attentive, conscientious manner, respected by colleagues for his insights and artistic hands, and held in awe by students for his teaching skill and the perfectionism he demanded in the operating theater.

Betty Goldman, though poorly educated, was a porcelain-skinned beauty with fine features and well-tended blond hair. Before her marriage, she had

9

worked as a model at a stylish downtown French fashion shop, and she always had an eye for appearances and a taste for fine things. She aspired to society, kept a live-in housekeeper, and loved to play the hostess once or twice a year at catered parties where uniformed waiters served drinks in crystal glasses and canapés from silver trays.

But behind the curtains of the rambling three-story English-style Goldman home, there were dark and shaming secrets. Betty was a tormented soul. She had spent three years of her childhood in a tuberculosis sanitarium. As an old woman she was diagnosed with chronic brain disease. As a young mother she often flew into unpredictable outbursts of anger and violence and would beat, threaten, or humiliate her daughters while ranting at them in vile language. The haunting episodes routinely followed on her drinking, which was considerable, and were often compounded by the ingestion of barbiturates that she used in repeated suicide attempts.

Preoccupied with patients and career, Dr. Goldman seemed powerless against his wife's behavior, and Dianne and her sisters learned to cope and to survive. "What mood is she in? What is she going to be like today?" was a constant concern, recalled Yvonne. "It was everpresent, superseding everything, every day, consciously, subconsciously, unconsciously."

Betty liked to hire professional photographers to come to her big house on Presidio Terrace to make portraits of her daughters dressed up in finery. These pictures lined the wall along a staircase that led from the entrance hall to the second floor—a gallery of formal family moments with the sisters posed in pinafores, frilly dresses, and Mary Janes on a well-upholstered couch or on the flagstone terrace.

Decades later, Dianne would keep one of those portraits in her own Presidio Terrace mansion—a richly appointed home directly across the street from where she grew up—and take it out to show a visitor. She would point out the sadness and the hurt around her eyes looking out from the picture frame, and recall that her mother had beaten her moments before the photographer arrived.

Having pushed away the childhood pain, or channeled it into her pioneering political career, United States Senator Dianne Feinstein would speak of those days only haltingly and with great emotional effort. "We lived in a great deal of fear," she said. "The part that was so hard was the unpredictability . . . "

"When my father met my mother," she sighed, "a marriage took place that probably never should have."

LEON GOLDMAN AND BETTY ROSENBURG came from two very different kinds of immigrant families tossed to the New World by Russia's revolution and expansion. Each family in its own way shaped Leon and Betty's oldest daughter through a paradox of values, attitudes, and behavior: Jew and Christian, reason and raw emotion, self-control and self-absorption.

The Goldman clan was big, convivial, and proud enough of its Jewish heritage to trace the ancestral generations in detailed family trees. The Rosenburgs were few in number, detached and distant. Their background and history were shrouded in mystery as thick as the clouds of incense that filled the Russian Orthodox church where some of them worshiped.

Leon's father, born Samuel Gelleorivich, is said to have stowed away at the age of fourteen on a ship bound for Boston. He was fleeing a pogrom in the town of Griva in a region of Russian-ruled Poland that was known in the nineteenth century as the Pale of Settlement. Leon's mother, Lily Kaflin, came from Vilna, near the border of Lithuania and Poland.

In America his name became Sam Goldman. A shoemaker by trade, he made his way to Sacramento and, in 1895, to San Francisco, where he opened a dry goods store on broad and dusty Market Street. Three years later he met and married Lily, and they moved into a Victorian house in the working-class Mission district, where she bore the first six of their eleven children.

On the morning of April 18, 1906, the family was shaken from its beds by the great San Francisco earthquake; it lost nearly everything in the fire that left the city in ruins. The Goldmans moved first to Berkeley and later to southern California, where Sam speculated in wildcat oil wells and worked as a retail merchant before finally returning to the San Francisco Bay.

An Orthodox Jew, Sam was active in Hebrew organizations and helped found several temples around the state, inculcating his nine sons and two daughters with the virtues of unstinting work, education, ambition, and achievement. While older brothers worked, the fifth-born Leon attended the University of California at Berkeley and the medical school at the university's San Francisco campus. He benefited especially from the labors of his elder sibling Morris, a successful businessman and streetwise gambler who would become a key influence on the young Dianne.

Leon's wife was enigmatic and traveled a harder immigrant road. She told her daughters that she was born Pasha Pariskovia in St. Petersburg and fled the revolution with her family as a child. Her father sold horses to the Czar's army, as the story was told, and the family escaped by hiding in a hay cart in which they made their way slowly across Siberia. With ways and means now lost in time and family silence, they came to the New World and traveled to Eureka, where Russian traders and trappers had made settlements on the rocky, fog-shrouded north coast of California.

Instead of finding fortune, however, the Rosenburgs found heartbreak and despair. Shortly after arriving in Eureka, Betty's father died suddenly at the age of thirty-two, leaving a bitter widow and four small children penniless in a strange land. Betty, who at first called herself Bessie, was a sickly child and spent several years in a sanitarium. Many years later, doctors using a CAT scan discovered extensive brain damage and speculated that the roots of her aberrant behavior lay in contraction of encephalitis in her youth.

Precisely what ailments, or primitive treatments, she endured in the institution was not spoken of to her own children. The Rosenburgs were not given to expansive discussions of the past. Betty's own mother never spoke a word of English, and rarely spoke to her grandchildren at all. "It was a really estranged situation," said Dianne, confronted with the many mysteries and unanswered questions about her mother. "As with many refugee families, you don't look back, you look ahead. Nobody wants to look back. And nobody wants to talk."

By the 1920s the Rosenburg family had arrived in San Francisco. Despite her illness, Betty's beauty had blossomed and she found a job modeling clothes at Maison Mendesolle, a boutique in the fashionable St. Francis Hotel that specialized in Parisian imports in the couture-conscious city.

One night, nursing a sick friend, Betty met a tall, bespectacled young doctor named Leon Goldman when he stopped to check up on the mutual acquaintance.

He was smitten by her looks. "My father fell in love," Dianne said with a shrug. "He always had an eye for beauty." The reaction of the families to the match, however, apparently was not a happy one; the couple eloped to Reno, Nevada, where they were married on June 19, 1931, by a Conservative rabbi named H. A. Opochinsky of Temple Emanuel. Until the marriage certificate was found in Reno during research for this book, Dianne and her sisters did not know that their parents were married in a Jewish service; Betty told her children she was Russian Orthodox, although she almost never went to church, as did her mother and her sister.

"This was one of the deceptive things," Dianne said. "My father thought my mother was Jewish. But she wasn't."

After their wedding, religion would be only one of many things to come between them.

BETTY BECAME PREGNANT the next year and gave birth to her first daughter shortly after midnight on Thursday, June 22, 1933.

Their child was called Dianne Emiel. The spelling of her first name was meant as a tribute to Betty's sister, Anne, but a clerk erroneously recorded it with a single *N* on the birth certificate, a mistake Dianne would legally correct after she achieved political prominence. Her middle name was after one of Leon's younger brothers who died in his early twenties.

She was delivered by Dr. Lois Brock, which was unusual not only because of the small number of practicing female physicians but also because Dr. Goldman did not believe that women should be trained in medicine. They were too likely to get married, bear children, and waste their education, he would argue. Although Dr. Goldman years later would become his eldest daughter's strongest supporter as she broke down gender barriers in another field, his opinion about females in medicine reflected widespread attitudes about the proper role of women at the time.

On the day Dianne was born, a glance through the hometown morning paper would not have been auspicious for her chances of becoming a trailblazing woman politician. The top political news that day was California governor James Rolph's call for state voters to endorse the repeal of Prohibition in the upcoming election; the following Tuesday they did just that, as San Franciscans led the statewide rum parade, with a smashing vote in the city of 127,665 to 8,975 for legalized booze.

A page 10 feature story in the morning *Chronicle* clearly reflected the place of women in the campaign. "Society and club women join in fight for big repeal vote," read the headline over a photo of a comely society matron smiling into a phone. "If a charming feminine voice telephones you to 'go to the polls next Tuesday,' you should do as you are told," the article began. "This is prefatory to saying that society and club women have combined in a speaking army to bring about the repeal of the 18th amendment."

Elsewhere in the paper, a report of a bitter intraparty feud within the city Democratic organization ended with the prediction of a political boss that "the boys will iron it out." This kind of tough-guy politics would all but shut out women from important elective office in San Francisco for decades to come.

Other news that fair and mild summer day focused on growing economic signs that the Depression was easing, and on the boycott of the World Economic Conference in London by the German government of Chancellor Adolf Hitler.

Dr. Goldman, who later would join an American delegation working to relocate Jewish doctors displaced by World War II, may have noticed a dispatch from Berlin, where Hitler gave a speech to sixty thousand storm troopers and sternly warned German parents that their children would be taken away and put under the authority of the government if they were not brought up to be good Nazis. "Youth is our future," the chancellor said. "If the older generation cannot get accustomed to us, we will take away the children and rear them in our spirit."

In San Francisco, there was evidence of big changes in the scope and appearance of the city. Coit Tower, soon to be a famous landmark in a city filled with them, was reported to be 75 percent constructed. And engineers of the Portland Bridge Company, which had just started building the most famous landmark of them all, admitted that underground blasting for foundation piers of the new Golden Gate Bridge was responsible for setting off earthquake detectors at the university.

Some things seemed like they would never change in San Francisco: at Seals Stadium, where Dianne's uncle Morrie sat behind third base and bet on every pitch of Pacific Coast League games with his cronies, a single by Joe DiMaggio in the bottom of the ninth inning led the San Francisco Seals to a six-to-five win over their city rivals, the Missions.

Behind the sports pages, the horoscope for June 22 predicted that "children born this day will be exceedingly independent and impulsive."

THE CHILD HAD BLUE-GREEN EYES, flawless white skin, and a radiant smile, a combination of striking features that would become perhaps her greatest political asset. Generations of San Francisco reporters later would invariably refer to her as a "raven-haired beauty," but in the first few years of her life Dianne was a bobbed and curled towhead, like her mother.

The twenty-nine-year-old Dr. Goldman and his twenty-seven-year-old wife lived with their daughter in a three-room apartment in a bay-windowed brick building just a few blocks from the medical school campus, where Leon was awarded a faculty position in surgery. The building offered a splendid view of the Pacific three miles to the west and, to the east, a lovely stand of fog-swirled eucalyptus trees. As an adult, Dianne would petition to save them from developers, thereby helping to spark a populist, slow-growth political movement in the city that she would battle against years later as mayor.

In 1936 a second child, Yvonne, was born, followed by Lynn in 1941. By then the Goldmans had moved to a duplex flat with a sunroom a few blocks from the Marina Green, a greensward of northern waterfront that had been filled with sand and landscaped for the 1915 Panama-Pacific International Exposition.

Dr. Goldman's career advanced with his increasing reputation as a teacher and clinician at the university and at San Francisco General Hospital. In 1946 the Goldmans moved into their own three-story home at One Presidio Terrace. One of the city's most prestigious neighborhoods, Presidio Terrace is a cul-de-sac of mansions with rolling lawns and spacious flower beds behind an iron fence and gate. Here Betty's demons raged.

Painfully discussing the long-hidden past, Dianne and her sisters all recall a childhood of almost constant anxiety and fear. "My mother was an abuser and a basher," said Lynn, remembering the day Betty forced and held her head underwater. "My first memory was of my mother trying to drown me in the bathtub. I was five, and my father pulled me out."

Her mother was "scary, distant, and forbidding," she added. "You never knew what was going to happen." For days, or sometimes weeks, Betty's madness might be stilled. She did not neglect her children, and always saw that they were well fed and clothed. With domestic help to run the house, she sometimes would spend much of her day alone in her bedroom. When her mood was good, she liked to garden, take her daughters downtown for lunch at El Prado, or invite them into her room for tea, lying on a chaise longue as she consoled them over a broken romance or a problem at school. Always conscious of other people's social standing, the semiliterate woman would have Dianne compose her thank-you notes, then copy them word for word in her own hand.

"She was a very beautiful woman and she had exquisite taste. I mean, she was the showstopper. She could walk in this room and you'd think she was perfectly fine," said Dianne. "And then fifteen minutes later, it would be the other way, a violent outburst. Something would anger her. And alcohol would exacerbate it."

The girls always walked on eggshells, in anticipation of the next ugly episode. Although often set off by her drinking, her anger might be triggered by a misplaced pair of sewing scissors, a dropped dish, a broken hair band, or seemingly by nothing at all. "We'd be doing our chores, everything would be fine. We used to sort of sing when we'd do the dishes," Dianne recalled. "And one thing, say we'd drop something, and that would set it off."

The sisters learned to sense a certain eerie silence in the house when they came home from school and to warn each other to be careful. Suddenly, their mother would tear out of her bedroom and start to pummel or slap around one her daughters, screaming obscenities or "little kike . . . little Jew"—epithets she also used against her husband.

Holidays could be especially dreary and sad. One Christmas morning Betty threw a tantrum and forbade her children to come out of their rooms to open presents. Since she had guests coming for dinner, however, everyone was summoned downstairs a few hours later and ordered to unwrap the gifts so that they could be properly displayed under the tree.

She liked Lynn to wear braids, but if a rubber band happened to break while she was fixing her daughter's hair, Betty would slap Lynn for it. Yvonne suffered from a chronic skin disease, for which she was blamed and sometimes punished. Dianne, who fled in fear when Betty chased her with a knife, was often singled out, as if her mother was jealous of the prettiest and most accomplished of her children. In many ways "Dianne bore the brunt of it," Yvonne recalled.

Barbara Isackson, a childhood friend of Dianne's who was one of the few children outside the family often in the Goldman home, said that "her mother had to have Dianne be everything she wasn't. But when Dianne did excel, I'm not sure there wasn't jealousy at the other end." Isackson added that "Dianne was the matriarch in her family as far as her sisters were concerned. Being the oldest, having superior strength, Dianne was protective of her sisters. She was very strong with her mother. Leon was not strong in the sense of home life."

Dianne recalled feeling "impotent—there's nothing you can do"—in the face of her mother's tantrums. "The smallest thing could set her off. You could not reason with her."

Still, she would try to intervene on behalf of her sisters. Lynn remembered being beaten in her room and Dianne rushing in to yell, "Leave her alone, stop it," diverting her mother's wrath to herself. "Dianne protected me," her youngest sister recalled. "She'd step in sometimes or say, 'Get out of the house, go out now.'"

Under early pressure to perform as a responsible adult against the violence of an abusive parent, Dianne grew up with many of the personality hallmarks of the oldest child of an alcoholic: an unstinting drive for achievement, control, and perfection, a heightened sense of responsibility, a desire to hide the secret and at the same time work to fix it. "You don't have a choice—things fall to you . . . you shoulder it," she said. At home Dianne was "in some ways mothering, in some ways dictatorial," said Yvonne, an apt summation of the personal and management styles her sister would later exhibit as a politician and a civic leader.

As a child she learned to "compartmentalize" her life, a word Dianne would use years later to describe her ability to cloak personal emotions in the crises that would shape and characterize her political career. She also developed a strong desire for privacy, even though she chose to spend her life in the spotlight of the public arena. "You sort of put it out of your mind," said Dianne, who is elusive and guarded in discussing broken fragments of her past. "Understand, you mask it."

Despite the sway that Betty's aberrant behavior held over their lives, it was long treated by the family and a few close friends as a shameful secret, locked behind a wall of appearances, pretense, and buried memories. "It was not supposed to be spoken of and was not, except by the three of us," said Yvonne.

Once, Lynn recalled, after Betty had overdosed on a sickening stew of bourbon and barbiturates, Dr. Goldman brought her home from the hospital, put her to bed, and left after putting a note on the banister for his daughters. "Your mother's all right," it read. "Let her alone."

IF CHAOS, CRISIS, AND CONTROL marked Dianne's relationship with her mother, she learned determination and perseverance from her father. "My father had a will of iron," she said admiringly. "He instilled in me the will never to be satisfied." By all accounts, Leon was an overriding influence on his daughter, and she drew strength, confidence, and esteem from his success. Watching him achieve in the world, despite the disastrous blunder of his marriage, she learned to transform emotional pain into fuel for her aspirations.

"Dr. Goldman adored Dianne and she was ecstatically proud of him," said Dr. Norman Sweet, who knew Leon as a student, colleague, and friend and as Betty's physician. "Dianne is really Leon Goldman in the garb of a beautiful woman."

Erudite, industrious, and proper, Dr. Goldman treated his wife's instability as a private burden to be endured in a life devoted to healing other people's illness. "I probably wouldn't have been half the doctor I am if it hadn't been for your mother," he would smilingly confide to Lynn, after the girls had grown and he had divorced Betty.

After receiving his M.D., he devoted himself wholeheartedly to the practice and teaching of medicine in a career that brought many honors and distinctions, including international renown for his contributions to surgery of the pancreas and parathyroid gland. He also served as physician to California governor Pat Brown, who would later launch Dianne's career in politics.

Despite his academic success, Leon made house calls throughout his career and often preached that "you treat the whole person, not just the wound." He routinely worked seven days a week, leaving the house before 7:00 A.M. and usually not returning for dinner at 7:00 P.M. "You gave all of yourself to it, there was no time for anything else," said Dr. Sweet, who met Leon in 1935.

Harry Goldman, a cousin who owned a San Francisco delicatessen, recalled that he once spoke to Leon about a customer who suffered from palsy. "Send him to see me," Leon said, even though he was told that the man had little money. Dr. Goldman diagnosed, then cured the patient through surgery but "never charged a nickel," Harry Goldman said. "And nobody ever knew about it. Leon was ambitious, not to have great wealth, but to be a healer."

Dr. Sid Foster, a San Francisco radiologist who was an early supporter and adviser to Dianne on health-care issues, said that Dr. Goldman wanted people to work at "150 percent, as he was doing. Hours meant nothing to him," he added. "If you ever met a perfectionist, it was Dr. Goldman. A lot of Dianne's drive comes from him."

Leon was a high school varsity football and baseball player and maintained a lifelong interest in team sports. One of his best friends was Benny Lom, an all-American halfback at the University of California who became a local sports legend when he stopped teammate Ray "Wrong Way" Riegels from running into his own end zone with a fumble during the 1929 Rose Bowl.

Dr. Goldman was known as "the coach" by UC medical students. As surgery department head and associate dean, he had a reputation for being a first-rate teacher who could explain the most complex matters of anatomy simply and methodically.

Despite his low-key manner, however, Leon's perfectionism could also flash in temper; he once threw a scalpel against the wall of the operating room, one of his daughters recalled, because some students were a few minutes late for a 7:00 A.M. surgery. "This patient doesn't wait for you," he snapped.

"Residents lived in fear of presenting a patient if they weren't prepared," said Dr. Foster. "But he was a good teacher."

He liked to take his daughters to the Playland at the Beach amusement park on Sundays, but more often invited them to accompany him on rounds at the hospital. And despite his early opposition to women doctors, he told his children that there were no limits to what they could accomplish through hard work and "mind over matter."

Each of his daughters revered and idolized him, none more than Dianne. "My father always believed I could do all kinds of things that I didn't think I could do myself. He always had high standards for me. And it was as if it was expected, not unusual," she said. When Lynn once complained that she was having trouble concentrating on homework, he advised her, "You have to bury yourself in the work." "He never put any pressure on us," said Yvonne. "But I think having only daughters . . . he pushed us to read, to work hard, to never just be sitting there."

"He was a very simple person who happened to be exceptionally gifted," said Yvonne. "He was a Jew and believed in it but he was extremely tolerant of other people. He was very much affected by bigotry and he was the first of his religion to do a lot of things. People would stop me in the street and say, 'You should be proud of your father.'"

While stoically accepting their mother's violence, the girls in some ways found it more painful to incur their father's mild-mannered displeasure. As a little girl, Lynn stole two spools of thread from the drugstore, one pink and one blue, because she liked the colors. Leon reprimanded her quietly and in private, then made her return the thread with an apology at the store. "It was worse to be talked to by my father in the study," she said. "Mother bats you, you put your hands over your head. But Dad says, 'Why did you do that?' and you always end up sobbing."

On a rare evening out, Dr. Goldman would accompany his wife to an opera opening or a ladies' medical auxiliary dinner, but only occasionally and nearly always in the company of another couple, most often Benny Lom and his wife. "I cannot remember my parents ever going out by themselves," said Lynn.

Far from resenting their father for not restraining Betty, his daughters often tried to shield him from the tyranny of her unpredictable behavior. They would pour Betty's liquor down the sink or cut it by adding water to the bottles. Sometimes they would not bother to mention it to Dr. Goldman when their mother blew up. They might even try to set off her anger before he came home, so as not to ruin dinner.

Despite the anguish in the marriage, Dianne said, "My mother always was in love with him. Although she was miserable to live with and all of that, there was no question that she loved him.

"And I think my father put up with it for us."

KING CREON OF THE CONVENT

Use your appearance to create an image of strength.

—*Dianne Feinstein's Rules for Getting Ahead*

STALKING THE STAGE in the garb of King Creon, seventeen-year-old Dianne Goldman pronounced a sentence of death upon the rebellious Antigone. "This girl has learned her insolence before this, when she broke the established laws," the high school Creon declared, condemning Antigone for daring to defy his authority. "When I am alive, no woman shall rule."

It was 1950, and the annual fall drama production of the senior class, always an elaborate affair at the Convent of the Sacred Heart, was under way. Sophocles' tragedy had gotten off to a shaky start when the high school girls playing the Greek chorus appeared on the stage in fake beards, drawing roars of laughter from the audience and sending a chill through the nun who doubled as dean of students and drama director.

But Dianne, playing a male lead as usual, lent a reassuring air of command with her enactment of Creon, the king who represents the established political order against an upstart young woman who challenges his rule on behalf of her family, with fatal consequences. Given the events that would unfold in her life over the next four decades, Dianne's self-assured portrayal of male dominion that evening was both ironic and apt. "The only Jewess in Catholic surroundings," as one of her high school teachers wrote, Dianne would carry out into the world not only a dramatic flair but also a special brand of self-discipline and polish instilled under strict supervision by the sisters of the Society of the Sacred Heart.

Dianne came to the "madames," as the Sacred Heart religious instructors were known, as something of a tomboy, an independent girl who escaped unhappiness at home by rising before dawn to ride horses and who navigated the city by cable and streetcar before she could read. By the time she left the Catholic academy for Stanford University four years later, she had learned invaluable lessons of "exacting persistence," as an early member of the society explained its mission, from her days inside the domain of cloistered women.

By then, Dianne also benefited from a very different kind of teaching provided by a jovial, savvy uncle who stirred an early interest in politics and was the first person to see that she was a natural on television, the medium that would later catapult her career.

When she arrived at Stanford in the fall of 1951, Dianne was primed for her first political campaigns. All that was needed was some cultural reeducation on campus. "We didn't struggle with identity crises or low self-esteem or being liberated," a female Stanford contemporary would write of the times. "The fifties woman knew her place and stayed there."

ONE DAY WHEN DIANNE WAS ELEVEN, she and Yvonne were walking to a lesson at Samuel Rudetsky's piano studio when a group of boys began to harass the girls on the sidewalk. As one youth made a move toward her sister, Dianne turned on him and snarled, "You hit her and I'll knock your teeth down your throat." Even Yvonne, who saw Dianne as "part mothering, part dictatorial," felt surprised at the aggressiveness of her sister. Already at this age, Dianne was not only the protector of her younger siblings but also a competitive tomboy who knew how to look out for herself.

She sought joy and refuge from problems at home by escaping on her bike or on the city's first-rate public transit system to explore what Robert Louis Stevenson called "the citied hills" of San Francisco, using buildings as landmarks before she could read the street signs along the Municipal Railway routes.

At an early age, she rode alone downtown and was thrilled on a trip to the orthodontist to see the famed San Francisco columnist Herb Caen standing on a street corner, wearing a camel-hair coat, a blond woman on each arm. She rode to Winterland, which would become the mecca of 1960s rock and roll, when it was still used for ice skating. More than anything else, she rode to the horses.

Her horse-crazed phase began before she was ten, when Dr. Goldman took her on a horseback ride in a sylvan Sierra setting near Lake Tahoe. In the summer the Goldmans sometimes vacationed at Tahoe Tavern, a popular destination for prominent San Franciscans that featured a casino and the world's largest springboard dance floor. Surrounded by the well-to-do, Betty was usually on her best behavior. She would spend her days by the pool while the girls rode or played tennis; Leon commuted up from work for a few days at a time.

In the city Dianne rose on Saturdays at 5:30 A.M. to catch the first bus to the St. Francis Riding Academy near the ocean to ensure she'd get her pick of horses for the first class of the day. On other mornings, she'd exercise polo ponies stabled there.

National Velvet came out in 1944, and the eleven-year-old Dianne sat in the dark at the movies with friend and neighbor Barbara Isackson, captivated by big-screen images of the coltish Elizabeth Taylor, whom Dianne resembled in coloring and build.

When she was a teenager, a man who kept horses at the academy asked Dianne to ride one of his at the Grand National Rodeo and 4-H exhibition at the Cow Palace, on the city's southern border. She won the equestrian competition for her age and was selected Queen of the Junior Grand National. This awarded her the honor of tearing out on horseback for the Grand Entry, carrying the American flag around the ring to cheers and adulation in which she reveled. "There's nothing more exciting than the show ring and all the pomp," she said. "I loved it."

Her triumph was a singular one, however, not witnessed by her family. She even had to sneak out on one night of the rodeo, when her mother forbade her to go. A sister recalled that Dianne said she would spend the night at a friend's and, when the ploy was discovered, received a rare rebuke from her father.

Horses were not the only animals that led to misadventure. A brief career as a female steer rider ended in instant ignominy when she was bucked. When she represented San Francisco in a cow milking contest at the fair in then-rural Solano County, thirty miles to the east, she came in dead last. "On a dare somebody said, 'I bet you wouldn't do it,' and I said, 'I will,'" she recalled. "People were holding down the cow. I had never milked before and the poor cow was in distress. I never hit the bucket."

When a pet turtle died, she put it in a matchbox coffin and quarreled with a friend who tried to decorate it with a cross for a somber funeral service. "No," she objected. "This is a Jewish turtle."

Amid its religious ambivalence, the family celebrated Easter. One year Dr. Goldman brought home two baby chicks, a rooster and a hen that the sisters named Curly and Pearly. Betty clipped their wings and, when they grew larger, put them in the backyard, where their barnyard noise drew complaints from the neighbors. They were banished from the city to a place down the San Francisco Peninsula owned by one of Leon's brothers. When the Goldmans went to Sunday dinner not long afterward, Curly and Pearly were served as the main course. "I left the house," Dianne said, "sat on the curb and cried and cried and cried."

She attended public primary schools during World War II, a war that seemed to be just something that grown-ups talked about, except for the days when she stood with thousands of people on the Marina Green to wave as troop ships sailed through the Golden Gate for the Pacific theater, or watched boats rig nets under the bridge to foil submarines that never came. Dr. Goldman belonged to the naval reserve but was not called; he served instead as neighborhood air warden, going out at night with helmet and flashlight to enforce the use of blackout shades around the block.

Dianne's early education was interrupted for a year when her father won a fellowship at Northwestern University in Evanston, Illinois. It was the only time she would live away from San Francisco for long until she was nearly sixty, and the bitter Midwest cold and motor trip across the continent left a lasting distaste for life away from the Bay Area. "It was the most miserable experience," she recalled. "It took us five days. I didn't eat either way, I was just so sick. Vomited all the way across the United States. And then vomited all the way back."

With Barbara Isackson she attended Grant and Winfield Scott public schools, went off to summer camp, and explored adolescence, poring through medical textbooks in Dr. Goldman's study for clues about sex.

One summer at Camp Talawanda near Lake Tahoe, Dianne slashed her finger, neglected the wound, and developed a painful infection. She was sent to Tahoe City where she had the finger lanced, bearing up with a stoic face. "She won an award for bravery," her friend remembered. "She always loved medicine and if there was an accident, Dianne always stepped in to help."

AN EIGHTH-GRADE TEACHER named Virginia Rider, who thought she saw something special in the girl, suggested that Dianne be sent to private Catholic school. Her mother didn't need much urging. While exposing her daughter to Christian beliefs, private school more importantly would admit her to the rarefied world of San Francisco's elite families.

Dr. Goldman, not a religious man despite his Orthodox upbringing, sent his daughters to Sunday school at Temple Emanu-el, where Dianne was confirmed, while enduring harangues from his wife, who kept threatening to have the children baptized but never did. Endorsing the notion of Dianne attending a quality private school, he agreed to her enrollment at the Convent of the Sacred Heart, one of the three most exclusive schools in the city.

There was talk within the family that Dianne was blackballed at the other two because of secret quotas on Jews, which may have been why Leon told her at the time that "no matter what you do, the world will always regard you as Jewish." But Dianne, coming from a home where constant tension was often expressed in hateful terms of religion, recalled that at the time she was "looking for something more in a faith."

"The Jewish religion is a very simple religion, there's not a lot of things you take on faith," she said. "There's essentially the Ten Commandments, as sort of a moral code. In Catholicism, the liturgy of the religion is much more developed. What is an act of faith? What is an act of contrition? It is a much warmer religion, which was very attractive to me."

Sacred Heart, with its precise codes of conduct and soothing ritual calendar of celebration—Lily Procession, First Friday Guard of Honor, May Crowning and Mater's Feast, Ring Ceremony, Wills and Prophecies, Senior Tea, Prize Day—offered escape from the unpredictable instability of home. Within the elegant marble "house of learning, refinement, and peace" that is the convent school, she thrived in the atmosphere of aesthetic nurturing, individual attention, intellectual challenge, material richness, and social discipline.

"For the sake of one child, I would have founded the Society," proclaimed Madeleine Sophie Barat, the nineteenth-century French reformer who founded the international Sacred Heart order to carry out the teaching of the "wholeness" of the child. Those who took Saint Madeleine Sophie's methods to San Francisco described their ultimate purpose this way: "Effecting change would require educating the children of the nobility to their social responsibility, for it was they who would someday assume positions of influence and have the power to shape and change society."

In a mansion built by a member of the local nobility, the madames taught Dianne and her classmates in a stately setting. The school was based in the James Leary Flood mansion, built on bedrock in plush Pacific Heights. Heir to the fortune of silver baron James Flood, one of the four famed "bonanza kings" who struck the Comstock Lode, its builder commissioned the lavish town house for his wife, who was traumatized by the earthquake and fire of 1906 that gutted her landmark Nob Hill mansion.

"I will build you a house of marble on a hill of granite," Flood promised his wife after the earthquake, and he did. Commanding a sweeping view of the Golden Gate and the bay, it combines Italian Renaissance, Rococo, Tudor, and Georgian interior designs—a dramatic entrance hall of marble, walls of satinwood, floors of teak, coffered ceilings, silver sconces, an Italian cortile, and a fireplace in every room. "The girls benefited simply by being surrounded by such beauty," said Sister Mary Mardel, mistress of Dianne's freshman class of thirty-eight girls.

In this sumptuous atmosphere, Dianne and her classmates wore starched uniforms and white gloves, observing strict rules of behavior as they marched silently in line from class to class and curtsied each time they encountered a religious instructor. This custom was celebrated in a contemporary newspaper interview with Miss Eveline McCullough, a then-ranking authority on British court protocol: "American women in general are not used to curtsying and the very idea terrifies them," Miss McCullough allowed, while passing through San Francisco. "The only exceptions are women educated in Sacred Heart convents, who learn the technique of the curtsy as children."

Years before Dianne came to Sacred Heart, Mother Janet Stuart of the society explained the underlying reasons for the discipline imposed on her students.

> The discipline in Schools of the Sacred Heart has met with a great deal of criticism. Why these moments of strict silence? Why this supervision?
>
> Why these exercises in behavior like formal parade? Why such exacting persistence as to manners? All, in the main, for the same reason: because they conduce to the training of character, they exact self-control, and attention, and consideration for others, and remembrance, not in one way, but in a hundred ways.

Leaving her tomboy days behind, Dianne enthusiastically applied herself to the regimen at school, adapting and advancing the lessons she had already learned at home about self-control. "We were sticklers for form and she took everything we had to give," Sister Mardel said of her prize pupil. "Many of the girls had been here before, but it was the first time Dianne had been in this kind of education. But she took to it right away."

In Dianne's first year, Sister Mardel assigned her class a project to photograph and analyze all the disparate architectural styles within the school. When each group finished its report, it was given to Dianne, who painstakingly copied it in her stylish hand to be bound in a book called "A Palace Beautiful" that is still cited at the school as a model work product.

She got all A's and B's and routinely walked the halls wearing gold medals pinned on green or blue ribbons, the Sacred Heart system's tokens of academic and social achievement. She also played guard on the basketball team, joined the riding club, and was president of the athletic association.

Dianne handled the publicity and finances for the senior class fall fashion show, a society event that drew fifteen hundred people. At the show she modeled a wool jersey top with a bold black-and-white skirt.

"The young San Franciscan is a hopeless clothes enthusiast," declared the program for the event. "The apparel she chooses must be strong. It should have character. Wisely conservative yet subtly smart. Just the right touch of the individual to make one remember that San Francisco is the city of well dressed women."

The value of a dignified appearance that she learned at Sacred Heart would remain with Dianne. After she had achieved recognition as a national political figure, she would tell an interviewer that good taste in clothing was "absolutely" necessary for women politicians. "People want to be able to look at a public official and say, 'You look terrific, I'm proud.' The sense of dignity you carry about yourself is the same sense of dignity you impart to the people."

But at Sacred Heart it was her stage performances that are still remembered by members of the staff, who have preserved them in scrapbooks filled with yellowing newspaper clippings and reviews. Dianne's height invariably typecast her as a strong male. Besides playing King Creon, she also starred as Prince Rupert in *A Waltz Dream,* as Peter Standish in *Berkeley Square,* and as Bassanio in *The Merchant of Venice.*

Meticulous in preparing for her characters, she would drive her own sisters, who also were educated by the madames, to near distraction. She would enlist Yvonne and Lynn in other parts to help her memorize her lines and would angrily banish them from her room when they started to laugh at her. For hours Dianne would stand before the mirror in her room and practice "every line, every gesture, every expression, every intonation of hands and body," one of her sisters remembered.

"The discipline I learned at the convent stood me in good stead," she said years later. "I'm now a pretty disciplined person in my work habits, in not falling behind, in getting myself to go the course."

Girls educated at Sacred Heart were "polished and coquettish," said another prominent San Franciscan taught by the madames: "You don't run downstairs, you float gracefully down the stairs. You've learned to handle others in society, always dress properly, and act ladylike."

The summer before her junior year, Dianne got her first job working at the basement notions counter of a downtown department store. Before she went to work, her father advised her what to do. "You get there early, you stay late. You don't take coffee breaks and take half the time allotted for lunch," Leon told her.

The same summer, Dr. Goldman spent two months in Munich with six other U.S. physicians tutoring and meeting with European doctors displaced by the war who wanted to come to America. On the trip, he contracted a chronic intestinal disease that would plague him the rest of his life, subjecting him to periodic illness that left him weak and in bed, vulnerable to physical attacks from his wife.

With a sense of tact and propriety, Dianne never mentioned the problems on Presidio Terrace to anyone at Sacred Heart. "Dianne and her sisters had a really unhappy childhood," a teacher would write later. "But they loyally kept up appearances and tried to hide the conditions at home."

DURING HER HIGH SCHOOL YEARS, Dianne came under the influence of another kind of mentor. Her uncle Morrie, a colorful San Francisco character in the style of *Guys and Dolls,* took his young niece under his wing and taught her a few lessons she would never learn in the convent. Morrie had worked so his kid brother, Leon, could afford to go to school. Fat, jovial, and Democratic, Uncle Morrie was also a few other things that Dr. Goldman was not.

In the wide-open San Francisco of the 1930s and 1940s, where politics, the police, business, and gambling intersected in after-hours clubs, barbershops, and bookie joints, Morrie was a player. A clothes manufacturer by trade, he owned a business called Miss California that marketed the first polo coats and pioneered new kinds of fabrics. By avocation, he was a gambler.

He lived in the Mark Hopkins Hotel on Nob Hill and held informal membership in the "Third Base Gang," a fraternity of bettors, bookies, and bagmen who sat behind the home-team dugout at Seals Stadium and tried to pick up intelligence from slugger Lefty O'Doul to gain an edge in the nonstop gambling. Uncle Morrie once wagered $20,000 on a single Seals game against the Oakland Oaks. He and his cronies "would bet on everything: the pitch—ball or strike—hit—fair or foul—or which side of the foul line a pigeon might land," recalled Herb Caen, whose columns of the time crackled with the exploits of the downtown gamblers.

In Uncle Morrie's world, the gang were guys who "went to the pocket pretty good," Caen wrote, who competed in "picking up tabs, overtipping waitresses, and pinching their bottoms," men who walked the streets in "polished nails, diamond pinky rings, double-breasted suits with padded shoulders, Charvet ties, white shirts with Barrymore collars, wraparound polo coats."

Sports and poker were not the only things that created action. "There was a place called Corbett's and there was a blackboard up there that would quote the odds for the mayor's race," said Henry Berman, a liquor wholesaler and pal of Uncle Morrie's who would become Dianne's campaign treasurer. "You'd back a candidate for two, three, five hundred and try to recover your money by betting on the opponent."

In the polite parlance of the newspapers, Morrie was often identified as a "frequent finance chairman" for local Democratic candidates. He knew how to raise a few bucks and was a pal of the notorious Sacramento lobbyist Artie Samish, a relationship that would lead him to a big fall and time in a federal prison.

But to Dianne in the late 1940s and early 1950s, Uncle Morrie represented fun and color. He liked to fetch the Goldmans in his LaSalle and take them to North Beach for an early Sunday show of Ted Lewis or Sophie Tucker. He liked to walk the streets with Dianne, introducing her to every merchant and hustler on Mission Street and telling his cronies that his niece would end up as mayor of San Francisco.

It was Uncle Morrie who got her hooked on politics by squiring her to what he called "Board of Stupidvisors" meetings. At the Monday afternoon sessions of the board of supervisors, San Francisco's equivalent of a city council, he would tell Dianne that he could fathom how members would vote by watching the city controller signal them with his cigar, and he would assure his niece that she could do better than these hacks. "Dianne, you get an education and you can do this job," he would say.

Morrie had an artistic side too. He had a trick of rhyming everything he said, including restaurant orders, and kept a little book of homilies and haiku-like poetry that he'd scribbled down. "Life is full of problems and woes, but I see plum blossoms outside my window" was one.

Always hustling, he put together one of the first television talk shows in San Francisco, a combination of politics, philosophical discussion, and cooking tips called "Food for Thought" that he hosted in the late afternoon. The program opened with an advertisement for his line of Miss California clothes. One of the models was his pretty niece, Dianne, who showed off the coats for viewers as she stood between Morrie's two pet dalmatians, who were also featured on the show.

"Morrie was grooming her like a Jewish Pygmalion," remembered Caen. "He was very proud of her. He'd say, 'Keep your eye on her, she's going all the way to the top.'"

THREE YEARS OUT OF HIGH SCHOOL, Stanford coed Dianne Goldman walked into the Phi Delta fraternity house on the leafy campus known as "The Farm." She was running for vice president of the Associated Students of Stanford University, the college student council, and her strategy this spring evening in 1954 was to campaign in the fraternity houses at dinnertime, when she could address the male students in large groups.

As she began her standard earnest pitch about improving the effectiveness and efficiency of student government, she was met with the usual combination of heckling, indifference, and snide comments from what she recalled as "a milling throng of insane humanity." All of a sudden a student stood up from a table and rushed her and before Dianne knew what was happening, hefted her slender frame over his shoulder. To the cheers of his fellow scholars, the student hustled her down the hallway and dumped her into a shower, where she was quickly and unceremoniously drenched. It was a wobbly first step on the road to the Year of the Woman in politics.

Dianne's response to the episode foreshadowed her approach to politics for the next forty years; rather than protesting or making a fuss about the offensive behavior, she accepted the humiliation as part of the game and promptly returned to her campaign rounds. Then she won the election and got her revenge.

As student body vice president, she exercised authority over permits for fraternities to have overnight parties on the autumn party weekend of the annual "Big Game" against the University of California. When the Phi Delts applied, they were turned down. "They couldn't get a permit because I gave them out," she said. "They had to get my permission. I was vice president. Until they came and apologized. That was the price—an apology."

Dianne, who scored 123 on an I.Q. test at Sacred Heart, was accepted for Stanford's class of 1955 despite an undistinguished showing on her College Entrance Examination Board tests. She got 901 out of a possible 1600 on the test; her verbal score of 538 was above the national average of 476, while her 363 for math was well below the average of 494. Her performance may be traced in part to her mother. In a rage because she couldn't find her sewing scissors, Betty locked Dianne out of the house the night before the test and she had to sleep in her father's car.

The Stanford campus to which she traveled, about forty miles south of San Francisco in Palo Alto, was idyllic and serene, except for the drunken brawls, water-bomb fights, and panty raids that marked weekend frolics. Male students outnumbered female students by a ratio of 3.3 to 1, and when a woman had a lousy date, she would invariably tell her roommates she "got the point three."

Conformity was in vogue, nowhere more than in matters of fashion. Young men dressed in button-down shirts, khakis, V-necks, and closely trimmed hair. The women wore skirts below the knee, cashmere sweaters, "a short strand of pearls . . . and fluffy bobs with forehead curls."

The San Francisco writer Merla Zellerbach, a contemporary of Dianne's at Stanford who later became a friend and neighbor on Presidio Terrace, described the times and the atmosphere on campus in an essay for *The Stanford Century* in 1991.

In the first half of the decade, life was calm and uncomplicated. Everyone seemed contented with a domestic role . . . Norman Vincent Peale's *The Power of Positive Thinking* came out in 1952 and became the pollyanna's bible. We were already pollyannas.

Johnny had come marching home again to be man of the house, Rosie the Riveter was back in the kitchen, Doris Day's virginity had made it through half a dozen movies, and we college freshmen, freshwomen, actually, had been programmed with two goals: get a husband and get an education—preferably in that order.

The family was all important and our roles sharply defined. Men had gone to battle and women, particularly educated ones, were expected to stay home and make babies. We would raise them with love and kindness and inspire them to rebuild a world that would forever be free of conflict.

Conflict kept impinging on campus tranquility, however. Students were distressed by the dispatch of troops to North Korea, by the knowledge that the Soviets had exploded a nuclear bomb, and by an undercurrent of news about French troops in a place called Vietnam. In Washington, Senator Joe McCarthy hunted communists on television, and the U.S. Supreme Court ignited the modern civil rights movement with its landmark decision in *Brown v. Board of Education*.

For Dianne's class of 1955, two years behind Merla Zellerbach's, such events were manifest in frequent earnest discussions about the United Nations and global government, and in the first twinges of inner conflict between traditional family roles and a nascent, idealistic desire to make the world a better place through political activism.

Years later, Dianne said of her Stanford days that "a girl had to get pinned, engaged, and married. If she didn't, society looked askance at her." But the former coed golfer also would recall that she was looking for a way "to put my divot back" in society. "I knew I wanted to do something where I could help people, for as long as I could remember," she said. "And I always believed an individual could make a difference."

As a freshman, Dianne made the acquaintance of three women with whom she would maintain lifelong friendships that she would largely keep from public view. The "roommates," as they dubbed themselves, not only had in common studies and activities but a particular family dynamic. "We were all first children and first daughters of high-achieving fathers . . . and beautiful mothers who stayed home," said Lurline Sampson Bickel, a San Francisco attorney. The fathers "wanted the daughters to occupy a position in life different than their own wives." The message was that "nobody was going to take care of you," she said.

Dianne, Lurline, Barbara Corneille, and Barbara Sokol all did their fair share of partying in Stanford's halcyon 1950s. But they also played active roles in campus political life and talked of how they "were going to save the world," in the words of one.

Sokol recalled her first impression of Dianne as "absolutely a raving beauty, with dark hair, big luminous eyes, perfect posture—every woman's dream of what she wanted to be." Dianne golfed, rode, played tennis, and drank beer on double dates on Friday nights at Rossotti's Alpine Beer Garden, an off-campus dive also known as "Zot's." Unlike several of her roommates, she dated only one person at a time and "had very good taste in men," said one friend.

She was pinned to Leon King, the center on Stanford's 1952 Rose Bowl team, which lost to Illinois 40-7. King would later become a Presbyterian minister. His relationship with the nineteen-year-old Dianne was a source of friction between her and Dr. Goldman.

As a friend Dianne was warm, engaging, and nosy, with a predilection for neatness, an underdeveloped sense of humor, and an episodic "enormous temper." "She has no sense of irony," said one roommate. "When you teased her, you had to tell her, 'Dianne, that's a joke.' Then she would laugh." Another recalled her as "a very meticulous person—God forbid if anything should be out of place."

Friends also recall her idolization of her father. "She adored Leon, a major role model, and was strongly connected to this man. She talked about him a lot," said Cynthia Wilder, a classmate who would play a cameo role in the first crisis of Dianne's adult life. "Her mother was very troubled and she was terribly frustrated by her mother's treatment," she said. "She was constantly being hurt and did not understand why. Her mother was erratic and rejecting, an attractive-looking woman, powerful in her own way."

In the summers Dianne worked as a model at I. Magnin department store and as the riding instructor at the fashionable Huntington Lake Camp for girls. One year she spent several months traveling with a group through Europe and, in Spain, saw "the enormous suffering of the people and the tremendous wealth of the Church," which left her disillusioned about Catholicism. "Religion was very confusing to Dianne," a roommate recalled.

Dianne majored in history and minored in speech and drama. An undistinguished academic, she carried a grade average that hovered around C+.

After she got into public life, Dianne would describe for countless profilers an epiphany that she said pushed her into government and politics. She came to college considering a career in medicine, she would say, but "got a D in genetics" her freshman year. Then she got "an A+ in American Political Thought," and that led to a life in public service. But her college transcript shows that while she did get a D in freshman general biology, she never got an A+ in anything. The only A's she received in four years were for courses in physical education, the "World Communist Movement," and "Marriage and Family."

Ventures into the practical side of politics were more successful. From the beginning Dianne emphasized pragmatism and moderation over ideology or settled beliefs. In an early race for a dorm office, her "first political consultant" was Lurline. "I remember us sitting on the bed, putting my hair up in curlers, talking about her speech the next day," her roommate said. "Dianne talked about effectiveness in office. Gender was not a factor and it's not a political factor naturally with Dianne."

Her successful senior-year campaign for campus vice president brought her the highest office to which women then aspired, given the unfavorable gender gap for women among the student body. Even before that race, she joined the daughter of onetime San Francisco mayor and congressman Jack Shelley to lead a campaign that rejuvenated the campus Young Democrat club.

"My father used to make great fun of us. He'd say, 'Dianne and six Democrats are having a cell meeting.' We were very small in numbers, but I got fascinated because the history showed it really was the party that responded to people's needs, and that saw government had a role in remedying some basic needs where the private sector couldn't."

It was through the Young Democrats that she met Hadley Roff, then the editor of the *Stanford Daily,* who would reenter her life at a critical time years later and go on to become her most loyal political adviser. "She was very earnest, very hardworking, very involved," Roff recalled.

As a leader of student government she provided a glimpse at her later political style, working with great energy on the nuts and bolts of social functions and big events on campus. "I always volunteered," Dianne said. "And I always found that if I didn't, I felt sort of guilty." When Barbara Sokol, a leader of the international student center, wanted money for a dance program for Asian, Indian, and other foreign students to learn the foxtrot and the jitterbug, it was Dianne who pushed the appropriation through the student government.

When Barbara Corneille was put in charge of decorating the student union for an event, she went before the council to ask for $1,800 but ran into trouble because the color scheme she had chosen was orange. The future centrist U.S. senator came to her rescue. "Orange was not what was popular, but it was what was on sale," her roommate said. "When people started to question my taste, Dianne spoke up and said, 'We're not here to tell Barbara what colors to use—we're here to debate the appropriation.'"

Upon her graduation, Dianne bought herself a year in resolving the conflict between career and family by winning an internship from the San Francisco–based Coro Foundation, which placed young people in political and government offices to gain practical experience. In applying, she told the interviewers that she had "planned to run for the Board of Supervisors this fall—but feels that a year with the Coro Foundation would be well worth the delay."

In a recommendation letter to the foundation, Stanford's dean of students wrote that her "only possible handicap is her idealism in political matters, which sometimes leads her to make judgments which seem a bit immature." One Coro board member wrote that she "seems to go too many directions at once," a sentiment echoed by a political science professor who wrote that "her one fault is to undertake more than anyone could handle."

Dianne's application contains a clear and early statement of her sweeping political ambitions, unusual for the times. "My future plans center around public affairs in that I plan to run for political office on a local and possibly a national level," the twenty-one-year-old woman wrote in the spring of 1955. "My experience in student government at Stanford, plus my observations of the need for stronger and better organized Democratic leadership within this state have turned thoughts into confirmed ambitions."

Her ambitions would soon be sorely tested.

3

FALSE START

Develop staying power.

—*Dianne Feinstein's Rules for Getting Ahead*

In JANUARY 1956, San Francisco district attorney Tom Lynch put Dianne's continuing education in the hands of a brash thirty-three-year-old prosecutor in his office named Jack Berman. She had just begun a stint at the Hall of Justice as part of her Coro internship and, after the introduction, Berman recalled, Lynch turned away with an optimistic prediction. "This will be a great match," he said.

He could not have been more wrong.

As Dianne stepped out of the sanctum of Stanford, fresh with hope and promise for the future, she quickly stumbled in the real world, repeating the painful pattern of her own parents' troubled union. Within a month of their meeting Dianne and Jack were involved in a whirlwind romance that would lead to an ill-fated elopement. Soon after the birth of a daughter, the marriage crumbled and, before the child was three, ended in long-lived bitterness.

In the years before *The Feminine Mystique* posited "the problem that has no name," giving voice to the anger and frustration of women trapped in conflict between demands of family and desire for career, Dianne confronted divorce, single motherhood, and the thwarted drives of an ambitious woman. With the persistence and industry with which her father had used a "will of iron" and "mind over matter" to achieve a brilliant medical career despite his family trouble, his oldest daughter resolutely overcame the wreckage of her marriage as she began to pursue her own chosen profession.

In the late 1950s and early 1960s, Dianne gained firsthand, practical experience in the retail bazaar of San Francisco politics, making contacts and forming relationships that would become crucial in years to come. The young single mother also set forth on a host of other pathways, from athletics to the arts, as she sought solutions to the social and financial conundrums faced by an independent woman struggling with an uncertain future in tumultuous times.

"It took me a long time to get a stable base," Dianne said, looking back. "The wonderful thing about life thirty years later is that you can choose to marry or not marry, to have a family or not, to work, to combine them both or just to have a career, and no one looks askance at you . . . In those days, if you got involved you got married."

JOHN MONAGHAN couldn't believe his luck.

A working-class Irish street politician, Monaghan had earned his reputation as a guy who could turn out campaign workers by organizing veterans after World War II, occasionally plying them with a taste from behind the seventy-foot-long bar of Monaghan's Ten Club, the saloon he owned and operated in the Mission district. In the 1950s the Ten Club was a mandatory stop for politicians seeking votes or favor with the blue-collar Catholic families who then populated residential neighborhoods that thirty years later would become predominantly gay.

At the time, even national notables like Senator Estes Kefauver and J. Howard McGrath, Harry Truman's attorney general, made Monaghan's saloon their second courtesy stop in San Francisco, right after calling on the archbishop. It was a bastion of support for Mayor Elmer Robinson, whom Monaghan and his cronies had helped elect in 1951, a few years before they helped defeat an up-and-comer named Phil Burton. Burton would go on to become San Francisco's most powerful politician as a member of Congress, but in his first state legislative race Monaghan and the boys helped beat him with a candidate who died a month before the election and was reposed in Holy Cross Cemetery when he won his final campaign.

"I'd made a lot of friends and could deliver the Eureka Valley and Duboce" neighborhoods, Monaghan remembered in a cigarette-and-whiskey raspy voice. "We could turn out the vote, but I stayed out of the papers. If you wanted those votes, you'd have to come into the Ten Club or we'd knock your cock off."

In the fall of 1955 the club was an active center in the campaign to succeed Robinson as mayor. Their candidate was a Democratic war-horse named George Reilly, who was in a battle with Republican businessman and supervisor George Christopher for the officially nonpartisan job of mayor. Reilly's camp had gotten a call from the Coro Foundation, asking if the candidate would take on a young intern named Dianne Goldman to give her a taste of what politics was all about. Tall and striking, she wore bright-red lipstick and had sparkling eyes. With her Sacred Heart manner and Presidio Terrace background, she seemed a bit of a snob, Monaghan thought, but "she kept it in pretty good."

"I didn't know Coro from a doughnut, but there was this good-looking young lady who was very affable and very nice, so we put her in the car with Reilly," he recalled.

A few months out of college, Dianne could not have been farther from the student councils of Stanford. No amount of Young Democrat caucusing or world-government colloquy could compare to the sights, smells, and tastes of politics as practiced on the streets of San Francisco. Perhaps the most international of American cities, San Francisco functions politically like a tiny nation-state. Both a city and a county, poised on just forty-nine square miles of peninsula, San Francisco cradles between its bay and the Pacific dozens of distinct neighborhoods, each like a little village with its own center of commerce, ethnic flavor, and, often, its own weather. Now, riding in George Reilly's campaign car every night, from Chinatown candidates' nights to Castro district church bingos, Dianne saw firsthand the spice and infinite variety of the city where she was born and raised, people and places that even Uncle Morrie hadn't showed her. "We worked to all hours of the night," Dianne recalled. "It was the rough and tumble old days of San Francisco politics. I learned how much I loved it."

The boys at the Ten Club had to hand it to her: the girl was okay despite her wealthy background. Without complaint she answered phones, stuffed envelopes, and did the other drudge work of the campaign. One night, when she saw some Christopher hacks tearing down Reilly's signs, a time-honored guerrilla tactic in city politics, Dianne's sense of fair play was offended. "Not only did I just go in and tell George Reilly, I picked up the phone and called George Christopher myself," she said. "Here I am, twenty-two years old: 'Mr. Christopher, my name is Dianne Goldman and I'm the Coro intern assigned to George Reilly's campaign and your people are taking down his signs and it's wrong.' And he got furious at me." Monaghan and the boys had a big laugh over that one.

But her political naïveté could backfire too. One night, with Monaghan performing duties of what would now be called an advance man, Reilly and his entourage moved through a typically crowded schedule and ended up in North Beach after midnight. They stopped in at the Hungry I café, where the candidate was warmly greeted and his entourage admitted free. "In those days, there was a lot of cash floating around campaigns," Monaghan recalled. The surfeit of cash was due in part to enthusiastic political supporters making spontaneous, on-the-spot contributions to the cause. Although technically illegal, such donations were made only in the interests of good government, of course.

On this night, a theatrical agent jumped up from his table as Reilly came in the door, walked over, and thrust five hundred dollars in twenty-dollar bills into the candidate's hands. No one much noticed or cared, except for Dianne. She watched the scene with shock and disbelief, mouth ajar, Monaghan remembered.

"Christ, she's going to pee in her pants," he thought, as visions of last-minute indictments and scandalous newspaper headlines raced through his head. But Reilly also noticed his young intern's surprised expression. With the practiced politician's quickness and timing, he turned at once to hand the money to his advance man. "Monaghan," he said, "see that that's properly recorded in the morning."

Dianne relaxed, and Monaghan breathed a sigh of relief.

ON ELECTION DAY Christopher overwhelmed Reilly to become mayor, but Dianne had little time to nurse any disappointment. After the holidays she moved on to a study project about the state criminal justice system, which began at the San Francisco district attorney's office. A few years later she would use the report on criminal justice that was produced during her internship to help her secure an appointment from Governor Edmund G. "Pat" Brown to a state job. But then, the focus was on more personal matters, specifically Jack Berman.

Berman, to whom Dianne was introduced that January morning, had joined the DA's office in 1947 when it was still run by Pat Brown, who had since embarked on a career in statewide politics. Eleven years older than Dianne, he had a sophisticated manner that made him very different from the college boys she'd dated at Stanford. With an easy grin and a sharp mind, Berman liked to squire beautiful women to the nighttime haunts of North Beach, where his knowledge of food, wine, travel, and all the inside dope about politics, cops, and courts made him a popular figure.

Born and raised in San Francisco, he had graduated from the University of California at the age of eighteen and gone on to Boalt Hall law school. He served as a Navy ensign during the war and as a lawyer in war-criminal trials that followed in the Philippines.

In the DA's office, Berman had a reputation as a hard-edged and flamboyant courtroom performer, with good convictions in some high-profile cases. Philosophically opposed to capital punishment, he unblinkingly would demand the death penalty for those whose heinous crimes he prosecuted, sparing no histrionic language in arguments to the jury.

He made headlines in a 1952 case with a forceful prosecution of an eighteen-year-old youth charged with the murder of a high school sophomore in a park adjoining Mission High School. The young man, Berman dramatically told the jury, was a "cold, callous, indifferent sadistic killer, who smoked cigarettes while the ground of Mission Park was still wet with her blood."

His prosecution of a grandmother for killing her husband, a California Highway Patrol officer whom she claimed had beaten and abused her, so inflamed the woman's twenty-one-year-old son that he leaped across the courtroom railing after a guilty verdict was announced and assaulted Berman, leaving him with a bloody lip. "I listened to Berman tell lies about my mother for three weeks," the tearful man told reporters after the incident. "I couldn't stand it any longer. I just blew up."

Now, as Dianne watched and listened to Jack prepare for another big case, sparks flew between them. "I had always known the all-American boy type, the athletes. And Jack was kind of the first departure from that. I found it interesting at the time," she said.

"She was infatuated with me," recalled Berman, "and I found it easy to be in love with her."

Dianne, who liked to date one person at a time, was much taken with Jack. Soon after they met she got a call from another young attorney in town, Quentin Kopp. Twenty years later Kopp would become her political archenemy, but now he was freshly arrived from New York and searching for a "nice Jewish girl" to date, he recalled. Given her name by a friend, he rang up Dianne. She said she couldn't go out because her father was sick. She said she would like to meet him, though, and invited him to Presidio Terrace.

"It was a helluva house," said Kopp, who has a beanpole for a body and a foghorn for a voice. "She offered me coffee or tea. Christ, I'm from Dartmouth, I wanted a drink. But I opted for the tea and we talked earnestly about world events," he added. "And she kept asking me, 'Do you know Jack Berman?' She seemed to consider him a great legal guru."

DIANNE REFUSES TO DISCUSS publicly the details of her marriage to Berman. "I don't want to talk about that," she said.

Berman's calendars for the period show the speed and social whirl of the affair. For their first date on January 28, his handwritten entry reads, "Dianne." By Valentine's Day he was simply writing "D."

He took her to the symphony and the opera, to the theater for *Silk Stockings,* to the movies for *Witness for the Prosecution,* and to North Beach for Mort Sahl. He took her to meet his parents over lunch and then lunched with Dr. Goldman and his pal Benny Lom at the Lake Merced golf club. He helped her find an apartment, and she treated him to a surprise party for his thirty-fourth birthday in March. They went to fine restaurants, to Nino's and Veltri's, the Papagao Room and Le Trianon. Everywhere they went, the owners, maître d's, and barkeeps would greet them with, "Hi, Jack, how are you" and usher the couple to a good table. "Jack in those days was very soigné," said Dianne's sister Lynn. "She fell in love just like that."

That summer, romance went on hold for a few weeks as Dianne's uncle Morrie went on trial on federal tax evasion charges. A few years before, the government had come after the legendary Sacramento lobbyist Artie Samish, after Samish foolishly posed for the cover of *Collier's* magazine holding a ventriloquist's dummy to show how he ran the California legislature. Uncle Morrie, a pal of Samish's, had been questioned in connection with the investigation but had refused to cooperate, friends recalled. Now he too was under indictment, charged with cheating the federal government out of $45,808 by siphoning a large amount of income into a secret bank account to hide it from tax collectors. At his trial the government proved that the money, which the clothier Goldman wrote off as "wool expenses" on his tax returns, was actually used to cover gambling losses.

On the stand Morrie freely admitted gambling "to a considerable extent. I was a loser, sir," he sorrowfully added, insisting that while he was guilty of "loose bookkeeping," he was not a tax cheat.

But in July he was found guilty on seven counts of tax evasion and later sentenced to six months in jail and a fine of $7,000. His conviction was splashed on the front page of the newspaper, but Dianne remembered that "he didn't want any of us to know. He was deeply humiliated by it," she said.

Dianne, then twenty-three, recalled that "I didn't understand, really, what was happening . . . the impact of it." But Jack remembered her speaking up for the uncle who had introduced her to politics, and her loyalty to the "stand-up guy" endeared her to him more. In the fall, on a ferry boat ride on the bay at sunset, Jack proposed and Dianne accepted.

Now all they had to do was tell her family.

MRS. GOLDMAN RITUALLY DISAPPROVED of the men in her daughters' lives, and she found forceful ways of expressing her displeasure. As a teenager, Lynn once quarreled with her about a date, then stormed out of the house, followed by her mother. Starting the car to back out of the driveway, Lynn checked the rearview mirror and saw Betty lying down behind the back wheels. Three times she got out of the car and dragged her mother out of the way, finally walking her back to the house. When Lynn got home that night, she found her mother comatose from another suicide attempt.

With such behavior as a backdrop, Dianne was faced with breaking the news of her impending marriage to her parents. First they told Jack's folks, who instantly approved, and planned to tell the Goldmans on Thanksgiving Day, when they would all be at Presidio Terrace for dinner.

With the family gathered around the holiday table, Dianne and Jack informed them of their intentions. Betty erupted with an angry tantrum, flinging insults at Jack. Dianne and her sisters "fled the room in tears," Berman recalled, and were trailed by Dr. Goldman. Berman tried to "settle everyone down" before he excused himself and left the house, he said.

He was surprised a few days later when Dianne's mother telephoned and, nice as could be, invited him to lunch. Not quite knowing what to expect, he showed up at the Plaza Hotel on Union Square and had a pleasant lunch with Betty. She was charming, except for the fact that she spent the lunch "excoriating and dumping on Dianne."

The following Friday, Dianne and Jack eloped to Los Angeles. After stopping at the bank and at City Hall for a marriage license, they caught an afternoon flight south. A rabbi in San Francisco had refused to marry them, and Jack arranged for them to be wed in the vestibule of a temple in Los Angeles.

In the temple but not of the temple, the ceremony was witnessed that Sunday by a pal of Jack's and by Cynthia Wilder, Dianne's old friend from Stanford, who opened her home for a small reception afterward. "I'd heard all about Jack," she said. "He was older and worldly, a mover and a shaker."

Worried that her mother would somehow manage to block the marriage at the last moment, Berman recalled, Dianne did not let her family know until the ceremony and reception were over and she was in San Diego, where Jack carried her across the threshold of a hotel room.

In the hours before she learned her daughter had eloped, Betty worked in the garden on Presidio Terrace with Lynn, as the girl's French poodle, Pierre, played nearby. Despite her pleasant, motherly mood, Betty seemed distracted and kept saying, "There's something wrong, I just know there's something wrong," Lynn said.

Dianne and Jack used his two-week vacation from the DA's office for a honeymoon in Mexico. At a resort called Las Cruces near Cabo San Lucas, they sunned and swam and were flown by the owner to a spot called Palmilla for some deep-sea fishing.

At one point, Jack thought to show his bride a more exotic side of Mexican nightlife. Several years before, he and a buddy had visited an establishment in Mexico City run by a madam called La Bandita, who was said to have been a lieutenant under Pancho Villa. Grander than a commercial house, La Bandita's place was a fashionable salon, said Jack, where prominent poets, bullfighters, and the muralist Diego Rivera had philosophical discussions over dinner and a gentleman could bring a lady on a date, or select one for the evening.

The newlyweds hired a cab and Jack instructed the driver to take them to La Bandita's. They soon were lost. The cab drove up to a house that didn't look like the right place and wasn't. When Jack went in to check it out, he said, the driver and his girlfriend sympathized with Dianne in Spanish, telling her it was terrible for her husband to do such a thing on her honeymoon. She tried to explain that they had it all wrong.

Dianne's family, while not happy about the marriage, tried to put the best face on it. Dr. Goldman, who disapproved more quietly than his wife, and Betty, concerned about appearances, threw a reception for the newlyweds with more than two hundred guests on Presidio Terrace.

"Leon Goldmans tell daughter's marriage," the Chronicle's social-page headline read on December 13, 1956. "Dr. and Mrs. Leon Goldman of this city are announcing the December 2 marriage of their daughter Dianne to assistant district attorney Jack Berman," the article said, briefly describing the Los Angeles ceremony. "The newlyweds currently are on a honeymoon in Mexico and on their return, will be honored by the bride's parents at a reception to be given at the Goldmans' Presidio Terrace home."

Betty insisted that Dianne wear a white dress for the occasion. After a quarrel, her daughter agreed. "She had to say the family approved, the little family is still sitting in the little house very happy," Lynn said of her mother. "But there was no joy in that occasion."

RETURNING TO SAN FRANCISCO, the newlyweds settled into a house they bought on an elevated cul-de-sac in the city's Upper Ashbury district. Equipped with a copper-hooded fireplace, the living room commanded a splendid view of the Golden Gate and of Temple Emanu-el, located just a few blocks from Presidio Terrace.

Among the lesser charms of their new home were seventy-one stone steps leading from the street to the front door. These became only seventy-one of many things over which they would quarrel.

With Jack back at the DA's office, Dianne got a job with the California Industrial Relations Department, helping to set up boards to determine a new minimum wage for women and minors in the state, and worked until late spring. On July 31, eight months after the elopement, their daughter, Katherine Anne, was born at the UC hospital.

The baby was beautiful, with dark hair like Dianne's. But her cries and needs clearly signaled the choice her mother had made of family over career. Jack was still the man about town, while Dianne tried to play the housewife, friends recalled. But her heart was never in it. 'They were a strange combination," said a mutual friend who visited their home for dinner. "Jack was an old-fashioned swinger type and Dianne was a prim presence. I could never understand that marriage."

When the baby was six months old Dianne turned away one day to get a fresh diaper. While her back was turned Kathy rolled over, all the way onto the floor, breaking her leg in the process. The infant was in a cast up to her hip for several weeks, which only added to the domestic tension, as Dianne wearied of climbing the cursed steps with a baby and the groceries.

One evening she cooked a pork roast for some friends of Jack's who came to dinner. When the center of the roast came out nearly raw, her husband with a smile suggested she put applesauce on it. Dianne stormed out of the room, which now happened with some frequency. "Jack was very stimulating intellectually, but there were evenings when he wasn't home. Dianne never liked housework and never liked to cook," said Dianne's old friend Barbara Isackson.

They employed a housekeeper to help out, while Dianne took a stab at getting involved in politics. Leaving the scenes at home behind the door, she would put on her public face and, with Kathy in the stroller, go out and meet the neighbors on behalf of various causes.

When she learned of a developer's plans to build apartments amid a twelve-acre stand of eucalyptus on Mount Sutro, trees visible from the apartment where she had lived as a little girl, Dianne circulated petitions and helped set off one of the early big development versus preservationist fights in San Francisco. From this 1959 battle, the dynamic would spread throughout the city's neighborhoods and shape its politics for the next thirty years.

One of the neighbors she met in that controversy was another active young mother named Sue Bierman. Bierman also had a keen interest in politics, but from the more traditional point of view that a woman's role was as a behind-the-scenes campaign worker. Three decades later, Bierman would run successfully for the city board of supervisors with the endorsement of Dianne, who was by then a candidate for the United States Senate.

During that campaign, Bierman would recall an evening in the 1950s when she invited Dianne and several other neighbors over to meet a Democratic candidate for the state assembly. The next morning, Dianne took Kathy to Sue's for coffee and to thank her for the invitation.

"What did you think of him? I thought he was pretty good," Bierman said of the candidate.

"He was all right, but I could do better," Dianne answered, surprising her friend with the passion in her voice.

"What do you mean?" Sue said. "Women don't run for office."

Dianne pounded the kitchen table with her fist and said, "This one does."

THE LITTLE HOUSE with the seventy-one steps wasn't big enough for two big egos, and things with Jack went downhill fast. It wasn't long after Kathy's birth that he found himself locked out so often that a neighbor friend had a key to his downstairs apartment made for Jack, he said, so that he could spend the night.

Dianne told friends she felt buried, misled, and stultified. Jack found her moods and outbursts increasingly unbearable. Amid frequent separations, they made stabs at reconciliation, visiting counselors and therapists, Berman said. Leon, detesting such pseudoscience, denounced it to Dianne as "a claptrap" while Jack spoke of the "Svengali hold" his father-in-law had on his wife.

After too many scenes and separations, the marriage broke when she refused to go on a Hawaiian vacation they had planned with another couple. Jack went with the others alone and, shortly after his return, they decided to divorce.

"I had enough of her temper. I was a controversial trial attorney and I wasn't interested in a tempestuous relationship at home. I didn't want to litigate at home," Berman, who remarried and became a state superior court judge, said thirty years later.

At the time of the divorce, Jack had left the DA's office for private practice. A street-smart lawyer, he decided to file the divorce papers late on a Friday afternoon when they might avoid getting the news published in the papers. It was April Fool's Day, 1960. As luck would have it, though, Berman bumped into a reporter with whom he was friendly on his way to file the documents. The next day's paper carried a brief item headlined "Divorce granted attorney Berman and his wife."

In the settlement, they agreed to joint custody of Kathy, who would live with Dianne while he had visitation rights. He would pay $100 a month child support and provide for Kathy's college education, plus $500 a month alimony to Dianne through March 1963.

At twenty-six, Dianne Goldman Berman, who had been trained "to assume positions of influence and power," found herself a divorced single mother when such a thing was still the stuff of gossip. She lived with her daughter in a rented house in a middle-class neighborhood. Kathy rose early in the morning, much earlier than her mother, who is not a morning person. One day the little girl clambered over the bed, grabbed one of her mother's favorite bright-red lipsticks, and drew all over the wall. Dianne hung a picture to hide it.

IN THE EARLY 1960s, few people used the term *day-care center,* and single mothers had few choices for help outside their families.

Dianne's alimony and child support payments from Jack paid for groceries and the $200-a-month rent on a three-bedroom Mediterranean-style house in the comfortable neighborhood of St. Francis Wood, with some left over for baby-sitters. Dianne also enrolled Kathy in a parent cooperative nursery school where, her daughter recalled, she "would always get other mothers to cover for her."

Torn by the conflicts between caring for her child, finding self-expression, and pursuing a career, she struck out in several directions. Even before the divorce Dianne had toyed with the notion of an acting career. Now she explored the idea more seriously.

She had enrolled in the Actor's Lab, a school for prospective players founded by an actress named Mara Alexander who taught the Stanislavsky method. At the age of fourteen in New York, Alexander had climbed up a fire escape and jumped through the window of producer David Belasco's office. She achieved her mission of getting a job and worked with many Broadway stars before opening her school in San Francisco.

"The method" is the science of theater art, an acting technique in which players build "the life of the human spirit" by isolating and focusing powerful feelings, systematically training the mind, will, and emotions. "There are no accidents in art, only the fruits of long labor," preached the famed Soviet director Konstantin Stanislavsky, a lesson that Dianne would apply, not in the theater, but in another career that would be marked by her emotional performance in real-life drama. "There are dramatic moments" in politics, she said. "It didn't hurt."

That would come later, however. In the early 1960s the budding actress failed to recapture the acclaim that had met her Sacred Heart theatrical efforts.

Shortly before the divorce, Dianne appeared in a local production of Ibsen's *The Master Builder,* playing the role of Hilda, the young woman who spurs the aging builder, Halvard Solness, to make towers and "castles in the air." Much of the drama focuses on the unrealized love affair of the two characters.

But Dianne's portrayal of the ingenue was panned by the San Francisco critic Paine Knickerbocker, who complained that the director "has permitted the graceful Miss Goldman to jar the atmosphere created by the others rather than to enrich it. In her attempts to present the coltish exuberance of youth, she becomes an attractive young girl trying to act like a young girl and her gestures are excessive and out of tune," he wrote, describing the antithesis of a successful Stanislavsky characterization.

Undaunted by the criticism, Dianne pursued the possibility of the stage. Not long after her divorce she flew to New York to browse the want ads and check out jobs and apartment prices, attending eight Broadway plays in five days in between her rounds. "I couldn't afford to do it," she said. "I would have had to work during the day, been able to do some off-Broadway at night. I would have had to have someone to take care of Katherine. By the time I finished with rent and baby-sitting or somebody living in, whatever work I could get there, it wasn't enough."

Back in San Francisco she continued to play the Renaissance woman, studying folk guitar with TV personality Laura Weber, then dropping by Sue Bierman's house to pass on her weekly lesson. "She was really interested in the arts," Bierman recalled. "That dramatic training and experience gave her confidence and helped her politically."

Dianne, who gave up riding when she went to Stanford, now took sailing lessons and encountered some thrills she'd never experienced from the back of a horse. She would take Kathy out on the tricky waters of the bay and drop anchor near Angel Island State Park, not far from Alcatraz. There she would secure the little girl on the boat and dive off into the frigid water. "I can't believe I did this, but I'd take her out in this little boat with me and we'd sail over to Angel Island and have a picnic or something," she said. "I used to trail a line behind the boat. I'd dive off the boat, catch the line, and pull myself back up on the boat."

In the spring of 1960 she lost the wind and got locked "in irons" while sailing a sixteen-foot sloop, and started drifting out the Golden Gate with the tide. Frantically, she waved a distress signal and was towed back in by a racing sloop owned by a man named Gene Gartland, who would become one of her closest friends and advisers. A year after rescuing her, Gartland got stuck when the wind died on the bay; Dianne by then had learned to sail, happened by, and returned the favor.

Through it all, she dabbled in politics. She involved herself in civil rights protests, working on campaigns for local candidates and for John Kennedy in 1960, building valuable contacts for the future. In the JFK campaign, she met Ann Alanson, a Democratic National Committeewoman and prominent fund-raiser who would become one of Dianne's key early supporters. "Dianne just walked in the door one day," she said. "I felt she had political ambitions. Besides being gorgeous, she had the brains."

She also met a bright young Democratic organizer named Rudy Nothenberg. Two decades in the future he would serve her loyally as a top City Hall staff member; now, he ate sandwiches that she prepared as a volunteer in a state assembly campaign. "She was enthused, bright, willing, upper-class, and well put together," Nothenberg remembered.

In the early 1960s, San Francisco, like other American cities, was fervid with civil rights activity. Blacks and whites together staged massive sit-ins at the elegant Palace Hotel and on the city's "Auto Row" on Van Ness Avenue, demanding equal access to jobs. Dianne made friends with a community street worker named Percy Pinkney, helping to raise money for his organization, which worked with gang members from tough neighborhoods like the Fillmore and Hunters Point. He would help her gather support in minority communities during her first statewide race.

In 1961 a builder of a new subdivision near Sutro Forest refused to show a model home to a flamboyant young black attorney named Willie Brown, who would go on to become one of the most powerful politicians in California. When word of the redlining against Brown hit the papers, Dianne showed up at a big protest at the subdivision site with Kathy in a stroller. "The picket line was slow and there was an incline and the stroller ran into the heels of the person in front of me, who was Terry Francois," she recalled. Francois was a firebrand attorney and leader of the local NAACP who soon would become another of Dianne's mentors.

And, within a few months, she would meet the most important one of all.

4

WORK AND LOVE

Specialize.

—Dianne Feinstein's Rules for Getting Ahead

ONE AFTERNOON IN THE FALL of 1961 Dianne was at home, grumbling about Kathy's morning habits to a former Stanford roommate, when the telephone rang. "She was complaining about how early Kathy always woke her up, how she liked to get up to watch the garbage truck," said her old friend Lurline Bickel. "Then the governor called."

It was Pat Brown on the line, and from Dianne's big smile and the way she kept saying "Yes, Governor," it was clear to Lurline that her friend's luck was about to change. The governor had called to offer Dianne a seat on the five-member board that set prison terms and parole conditions for women felons in California, a patronage post that offered her both financial independence and a chance to make a start in public service.

Over the next five years she made the most of it. Immersing herself in the policies and practices of the criminal justice system, she built a portfolio of expertise on a high-profile political issue that would launch her into elective office in San Francisco. Along the way, she would encounter for the first time some of the most difficult questions in public life—crime and punishment, murder and abortion—issues that would continue to shape politics in California over the next three decades.

Her entry into public life in the early 1960s coincided with a major turning point in her personal affairs. Shortly after accepting Brown's offer, she met a courtly neurosurgeon named Bertram Feinstein who would become the love of her life. Through triumphs and tragedies to come, she would take and keep his name, and be encouraged, nurtured, and supported by him in the formative years of her quest to make political history.

It got started because of Kathy.

SEVERAL WEEKS AFTER her call from the governor, Dianne took her daughter to a Christmas party at the elegant home of June Degnan, a socialite friend. At one point in the evening, the four-year-old wandered off among the wool-suited legs and velvet dresses of the crowd. Dianne finally found her in animated conversation with a handsome man with salt-and-pepper hair who was sitting on a window seat.

In his well-tailored British tweed suit, Dr. Bert Feinstein had an engaging continental air that Dianne found immediately attractive, despite the fact that he was nearly twenty years older than she. Although she did not know him, he recognized her right away. Nearly ten years before, Feinstein, a Canadian-born neurosurgeon, had been in the office of Dr. Leon Goldman interviewing for a teaching position at UC when Dianne happened to be visiting her father. Feinstein, a bachelor, was taken by her looks but put off by the fact that she was too young. Now the girl had grown into a striking young woman and Bert Feinstein's interest was piqued again. "It turned out that Bert had met me, which I did not remember, in my father's office when I was eighteen," said Dianne. "And he thought of asking me out then, but he told me later he thought I was 'jailbait.'"

A native of Winnipeg, Manitoba, Feinstein had been in his second year of medical school the year Dianne was born. He'd practiced briefly in Canada before going to England, where he spent World War II as a surgical resident at the Radcliffe Infirmary at Oxford. When the war ended, he went to Berkeley, where he lectured in anatomy and neurosurgery before becoming an assistant professor at UC in the early 1950s.

Now he was assistant chief of surgery at San Francisco's respected Mt. Zion hospital. Charming, warm, and witty, he was every inch a distinguished gentleman. His first job had been playing the piano for silent movies, and he had an extensive jazz repertoire heavy on Fats Waller tunes. He swam and played tennis regularly, collected vintage automobiles, had abiding interests in fine art and in Japan, and showed a knack for keeping people loose and laughing.

He set his sights on Dianne. A few days after the party, he called her for a date. He suggested dinner. She suggested lunch. He suggested a late lunch. She accepted and he said he'd pick her up around 7:00 P.M.

Later, he would tell Kathy that he took Dianne that night to a romantic French restaurant in Marin County, just north of the Golden Gate Bridge. After a few glasses of wine, he confessed that he was in love with her and proposed marriage.

"You're crazy," Dianne answered.

"I didn't ask you for a clinical opinion," he told her. "I asked you to marry me."

Dianne demurred. But while barhopping with her old friend Barbara Isackson not long afterward, she talked about how much she liked the soft-spoken doctor. "I said, 'You don't want somebody who's so old,'" her friend recalled. "But Bert gave her everything she wanted. He was a lot like her father."

In early January 1962, a month after the couple met, Dianne was preparing to fly to southern California to start her new job on the women's prison board. She was having a hard time. She was upset about leaving Kathy for ten days, and Kathy was inconsolable. Bert helpfully offered to take Dianne to lunch and then drive her to the airport.

On a previous date, he had picked her up in an old Chevrolet that Dianne recalled as so shabby that it had "penicillin growing in the backseat." Later she learned that he liked to buy and restore old cars and it was one of his works in progress. On this day, he drove her to the airport in a gray 1943 Phantom II Rolls Royce.

But all the way to southern California, Dianne's stomach was in knots with misgivings and self-doubt, worrying about the job, her daughter, and the difficulty of trying to balance family and career. She was distraught by the time she arrived at the Biltmore Hotel, where her "state-rate" room had a view of a brick wall. She checked into the hotel, went to her room, and, twenty minutes later, was surprised to hear the phone ring. It was Bert Feinstein calling, just to see how she was doing.

"That broke the barrier," Dianne remembered. "I was very lonely and I'd never been away from Katherine. I was away for the rest of the week and he called every night and we probably talked for two hours a night on the phone. And when I came back, I knew him. It was a relationship. We just broke all the barriers on the telephone."

WHEN PAT BROWN informed his staff in Sacramento that he planned to appoint Dianne to the $600-a-month post on the women's prison board, legal affairs aide Bill Coblentz was not the only one who objected. "Who is she?" Coblentz, an attorney who would become one of San Francisco's most influential power brokers, remembered asking Brown. "A woman, and a woman with little or no experience."

Years later Dianne would say that Brown appointed her because of her Coro internship report on the criminal justice system. The report, which was a group project produced by her entire Coro class, was duly sent to the governor in 1956. It may have helped Dianne get the job, but she also had a few other things going for her. The governor had been a patient of Dr. Goldman's and one of Brown's daughters had been a classmate of Dianne's at Sacred Heart. She also got a well-timed plug from Ann Alanson, the well-wired Democratic fund-raiser, among others who knew Brown.

So Brown was not dissuaded by the staff's objection to Dianne's appointment. "She's going to be great," he told Coblentz that day.

Dianne started her new job on Monday, January 15 and was identified in the meetings' minutes as "Dianne G. Berman." Within a few years she would start omitting her marriage to Jack from her campaign and official biographies, but for several years after the divorce she continued using his name.

Over the next five years Dianne would hear and take official actions in more than five thousand cases involving women caught in the machinery of the California criminal justice system. Working ten days a month, most often at the prison near Chino, in San Bernardino County, she would encounter a new world, a closed society of losers and wrongdoers, far from the openness and freedom of San Francisco and the havens of privilege where she had been educated. In institutional buildings surrounded by acres of southern California farmland and concertina wire, she would meet and mete out punishment for abortionists, alcoholics, arsonists, burglars, car boosters, check kiters, drug addicts, embezzlers, fences, forgers, murderers, scofflaws, swindlers, and thieves.

"I learned a great deal, about people, about motivation, about criminality," she said. "I certainly learned the police perspective. And I learned how to handle it so that I could make a decision. I was very apprehensive. I found sitting in judgment of another human being very difficult. I lost twenty-five pounds the first year on the board. At twenty-eight these are not easy decisions."

When Dianne started on the five-member board in 1962, it was known as the Board of Trust of the California Institution for Women. The name was later changed to the California Women's Board of Terms and Parole. The women's prison where it convened was the only institution for female felons in the state penal system and the largest such facility in the United States, with more than eight hundred inmates. Board members had responsibility for setting the actual term to be served by each woman who was convicted of a crime.

At the time, California's penal code was based on the indeterminate-sentence system. Under it, convicted criminals received a sentence after their trial that ranged from a minimum to a maximum period of incarceration. Responsibility for deciding how long a convict would actually serve rested with the prison boards, which had wide latitude in setting sentences of "not less than . . . nor more than. . . " according to the circumstances of each case.

In 1978, after Pat Brown's son, Jerry, became governor, criminal statutes were rewritten and a fixed-term, "determinate-sentence" system was put in place, fueling a long-running political controversy in California that would become an issue in Dianne's statewide campaigns in the 1990s.

Voting as a panel, Dianne and the other board members had broad powers to set the length of term, based on the crime, a prisoner's behavior, psychiatric evaluations, and other considerations. At periodic hearings, the board evaluated the fitness of women felons to be granted parole. It also established rules and conditions by which parolees could live in the community and returned women to prison for violating conditions of parole. The board also exercised authority over women while they were in prison, punishing them for infractions such as fighting, drug use, or talking to a friend at a time or place forbidden by the rules.

While serving on the parole board, Dianne viewed several important criminal justice issues differently than she would later. Years after leaving the board, her support for the death penalty would become a crucial part of her political image. But in those days she staunchly opposed capital punishment. "Though you may owe it to your fellowman to put a criminal out of commission, there is no moral or religious ground that gives you the right to terminate the life of another human being," she wrote at the time.

In the 1960s, capital punishment was a hotly debated issue in California. Governor Pat Brown, a foe of the death penalty, suffered serious political damage amid months of legal maneuvers on a clemency plea for Carryl Chessman, a robber-rapist known as "the red-light bandit." Chessman was finally executed in 1960 after high-profile, anti-death-penalty demonstrations that drew thousands of protesters, including Dianne, to San Quentin prison in Marin County, where California's gas chamber is located.

In 1967 murderer Aaron Mitchell was put to death, the last execution in the state until 1992, as a series of federal and state court rulings on the constitutionality of capital punishment halted the carrying out of the death penalty for twenty-five years. By then most Californians, including Dianne, had changed their minds and supported the death penalty.

The evolution of her views began on the prison board, she said, when she heard the case of a woman convicted of robbery who had carried an unloaded weapon for the crime. When Dianne asked why it was unloaded, the woman answered, "So I wouldn't panic, kill somebody, and get the death penalty." Although it would be several years before she would publicly change her position on the death penalty, the case would stick in her mind as she began to rethink her ideas on the issue.

Another difficult issue that she faced at the time, and that would transform political debate decades later, was abortion. Thirty years later she would campaign as a fierce protector of abortion rights as outlined in the Supreme Court's 1973 *Roe v. Wade* decision, presenting herself as a woman who had been "always pro-choice." But on the prison board she set sentences of between six months and five years for those convicted of performing abortions, many of whom were black or Hispanic according to prison records.

At the time, abortion was illegal in California and other states. As with the death penalty, though, there was furious public debate about the issue. With more than one million abortions estimated to have been performed each year in the country, botched abortions performed with coat hangers, castor oil, gasoline, and soap solution were reported to be the largest single cause of maternal death in the United States.

By 1962, the year Dianne joined the prison board, reform of abortion laws had been triggered by the American Law Institute. The institute approved a model penal code permitting hospital abortions under certain conditions, such as when pregnancy had been caused by rape or incest, endangered the life of the mother, or was likely to produce a defective baby. This code was embraced in California by abortion reformers who began trying to pass a modified abortion law in Sacramento. Their efforts failed until an epidemic of German measles (rubella) struck between 1963 and 1965.

The epidemic infected an estimated eighty-two thousand women during the first three months of their pregnancies, when the virus could make a fetus blind, deaf, deformed, or retarded.

As the number of rubella-defective babies born increased, some doctors' wives became infected and, by 1965, some hospitals began performing abortions on women with rubella. This brought the issue to a head. In 1966 nine doctors in San Francisco were charged with unprofessional conduct by the state Board of Medical Examiners, leading to an outcry by much of the medical establishment. The following year the legislature passed and Governor Ronald Reagan signed the state's Therapeutic Abortion Act, which began to ease state abortion laws established in 1872.

At the time of this debate in the 1960s, Dianne said, her political views on abortion had not "crystallized." At Stanford, she recalled, she

> contributed to somebody so they could get an abortion, without really knowing any of the details of where. Passing the plate. You never wanted to know too much because you knew it was against the law. There was a whole subterranean grapevine that existed, that you could get into if you had need of. But you asked no questions if you didn't.
>
> I personally never would have had one. I wouldn't have had one myself, but I always felt that there could be a circumstance, something could have happened and I could understand how it happens and I wouldn't cast any judgment. I don't think any less of a woman who does than one who does not.

But she recalled that as a member of the prison board she did not view abortion as a political issue. "These were, for the most part, when they came to state prison, all illegal back-alley abortionists. Many times, the women that they performed an abortion on suffered greatly. I really came to believe that the law is the law." Reflecting on the abortion cases she heard on the prison board, she said, "I had occasion to read the case histories and saw the morbidity and the mortality, and the suicides and the tragedies. And I think we can never go back to the way it was thirty years ago, because thousands of women are going to die unnecessarily."

ALTHOUGH DIANNE COULD BE with Kathy most of the time, she was still away from her young daughter for long stretches when the board was hearing cases. The Monday mornings when she flew to Los Angeles became a heartbreaking ritual, as her little girl sobbed and pressed her face to the leaded-glass window of her bedroom, screaming "Don't leave me" as her mother's car pulled away from the curb. "She was the only mother who was divorced and the only mother who worked," her daughter recalled. "I hated it."

Dianne sometimes left Kathy in the care of Lynn. The sisters "would have long talks about raising a child by yourself," Lynn recalled. Having been brought up in the painful atmosphere they had, Dianne "was very philosophical and thought it better to have one parent who loved you than a couple who was fighting all the time. She wanted to be the perfect mother and the perfect provider," her sister said.

Dianne also engaged the services of a series of live-in housekeepers to whom she entrusted Kathy, with occasional frightening consequences. One of her baby-sitters was an alcoholic who would begin drinking Dianne's liquor out of her china teacups almost as soon as she was left alone with the child. Kathy hated the woman and often fought with her. One day the baby-sitter slapped the child. The five-year-old girl, who had an independent streak of her own, ran away, down the block and across a busy thoroughfare to a gas station, where she called a friend of Dianne's to come and get her. "It was a very sad case. I had to let her go," said Dianne.

If things were sometimes rocky with Kathy, they went more smoothly with Bert. "Bert just worshiped her," a mutual friend remembered. "With him, Dianne became a very capricious little girl. He gave her everything she wanted. He was tender, understanding, loving. Whatever her whim, her likes, her dislikes, he was there giving and giving in."

When Dianne was home, Bert was often around, with early mixed reviews from Kathy. One morning she asked her mother, "Who is that man?"

"What man?" Dianne answered vaguely.

"The one whose feet are sticking out under the shower curtain," Kathy said.

When Bert invited Dianne on a weekend away in Carmel, on the spectacular Monterey Peninsula south of San Francisco, Kathy was left at home. She was angry, until Bert delighted her with a gift of a little stuffed dog equipped with a secret pocket for her pajamas.

At times it seemed that Bert courted the daughter as much as her mother. He took her everywhere—out to lunch, to book and music and toy stores, to the tailor, where he let her pick out gaily patterned linings for his suits, to the auto body shops he haunted on behalf of his fleet of foreign cars, to the optometrist, where he would select designer eyeglass frames for Dianne, with pink hearts and purple scallops on them.

Jack was a faithful weekend father, but Kathy sometimes objected to going out with him on Sundays, one sign of what would become several years' worth of bitter custody battles. "Why do I have to go with him?" she remembered snarling at Dianne. "I didn't marry him."

By the fall of 1962, less than a year after they began seeing each other, Dianne and Bert had decided to marry. Dr. Goldman, as he had with Jack, objected to Bert. "My father urged me not to marry him," she said. "He said there was a nineteen-year difference in our ages and that bachelors are not flexible. But Bert turned out to be the most flexible human being I ever knew."

Leon was not in a strong position to dispense marital advice. After Dianne moved out of the house, he had increasingly become a target of Betty's rages when suffering periodic flare-ups of his illness. In June 1962, after yet another episode, Lynn half carried him from the house on Presidio Terrace, she said. He was never to return. After three decades of keeping up appearances, Dianne's parents finally divorced the following March.

"Late-blooming incompatibility ended the 31-year-old marriage of Dr. Leon Goldman, 59, chairman of the surgery department at University of California medical school," the morning paper reported, with no hint of the years of pain and anguish that lay buried beneath the bare facts.

Dr. Goldman remarried the following year, but his second marriage proved nearly as disastrous as the first. According to his statements in court records, his new wife at various times attacked him with a knife and a lead pipe, attempted suicide, and took quantities of painkillers. This unhappy saga ended quickly in divorce.

Despite Dr. Goldman's doubts, Dianne and Bert were wed by a rabbi on November 11, 1962, at the rented house in St. Francis Wood. "It was a very small wedding," Dianne recalled. "What I remember is I had a dress made for Katherine that was a replica of my dress, sort of an ivory, long dress. She stole the whole ceremony. She stood right up there with us. She was ready to participate in it."

Among the forty witnesses were her parents, then living apart. With many of those present on pins and needles over what might happen, Betty kept her temper in check, one witness said, except for berating one of Dr. Goldman's brothers for not helping her get her husband back.

Bert gave up his own apartment and moved into St. Francis Wood. Yvonne had married and moved to Seattle, but Lynn, with her own little girl from a failed first marriage, would pick up Leon on Sundays and the three of them would go to the Feinstein home for burgers or pizza and "The Ed Sullivan Show." "It was the closest we ever were as a family," Lynn said.

Bert was "secure and serene," a friend remembered, and he and his new bride were affectionate in public and rarely in different rooms when at home. He had a talent for making everyone feel good and relaxed, and not only because he liked to mix the drinks strong.

"For the first time now, my personal life was secure, stable," said Dianne. "He was the sun, the moon, and the stars. It's fair to say that as a marriage, it was a ten. We just never were apart."

In 1966 Dianne, Bert, and Kathy moved into a thirteen-room house on Lyon Street in Pacific Heights, not far from Presidio Terrace. Over the next twenty years it would be the site of countless campaign meetings, late-night strategy sessions, sky-high celebrations, excruciating pain, and agonies of mourning.

BY THE TIME THEY MOVED into the new house, Dianne was in her fourth year on the prison board and served as its vice-chairman.

Governor Brown, still smarting from the damage inflicted by his handling of death-penalty cases, now had a new political problem on his hands: unrest on the campus of the University of California. Televised images of thousands of students in the Free Speech movement holding police at bay had reinforced Brown's image as a waffler, and handed a big campaign issue to Ronald Reagan, a B-movie actor whom the Republicans had nominated for governor.

Working on the doomed campaign to elect her mentor to a third term in 1966, Dianne was often absent from the board that year, missing more than thirty meetings before she finally resigned "for personal reasons" in December. "The commute had become very hard for me," she said. "I thought, I'm going to kill myself if I keep doing this. And I didn't want that separation."

Back in San Francisco, the expertise she had gained had helped her win public attention on the local political scene. With the help of friendly editors at the *San Francisco Examiner,* she published in the summer of 1965 a splashy series of articles about her prison experiences that ran three consecutive weeks in the well-read Sunday paper. The series included a flattering, full-length photograph of Dianne wearing a Jackie Kennedy bob and dress and leaving "her St. Francis Wood home, bound for a woman's parole board session." Her articles provide a capsule view of her more liberal ideas and theories on crime and penology at the time, along with a few personal glimpses of the author.

In one part she presented the arguments for community-based "halfway houses" as an alternative to straight parole, a pet project of hers on the prison board. Among the case histories she cited was a woman she gave the pseudonym of "Betty," who had a serious drinking problem and would often be "sprawled unconscious" in front of her little girl, whom Dianne called "Kathy."

The series began with a sympathetic account of "Joanne Elwood," a woman who had been convicted of second-degree murder for slaying her abusive husband and who appeared before the board to have her sentence set and first parole hearing scheduled.

> The product of a broken home, she was reared by her mother, remembers her father only as a person who expressed no affection toward her and responded indifferently to her constant effort to please him. Hungry for love and affection, she married in her teens, was divorced soon after and later remarried. Almost deliberately, Joanne seemed to seek out a mate so abusive and brutal that her life with him became a nightmare. When she could bear it no longer, she killed him.

Dianne and the board set sentence at ten years and decided the woman could come before them again in fourteen months for consideration of parole. This meant she might be out of prison about three and a half years after the killing. Sounding defensive in print, Dianne offered a long explanation for the decision. "Should this appear lenient in the extreme to some, let me present the case of Joanne's early parole," she wrote, noting that the woman had no prior arrest record, that she was mother to three children, and that "all available research" suggested that she would not violate her parole.

Elsewhere in the series, Dianne endorsed other liberal reform ideas, such as lighter prison terms for narcotics offenders, calling for "the punitive approach [to be] replaced with rehabilitation programs."

"In those days I saw the criminal justice arena very differently than I do now," Dianne said of her liberal views in the 1960s. "The nature of the problem has changed. I think my perspective is very different. I was very young and what you see in the world plays a real role in how you come to view things."

Dianne's newspaper series attracted considerable attention, both for its dramatic tone and for the contrast between the genteel author and her subject. The summer that the series appeared, Dianne was honored for her work on the prison board when she was selected one of five "distinguished women" at a luncheon sponsored by the Western States Democratic Conference. A few days before the award was presented, she was profiled in the *San Francisco Chronicle* in an article headlined "A pretty expert on crime" that captured the tone of the times and the cultural obstacles she still faced in her career.

"San Francisco's Dianne (Mrs. Bert) Feinstein is a raven-haired, blue-eyed beauty who looks more like an actress (which she has been) than an expert on California criminal justice (which she is)," the article began. Dianne was quoted at length about her criminal justice views, including her strong belief that the death penalty should be abolished. "States with the highest homicide rates are those that have the death penalty," she said, arguing that capital punishment could never be fairly enforced because "very few people with good paid defenses have gone to the gas chamber."

The following summer, in 1966, Dianne obtained an appointment from Terry Francois, the civil rights attorney whom she had befriended and who was by then on the board of supervisors. Francois put her on the newly formed Advisory Committee for Adult Detention, which had authority to inspect and report on the condition of the city and county jails. This made her a player with portfolio in local politics.

Secure in her marriage, with a deeply supportive husband standing behind her and a full-time housekeeper to look after her home and child, Dianne now threw herself into her new position as chairwoman of the committee with characteristic earnestness and industry. Over the next nine months, sometimes with other committee members but often alone, she repeatedly inspected the city and four county jail facilities, along with local prisons in five neighboring counties, writing up her reports on a portable electric typewriter in the study on Lyon Street. The committee's findings, complete with field reports, were submitted to Mayor Joseph Alioto in 1968 and had considerable political impact.

With the zest for firsthand observation, sensory description, and infinite detail that would become trademarks of her political style, Dianne examined and reported on every conceivable aspect of local jails, from bedding, budgets, and clothing to commissaries, sanitation, and showers.

"The vermin problem is complicated by inmates, often dirty and unkempt, spreading vermin from their clothing into the bedding and throughout the facility. The committee personally observed arms and backs marked by numerous bites allegedly caused by vermin," she wrote after one inspection. After another she reported:

> The meal served was a glutinous mass of noodles with gravy containing chicken gizzards, cabbage, three pieces of bread and coffee. The large pot of gravy was examined with a ladle and revealed no more than 20 gizzards in the pot to serve the block of some 60 inmates.
>
> The chief cook indicated there were some 450 pounds of gizzards in the gravy we observed. Subsequently, it was indicated that there were no checks on staff in the kitchen and no way of ascertaining whether 450 pounds of gizzards were ordered or they actually went into the preparation of the meal.

Dianne soon became a familiar visitor in the jails, wearing her I. Magnin outfits and clicking through the stone corridors on her high heels. But she was not always a welcome one. On one solitary and, supposedly, surprise inspection, she observed isolation units in both the women's and men's facilities.

> All isolation cells were empty. I was taken to see the psychiatrist, who asked to see my credentials and indicated a sensitivity to "unjust criticism." I responded that, "if the criticism is unjust, why worry?" The captain then indicated that I probably didn't know much about jails. I thought I had better leave and did.

When her committee's report was issued in March 1968, it created headlines with its descriptions of deplorable conditions in the jails. After the report appeared, Dianne received an appointment from Alioto to a blue-ribbon crime committee. This group followed up Dianne's first report with a stinging censure of the sheriff in charge of the jails, who had admitted to a drinking problem. He was defeated at the next election.

Within a few years, Alioto would think differently about his appointment of Dianne, after she emerged as a political rival and challenger to his own re-election.

His introduction to Dianne came when she visited his home, a few doors down from her childhood residence on Presidio Terrace, bearing an unusual gift: a can of mace. She had recently learned of the effectiveness of the noxious spray as a crime-fighting tool and wanted to bring it to the mayor's attention. "She was an intense young woman, avidly searching for knowledge and experience," Alioto recalled. "I'll always remember her sitting there in my living room with this damn can of mace."

With the publicity she received from her crime studies, Dianne was poised to take the plunge she had been planning since her afternoons at City Hall with Uncle Morrie. By then she had made a few more important connections. In 1967 she had been asked to head a special women's committee in support of state senator Eugene McAteer, who was running for mayor. But McAteer died suddenly, throwing local politics into turmoil. His death drew Alioto into the race and left a young McAteer aide named Bob Mendelsohn in search of a future.

Mendelsohn decided to run for the board of supervisors and asked Dianne to lead his own women's campaign committee. At the age of twenty-nine, Mendelsohn was elected the youngest member of the board ever. In the process, he joined Francois, both as a supervisor and as a political mentor for Dianne.

In the months that followed, Dianne, with Bert, with Francois, and with Mendelsohn discussed over and over again the pluses and minuses of running for the board herself. Finally, late in 1968, Francois threw up his hands and gruffly told her, "If you're going to do it, do it, and just stop talking about it."

5

DARK HORSE

Don't wear your sex like a badge on your sleeve.

—*Dianne Feinstein's Rules for Getting Ahead*

SHORTLY AFTER NOON on election day, 1969, Dianne sat sullen and exhausted in an overstuffed chair next to the crackling fireplace in the Russian Hill living room of friend and fund-raiser Ann Alanson. In the next room, her father, husband, and sister gathered with glasses of champagne before the view window, peering in vain for the Vote for Dianne skywriting they had commissioned. It was obscured in the thick white banks of cold November fog that hovered above the bay.

Dianne was in no mood for celebration. Several hours before the polls would close her first political race, all the insecurity behind the smiling face she had worn in public for nearly a year suddenly broke through. "I know I'm going to lose and let all of you down," she groaned.

Alanson would not hear of it. "You're right, Dianne, you do have a terrible problem," she said. "You're going to come in first and be president of the board, so you'd better be prepared for that." A few hours later, the political pro was proved right as Dianne pulled off one of the great electoral upsets in San Francisco history. Conquering both precedent and her own self-doubts, she finished first in a crowded field for the board of supervisors, confounding the pundits and shocking the town.

The electrifying win of the attractive Jewish mother was just one part of a panorama of change in San Francisco that fall. A center of campus unrest and the peace movement, the city had become a national depository for the far left and the capital of cultural fallout from the anti–Vietnam War political crusade. Cells of alphabet-soup terrorists composed "communiqués" of wooden rhetoric to justify murder, mayhem, and bombings plotted in secret "safe houses." Hippie casualties roamed the streets with tombstone eyes, and late arrivals for the long-gone Summer of Love just kept on arriving.

San Francisco was in flux. The grip the Irish held on City Hall for generations had been broken. Many conservative white ethnics fled to suburbs across the bridges of the bay—or stubbornly dug into the neighborhoods where they were born and raised—as immigrants from Asia, Central and South America, and elsewhere brought new kinds of demands upon the city. The new immigrants "learned in the 1960s what had taken the already arrived minorities many decades to master: the means of obtaining political power," the political scientist Frederick M. Wirt wrote in his landmark study of San Francisco in 1974. ". . . the former quiescence of Negroes, Latin Americans, Orientals and Indians had become the turbulent challenge of blacks, Chicanos, Asians and Native Americans."

The soon-to-be majority of ethnic minorities was joined by another group demanding equal rights and opportunity under the law—lesbians and gay men who fled less tolerant climes for the city of St. Francis, where they established a large and vocal presence that soon evolved into political clout.

The economy of San Francisco was changing too, as a powerful coalition of big business and big labor joined with local and regional government to forge a transformation from a blue-collar, port trade, and manufacturing base to an international, "Pacific Rim" center of white-collar financial services and tourism.

The economic changes also transformed the physical landscape and scale of the city. Fighting "Manhattanization" became the rallying cry for an aggressive new slow-growth movement based in San Francisco's neighborhoods, which fought against forests of high-rise towers that sprouted and sprawled in the downtown business district. "Behind that dramatic infusion of steel, concrete and glass lurk more profound changes that threaten to destroy what the city has been for one and a third centuries," the urban planner Chester Hartman wrote in *The Transformation of San Francisco* in 1983. "There is a pervasive sense that much of what is good in San Francisco is on its way out."

In this turbulent, changing city, teeming with political gossip, Feinstein had suddenly become a central figure, an instant celebrity whom voters and headline writers alike referred to simply by her first name. Her elected job was then considered a part-time position, held by people who worked full time in business or the professions. It paid only $9,600 a year and was only one seat on an eleven-member legislative board in a city government where power is straightjacketed by an anticorruption charter and authority diffused among the board, a mayor, a city manager called the chief administrative officer, and a bureaucracy so byzantine that Wirt dubbed it "a government of clerks." But Dianne remade the job, using her political independence, media skills, and energy to accumulate power and set her own political agenda as she became San Francisco's first full-time supervisor.

She had learned tough lessons about leadership at home; her father had taught her that the purpose of life was to matter; Sacred Heart had primed her "social responsibility to shape and change society"; and her Stanford days had left her with a core belief that an individual could make a difference in improving the world. For nearly fifteen years she had sought to get her personal life in order while gaining a foothold in public service. Now, at the age of thirty-six she began a starring role she would play for twenty years' worth of San Francisco's civic dramas, follies, and tragedies.

MARGARET MARY MORGAN was a suffragette, the tough and independent owner of a print shop in the brawling South of Market district, when she became the first woman ever elected to San Francisco's board of supervisors in 1921. "Remember," she said, as she left office just two years later, "a woman has to work harder than a man and have more patience in order to achieve success." No one knew at the time just how patient women would have to be.

For as Feinstein began the task of assembling her 1969 campaign, Margaret Mary Morgan held the distinction of being the last woman elected supervisor without benefit of appointment to an empty seat on the board. In the intervening forty-eight years there had been exactly two other women supervisors, and both of them had been first appointed to a vacancy by a mayor. One was Clarissa McMahon, and when she retired in 1966, the "woman's seat" on the board was given to a tax attorney and single mother named Dorothy Von Beroldingen, who would seek election on her own for the first time in 1969.

If Dianne needed any reminders of why women had been all but shut out of local politics for most of San Francisco's history, she got them in a hurry. She made the decision to run after a family meeting in the living room at

Lyon Street. Bert, Leon, and Lynn all enthusiastically pledged to help her. Then she started making the rounds of power brokers.

First, she went to several dozen downtown businessmen whom she had interviewed for a Coro project. Almost unanimously, they advised her against running. She went to lunch with former mayor Elmer Robinson. "Don't run, Dianne," he told her. "People will never vote for another woman." At the behest of Dr. Goldman and Uncle Morrie, she received an audience with Ben Swig, owner of the Fairmont Hotel and a prime mover in politics and the Jewish community. He agreed to phone his friend the mayor on her behalf. "So I talked to Ben Swig about talking to the mayor and he called me back, and he was all excited and he said, 'The mayor committed to give you the third vacancy he might have on the board.' Not even the second, but the third. And of course there would never be three." So Dianne decided to try it on her own.

San Francisco's eleven supervisors ran citywide for staggered four-year terms, with six seats up in one election and five the next. In 1969 all five incumbents whose terms were ending sought reelection and, in a total field of eighteen candidates, all were favored to win. With Feinstein still a virtual unknown, despite her work on the crime and jail committees, even some of her friends were less than sanguine about her chances. Socialite Charlotte Swig, who years later would become an important behind-the-scenes player when Feinstein was mayor, told her, "You're not well-known enough to win, but at least if you run, you'll get yourself known," she recalled.

At one point Dianne sought advice from writer Merla Zellerbach, the chronicler of Stanford life, and her husband, radio broadcaster and author Fred Goerner. "I told her the incumbents had it locked up, not to mention her being a woman and being Jewish," Goerner recalled. "I thought she was absolutely going to lose and be lucky to finish twentieth. But she had made up her mind to do it."

As generations of advisers, allies, and enemies would learn, telling Dianne she could not do something was the best way to ensure she would try. "Everybody believed I couldn't win. It was impossible," she said. "But I knew I wanted to do it and I made up my mind."

Nearly three months before she formally announced her candidacy, word that Dianne would run was slipped into a favorable profile in the Sunday *Examiner.* One of a long series of articles that got the color of Dianne's eyes wrong, the piece nevertheless gave her a running start in her uphill battle. It began:

> Tall and slim, with luminous gray eyes and an obvious sense of style—the sort of woman one pictures in the gentle ambience of the drawing room—Dianne Feinstein paradoxically is no stranger to crime and punishment.
>
> She has "heard the groans, smelled the stench, seen the hate and despair." She knows first-hand about men and women behind bars.
>
> And she also has moved in the rough, tough world of politics.

Noting the historic challenge she was facing, the article posed the rhetorical question, "What makes Dianne run?" In her answer, the candidate for the first time publicly articulated her vision of politics and leadership as a woman trying to break down barriers of exclusion. As she would throughout her career, she cast her crusade in terms that threatened neither men nor the status quo. Far from women's liberation, her words echoed more with the noblesse oblige ideals of Sacred Heart and the women's good government, "municipal housekeeping" civic club movement of the Progressive era.

> If women with the time, the interest and the background do nothing, how can we expect anyone else to? If the silent majority—generally those in comfortable circumstances who feel they have satisfied the traditional obligations of citizenship—does not mobilize to permit everyone to share, we can only come to tragic failure.
>
> I think a woman can cut through to the core of a problem with a special flair and enthusiasm to put action into government. She can serve and still fulfill family responsibilities.

YEARS LATER, Feinstein would portray her 1969 upset victory as the result of an amateurish, plucky, little people's campaign. And, in the beginning at least, it did have a distinctly family flavor. Her first headquarters was the third floor of Lyon Street, and Lynn was her first paid operative. Working on phones set up on a Ping-Pong table in a big open room between the guest room and a bath, they started calling people on lists of potential donors and supporters provided by Ann Alanson and Bob Mendelsohn. "When I decided to run, I knew it was an uphill battle and that the odds were not great.

I decided just to give it a full year and do the level best I could. So I started early, went out and asked people to support me, and put together a good little team."

Dr. Goldman hosted her first fund-raiser, a luncheon at the St. Francis Yacht Club. The guest list was drawn largely from his and Bert's medical profession networks.

Bert took charge of house signs, an important part of making a campaign visible in the grass-roots neighborhood politics of San Francisco. With Kathy in tow, he spent his Saturdays climbing up and down ladders, despite an inner-ear disorder that affected his balance, taking pride in the perfect surgical knots he tied in the wires and cords to affix bold red "Dianne" signs to buildings and homes all over the city.

Her first volunteer was Bruce Kennedy, a young Episcopalian priest who had worked with Dianne in the local office of Robert Kennedy's 1968 California presidential primary campaign, which had ended in victory, then assassination. When Bruce read in the paper that Dianne was running, he called to offer his services. She gratefully accepted and he was quickly enlisted as scheduler, speech writer, gofer, and chauffeur, grinding the gears on Dianne's Jaguar as he drove her to campaign events. Within a few years he and Lynn would marry.

Despite such homey touches, however, the Feinstein campaign soon took on a serious and professional dimension, beginning with the hiring of a full-time campaign manager named Sandy Weiner. Weiner was a chain-smoking, irreverent ad man who was a local pioneer in what would later become known as the political-consulting business. It was his idea to run the candidate as "Dianne," a tactic that instantly separated her from the pack, and to print all the signs and campaign materials with her first name boldly splashed in red and her last name less prominently displayed in black. "Calling her 'Dianne' gave her automatic name identification," Kennedy recalled. "She was the only Dianne in the race."

Under Weiner's guidance, her campaign had all the earmarks of those that would follow: money, especially family money; skillful use of media; emphasis on themes of effectiveness and independence; and a temperamental candidate.

In the end, Dianne would outraise and outspend all her rivals in the race and forge an impressive network of supporters and donors, skillfully interweaving family and political connections she had made in years of good-government and campaign drudge work. Although published reports vary, she spent something on the order of $100,000, at the time a huge and unprecedented amount for a job that paid $9,600 in a race with a total of about 200,000 voters.

"Money was no object," said then-supervisor Robert Gonzales, who watched Dianne's glitzy campaign in awe. "At that time, it was astronomical to spend $50,000, so it had to be the most expensive campaign in the history of the city."

Ann Alanson, the Democratic National Committee member and fundraiser who had become friendly with Dianne when both volunteered in other campaigns, was a major asset. She recalled that "Leon Goldman brought in a huge amount of money" while she herself "put everything on the line for that campaign."

A big fund-raising event of the campaign was a silent auction, held at the Huntington Hotel. Dr. Goldman donated a free surgery, Bruce Kennedy offered a free wedding service, and Alanson's first husband, a meat wholesaler, put up a side of beef, plus the filets mignons served to guests. Ann donated some of her Amari porcelain, along with a portfolio of twelve natural studies by the famed photographer Ansel Adams. The photographs, worth thousands of dollars, were auctioned for $400 to a local physician.

"Ansel said, 'Ann, don't do that—give it to the museum and you'll get a big tax write-off,'" she remembered. "But I didn't want a write-off, I wanted to help Dianne."

In addition to Leon and Bert's connections, Alanson and Bob Mendelsohn, the crafty young supervisor and Feinstein mentor, helped her court key players in the Jewish community: Bill Coblentz, the influential attorney and former Pat Brown staffer; Mel Swig, Ben's son, who became her campaign treasurer; and perhaps most significantly, Morris "Mighty Mo" Bernstein, an avuncular and wealthy businessman and major City Hall power broker.

A pal of Uncle Morrie's, the bald and impish Bernstein had various financial interests, but his real business was politics. It was not uncommon for him to be on several sides of issues and political races simultaneously; in his years as a fixer and local political institution, Bernstein raised money with a few phone calls, liked to be in the know, and was not shy about brokering deals among the many city officials he had helped elect. He became a Dianne booster, calling her "my little girl" in conversations with others. He would play an important behind-the-scenes role in helping Feinstein advance to the highest levels of city government. "Mo shepherded her around," Coblentz recalled. "He was her political mentor."

Terry Francois, her mentor from the civil rights movement, helped in the black community, as Dianne won endorsements from Eloise Westbrook, an important community figure in the troubled Hunters Point district, and Willie Brown, the up-and-coming state assemblyman who was the only elected officeholder to endorse her.

Former governor Pat Brown was the honorary chairman of her campaign, and the political establishment was represented by Brown's son-in-law Joe Kelley, an attorney, by Democratic county committee chairman Agar Jaicks, and by Dave Jenkins, an old-left longshoreman and major player in Alioto's labor-business coalition.

At the same time, Feinstein cultivated two outsider groups that were just beginning their rise to power in local politics—the slow-growth, neighborhood environmentalist movement that arose in opposition to Alioto's Manhattanization policies and the gay community, which she and Weiner foresaw would become a major voting bloc.

As Dianne had learned first in the George Reilly campaign, running for office in San Francisco is traditionally a nonstop round of shaking hands and passing out literature at bingo games, bus stops, candidates' nights, church basements, ethnic parades, living room coffees, and trade union halls. Both Francois and Mendelsohn had been through the ordeal themselves and lectured her about handbills and house signs. "We'd tell her, 'Raise what money you can, but the most important thing is to get out and meet the people at bingo and bus stops,'" Mendelsohn said. "It's like jumping into the cold ocean, but she did it."

As a practical matter, however, such retail politics in 1969 looked like a ticket to defeat, for no matter where she went, the five better-known incumbents seemed always to have been there first. But Dianne had money and that money allowed her to do something no one else had done in a supervisors' race—run a TV campaign. "It was Sandy's idea," said Lynn. "She was killing herself going to coffees."

The conventional wisdom in San Francisco was that television advertising was not effective because it cost too much to run in one of the nation's most expensive media markets. Because the city is nestled in the center of a vast metropolitan area of several million people, only a fraction of the audience who viewed the ads were actually voters.

The conventional wisdom was wrong. For several days, Weiner had the candidate shadowed by a camera crew and cut a series of quick spots with Dianne on location around San Francisco: Dianne with Kathy, talking about schools; Dianne at the bay, talking about the environment; Dianne walking about Telegraph Hill, talking about accountability.

The impact was sensational. As Uncle Morrie had long ago understood when he used his attractive niece to hawk Miss California coats on his pioneering afternoon talk show, Dianne sparkled on television. The combination of images of the lovely woman and her lovely city underscored the message of a fresh-faced outsider who stood for change, and the "Dianne" tag line hammered it home.

"The basic theme was, 'Here's a person you never heard of before and here's what she stands for,'" recalled Bruce Kennedy.

WITH BERT AT HER SIDE, Feinstein formally announced her candidacy at the end of May. At her press conference she wore a wide-belted, jacketed wool suit tailored sharply enough for a model. She also wore a clenched-jaw expression intense enough for a linebacker. In a sweeping indictment of City Hall, she promised to address the "increasing frustration among our citizens who find they are helpless in changing their destiny." Then she ticked off a list of good-government priorities—lowering the crime rate, "responsible budgeting and tax reform," education, and the environment—that would remain her basic agenda for the next thirty years.

Rather than offering programmatic solutions, she promised she would solve civic problems through industriousness, improved efficiency, the advice of experts—and the force of her personal character. "I will be a full-time supervisor to keep in constant touch with citizens who want help," she said in a statement of candidacy, where she selected "Member, Mayor's Crime Committee" as her ballot designation. "I will work to improve the effectiveness of the board by sponsoring major revisions so that the board may be more responsive," she said.

In what would become a hallmark of her governing style, Feinstein also vowed to appoint a blue-ribbon study group, in this case a "committee of tax experts." The committee was to recommend alternatives to the residential property tax, the growing burden of which would snap within ten years into the backlash of California's Proposition 13 tax revolt. In 1969 her proposal allowed her in the campaign to declaim foursquare against property-tax increases without the need to propose alternatives.

A few days before the election, she got a rare snippet of news coverage with a populist suggestion that voters take their tax bills to the polls: "Everyone is wondering again why the property owners of this city continue to be strangled by increased taxes every year while the downtown business community remains blessed by a majority of our current board of supervisors," she said. This statement would resound with irony within a few years.

While she spoke often of her effectiveness as a professional public servant, Feinstein rarely mentioned gender, and then usually only when asked. In interviews during her early years in politics, she at times displayed a lack of sensitivity to the problems of women not as well off as she. Shortly after her first campaign, for example, she argued that women made superior public servants because they were untainted by the need to make a living:

> A woman does not have to make decisions based on the need to
> survive. She can cut through issues, call shots as she sees them. Many
> bad decisions are made by men in government because it is good for
> them personally to make bad public decisions.

She also noted that "there will be times in a woman's life—when her children are small or in a new marriage—when she can't serve, but she can use this to prepare herself. Then she must have a husband secure in his own field who will be proud of her efforts," she added.

Before long the Junior League tone of such public comments, along with her stylishness, would lead to her being tagged as a "Pacific Heights matron" and contribute to a reputation for being out of touch with working women that became a political liability in San Francisco and took her years to overcome. In the 1990s she would use gender politics as a foundation of her election to the U.S. Senate. But in 1969 she cast the issue not in terms of equality and fairness but rather as another example of her independence, the overarching theme of her campaign.

At one point in 1969, she endorsed a two-term limit for local legislators, as a way of renewing the energy of the political system. Many terms into the future, the political outsider turned insider would renounce the idea of term limits.

Her political positioning was helped by the fact that, despite years of volunteerism in Democratic politics, she genuinely belonged to neither of the two warring camps in local Democratic party politics. At the time, the liberals were led by Phil Burton and the more conservative forces, allied with the late state senator Eugene McAteer, were led by an ambitious young politician named Leo T. McCarthy, who would become a major Sacramento player and resurface in Dianne's first try for statewide office.

When Phil Burton's brother, John, ran for the legislature in 1967 against a popular Republican incumbent, the Burtons asked Dianne for her support. Already pointing to her own 1969 race, she told them she "had to look to her own thing," according to John. "Dianne wasn't in politics, she was in government," he said.

"She was never a major player in Democratic politics in San Francisco," said veteran political analyst Rollin Post of television station KRON. "That was one of the things that made her unique at the time. She walked through Democratic politics, which was full of land mines, and never stepped on one. Neither side could figure her out."

FROM THE BEGINNING, Dianne was a mercurial candidate in private. In a business where prima donnas play for table stakes, she earned a reputation as a diva—extremely demanding of her staff, volatile of mood, and often wracked by self-doubt. Striving for tight control of every aspect of her public image, she insisted upon personally reviewing the smallest details of logistics and strategy. Capable of the most thoughtful and touching private gestures to aides and staff in campaigns and government, she sometimes also scolded them like children or embarrassed them in front of others.

"In one sense, you're a member of the family almost. You'll do anything for her," said one former City Hall aide. "But I've never seen anyone treat people as rough." Said Bruce Kennedy, "Like most perfectionists, she isn't perfect."

Feinstein acknowledged that, "I am demanding of staff. I'm demanding of myself, though, too . . . I really believe that we should perform to the very best we possibly can, and that's hard to do. And, I'm not saying this for excuses, but it's harder for a woman than it is for a man. There's a constant testing of a woman."

In the 1969 campaign, when Dianne wanted to approve every expenditure, she would go through stacks of checks that Sandy Weiner and Lynn had prepared for her signature. Hoping to avoid confrontation, they would stack the small checks at the top of the pile. When Feinstein had worked her way down the stack, one of them would distract her in an effort to divert her attention from the big ones on the bottom.

When the campaign was over, Weiner vowed to Rollin Post that he would never again work for a female candidate, putting the matter somewhat less delicately. "She often got nervous and upset," Alanson recalled. "Sandy used to say it was a woman's thing." When she was "nervous and upset," Dianne would collapse on a couch or bed, emotionally insist that she had no chance of winning, or threaten to quit the race.

"Dianne needed to be constantly reassured, to a far greater extent than other insecure politicians," said a political professional who worked closely with her for years. "As a candidate, she was sure she was going to fail, rather than sure she was going to succeed. It was always, 'People don't like me. I'm not going to get this done. I'm going to lose.' You couldn't talk about problems—you had to fill gaps."

As a candidate, Dianne said, "I may grumble that I want to quit and I may want to quit, but I don't quit . . . I'm a far more confident person today than I was then. But I never feel that I do as well or as much as I should. Never satisfied. I give a speech and I always have a feeling of inadequacy. I suppose what I attribute it to is never quite feeling I belong and striving mightily to have to try to, or to prove something."

Kennedy recalled that when Feinstein in 1969 would say, "'I can't do this, I can't handle this, I just can't do this anymore,' then Bert was the only person who could get her going again." Besides supporting her financially and through his house-sign labors, Bert in many other ways was the perfect political spouse, at a time when it was unheard of for men to play such a role for their wives. When she despaired or suffered a crisis of confidence, he would be the one to soothe her, massage her, make her laugh, and get her going again. If she offended a friend or volunteer campaign worker, he would be the one to smooth it over and keep everyone happy.

"One of her greatest strengths in his quiet way was Bert Feinstein," said political reporter Post. "Everybody liked Bert, he stayed in the background but had a large amount of influence on her."

DESPITE HER STRONG CAMPAIGN, Dianne rarely broke into the press coverage of the supervisors' race, which was focused on the running battle of tit-for-tat attacks between two incumbents, Roger Boas and Peter Tamaras, who were believed to be leading the pack. The contest was significant because the top finisher in the field was traditionally elected board president by his colleagues, a position with a public profile second only to the mayor's in town. By Labor Day, however, both Weiner and Francois were talking privately about the possibility of Dianne finishing first. She refused to hear about it and impatiently dismissed the notion.

By election day she was exhausted. When she, Bert, Leon, and Lynn arrived at Alanson's for lunch, Ann recalled, Dianne was upset because she was being followed by a reporter and photographer assigned to do a feature story in case she managed to win. "Please, get these people out of here," she whispered to Alanson as she arrived, heading directly for the bathroom. When Dianne finally emerged, she did not join the others who were looking for the skywriter Bert and Leon had hired, but sank down in a chair by the fireplace where Ann made her prediction.

As the returns started coming in that night, with Dianne, Bert and Kathy, and several of the roommates waiting at Lyon Street, it soon became clear that a big local story was unfolding. Dianne was not only winning, she was topping the ticket, an unheard of showing for a nonincumbent, let alone a woman.

As continuing returns showed her triumph inevitable, Feinstein still resisted going to her headquarters, which had been moved from Lyon Street to a storefront adjoining a delicatessen owned by Leon's cousin Harry Goldman. "It's only 98 percent of the vote," she was heard to remark at one point. Finally, with family and friends in tow, she made her way to the headquarters, where she was thronged by an emotional crowd.

"City Hall, ho," yelled Weiner, and supporters formed a car caravan to City Hall, where returns were still being tallied in the basement.

"We joked about painting City Hall pink," remembered Bruce Kennedy.

Inside the building, with its Beaux-Arts design and 307-foot, six-inch high rotunda, the Feinstein forces were jubilant. That night Dr. Goldman told a radio reporter he had "never been so proud."

THE NEXT DAY the new supervisor was swept up in a whirlwind of excitement and publicity, as both major dailies led their front pages with accounts of "Dianne's" big upset. Having largely ignored her during the campaign, the press now stampeded to her door. The *Chronicle* dispatched Carolyn Anspacher, a grande doyenne of San Francisco journalism and the only woman reporter on its cityside staff, to Lyon Street to profile the winner.

Her interview with the "dark-haired, blue-eyed beauty" captures both the flavor of the times and the view of Dianne that quickly settled into the public mind:

> If her elegantly, superbly decorated English home is any indication, quiet and order will be keystones of Mrs. Feinstein's political career. Long stemmed American beauty roses were everywhere, in proper containers on highly glossed antique chests and tables. After an election day that ran better than 20 hours, Mrs. Feinstein was serene, impeccably groomed and fully in command of a situation that might have driven a male counterpart to tipple.

The story noted Feinstein's teenage aspiration to the board, and quoted her as saying she "never wanted to cook." "I'm fortunate enough to be able to run a home and have a husband so secure in his own profession that he enjoys my being active," she told the reporter.

Anspacher also took note of the supervisor's preteen daughter and joked that in light of Dianne's triumph, it is "not at all strange that 12-year-old Kathy is mapping out a career that will put her into the mayor's office."

"Each generation does better than the one before," Dianne said.

Almost lost in the buzz about Feinstein was the equally surprising victory of another newcomer, a conservative Republican real estate man named John Barbagelata, who finished fourth in the crowded field, as William Blake and Jack Morrison, two of the heavily favored incumbents, were forced from office.

One political analyst noted that while both new supervisors had promised "a new direction" in city government, "their opinions on that direction are likely to differ." Described as an "attractive, 36-year-old brunette" who had worn a "fashionable blue Norell original with a bolero top and wide white belt" on election night, Dianne interpreted the vote to mean "a new era, a different kind of politics working strongly for change." Barbagelata, whose salt-and-pepper hair and dark suit were not described in the article, said that, in his view, San Franciscans had voted to "get the city turned around and bring it back to what it used to be."

No one knew it at the time, but the two political unknowns would become leading antagonists in a decade of bitter debates, strikes, and terrorism to follow. Their competing visions for San Francisco—one from a Jewish woman who had courted environmentalists, gays, and minorities, the other from a strict Catholic father of eight who spoke for old-line, white ethnic families—reflected strains that would grow deep and broad beneath the surface of City Hall politics for the next ten years, like the powerful and hidden earthquake faults that constantly but silently threaten the city with disaster.

It wasn't long before Feinstein's new archnemesis struck the first blow.

Part Two

STORMING CITY HALL

6

FAST START

Put in more time than anyone else.

—*Dianne Feinstein's Rules for Getting Ahead*

SHORTLY AFTER 2:00 P.M. on Monday, January 9, 1970, newly installed Supervisor Dianne Feinstein was nominated by her only woman colleague to be president of the city's eleven-member legislative board. "A
young woman who, with her eloquence, sincerity, and charm, swept San
Francisco to her heart," she was described by Supervisor Dorothy Von
Beroldingen, who in the November election had hung on to her appointed
seat and given the city the unprecedented number of two women lawmakers.

After the speeches, all that remained was a pro forma vote for Feinstein to
become board president, the first woman ever to achieve the ceremonial but
powerful post traditionally afforded the first-place election winner. After her
upset win, some conservatives had loudly grumbled that she should do the
"statesmanlike" thing and step aside in favor of a more seasoned colleague.

The grumbling quieted as, with the help of Supervisor Francois, Dianne
locked up her votes behind the scenes. Now the clerk called the roll in al-
phabetical order, starting with freshman John Barbagelata. He drew an audi-
ble gasp from the crowd packed into the formal, carved Manchurian oak
chambers by departing from decorum and unexpectedly voting no.

The lone dissenter to Feinstein, Barbagelata said later that Dianne was not
qualified for the job because she had "no real-life experience." But as Dianne
took over the gavel after the ten-to-one vote, she noted that Barbagelata's
wife and five daughters were in the audience: "With all those women in the
family, how can you be opposed to a woman as president?" she asked him
with a smile. "The truth is," he answered, "that's the reason."

It was a wry conclusion to the first skirmish in a nasty and long-running political battle in San Francisco, as Feinstein and Barbagelata time and again would clash as bitter enemies, both personal and philosophical. A bottom-line businessman with an instinctive distrust of government, Barbagelata was appalled in watching Feinstein enact her campaign promise to become a "full-time supervisor."

When Feinstein took office in 1970, she changed at once the political dynamics at City Hall. All her colleagues had outside jobs that took much of their time, according to the traditional practice of supervisors being professionals who brought their expertise to bear in part-time public service.

The single-mindedness and self-discipline she took to the board of supervisors set a pattern for every public position she held afterward. Every morning she would leave Lyon Street in her Jaguar and show up bright and early at City Hall. Dominating the legislative agenda, she crafted reams of legislation, convened citizen advisory committees, performed ceremonial functions, demanded reports from bureaucrats, and got her name in the papers day in and day out.

At Stanford, Dianne became a Young Democrat because she felt that government has a major role in "remedying human needs." As a supervisor, she was burning up with ideas that she thought would help the people of San Francisco on matters large and small—from putting more policemen on the streets and shaping how the city would grow, to prohibiting restaurants from serving frozen foods without a menu disclaimer and permitting neighborhood Chinese laundries to increase the capacity of their washers.

Before long, one pressroom wag was comparing her to a busybody character made popular by radio personality Henry Morgan. "Violet Ray," he would intone in a raspy voice, "the story of one woman's fight to meddle in other people's business."

Of her own early days at City Hall, Feinstein reflected that, "At the time, I was sort of intoxicated with my win. I had done something that hadn't been done before. I didn't understand what loss was like in the arena."

FEINSTEIN'S SWEARING IN was a major media event that drew a bank of TV cameras and a standing-room-only crowd of more than three hundred to the supervisors' chambers, up a splendid marble staircase from City Hall's rotunda. Indicative of the times, the style of the young woman taking on the important civic post created more interest than the substance of what she had to say. "Dark haired Mrs. Feinstein, a strikingly attractive woman in her crimson, Originala knit suit with lizard belt and buttons, accepted the gavel," read one account the next day.

With the chambers fragrant with hundreds of flowers from friends and well-wishers, Dianne received a gavel crafted of white carnations. In her inaugural address she said, "We must work to see that this is a decade of magnificence for the city we love. I take the faith of those who voted for me as the highest trust of my life. I will try to be fair and impartial as we come out of a dismal decade and enter into a very crucial decade."

Despite her earnest tones, it was Dianne's tall and striking appearance that continued to fascinate, a reflection of the unaccustomed strain of taking seriously a woman in the political arena. A few weeks after she took office, the influential Barristers Club invited her to address its members. In her speech, titled "A Time and Place for Urban Solutions," she called for San Francisco to become "another Camelot." "Mrs. Feinstein was sufficiently eloquent to divert the minds of the mostly male members of the Barristers Club from her stunning good looks," noted the *Chronicle* dispatch, which was light on details of her proposals.

In other forums where she spoke without the filter of the news media, Feinstein sounded a political voice that would remain largely unchanged over the next twenty-five years as she worked her way from local office to the U.S. Senate: commonsense concerns for day-to-day human problems, expressed in the language of a pragmatic technocrat. "Mine is the dream of a wife and mother," she wrote in an opinion piece shortly after her election. "I want to see our city become a place where my daughter can walk to the store or ride a bus downtown without my worrying about her safety. My dream is to help continue constructive problem solving where it has begun and to begin where it has not."

She saw no absence of problems to solve. San Francisco's byzantine charter defines the supervisors' role as setting forth broad budget and policy guidelines and legally prevents them from interfering in day-to-day operations of city departments. But Dianne soon expanded the scope of her job. She hired the board's first professional budget analyst to cut through the obfuscations of department bureaucrats and give the supervisors more clout in budget battles with the mayor. She made a personal crusade of pushing for an increase in the number of beat patrol cops and fought for reforms in the jails, youth facilities, and probations procedures.

Her impact on City Hall was both quantitative and qualitative. In the two years of her first term as board president, the supervisors dealt with 2,261 ordinances and resolutions, along with more than three dozen measures that they placed on the city ballot. This was a record-shattering legislative pace.

The board's weekly Monday meetings began routinely to run late into the night, which did not entirely displease some members, who took to dining at fine restaurants at taxpayers' expense during the dinner recess. When they returned, some of the supervisors were often in good spirits, which they maintained by ordering their aides to "fill up my coffee," a euphemism for fetching a cup laced with brandy, a practice in which the prim Dianne did not indulge.

A few months after Dianne took over as board president, the *Examiner*'s veteran City Hall reporter, Russ Cone, wrote a memo to his bosses asking for more help because of additional work load, brought on both by the ambitious, ebullient Mayor Alioto and by "the supervisors . . . holding more and more meetings," which he calculated at fifty-two in the preceding forty-two days. "Dianne was in the best sense an honest person, never influenced by personal gain," Cone said years later. "But a make-work ethic took hold with her election. They started playing full time at being supervisor and turned it into a business."

Her single-minded commitment to public business was recalled at one point by the late Frankie Aiello, a longtime aide to the supervisors who drove Dianne around in the town car to which she was entitled as board president. "Everything was political with Dianne," he said. "She just lived politics. We didn't carry on too much conversation; she'd be thinking political all the time—you could see things registering in her head. Sometimes she would talk into a recorder while I drove."

As board president Dianne not only wielded the gavel at meetings and stood first in line of succession to the mayor, she also had the power to appoint all board committees. Under the tutelage of Francois and, especially, Mendelsohn, whom she credited with teaching her "to count to six"—a euphemism for working votes on the eleven-member board—she duly rewarded her friends and punished her enemies.

Von Beroldingen, a tax attorney who had resisted efforts by campaign reporters to be drawn into a woman-on-woman public battle with Feinstein, kept her post as the chairman of the powerful Finance Committee. Not surprisingly, Francois and Mendelsohn got the other two seats on the committee, which approved every penny of city spending. Barbagelata, by contrast, was banished to the largely irrelevant Cultural Activities Committee.

Most other members of the board found her "very collegial," recalled Von Beroldingen, and were impressed with her charm, energy, and earnestness. Dianne and Bert also sometimes hosted other supervisors for receptions or dinners at Lyon Street. A colleague recalled one party at which Dianne provided a dramatic reading of "The Raven" by Edgar Allan Poe. "I never read 'The Raven,'" Feinstein insisted.

But colleagues also felt annoyance at her imperious streak. "Her first-place finish was not necessarily a good thing," said a political ally of the time. "She always felt that she was ordained and this was solidified by running number one. However bright and pleasant she might be, she had never run a business or had a real job, but no one could tell her anything. She was quick to leap to conclusions and then would never change her mind."

Another close adviser from the time said that the flip side of Dianne's political independence was that "There wasn't the sense that, 'I have to do these things because my constituency wants me to,' but rather, 'What should I do because I'm an anointed leader. I'm anointed to do what's right.'"

BESIDES THE AGENDA for action that she developed on her own, Dianne also enlisted the help of a group of bright, accomplished San Francisco professionals that she dubbed "the think tank." The group was the brainchild of a young attorney and Stanford graduate named Jim Haas who had an interest in good government and city planning. Disillusioned with Alioto, whose ambitions and ethics were brewing political trouble, Haas made a breakfast date with Dianne the month after she was elected and proposed putting together a group of planners, architects, accountants, and lawyers to help her develop policy ideas and legislation. She embraced the idea at once.

Meeting both at City Hall and at Lyon Street, the group of several dozen people, largely male, formed committees to research issues, supply Dianne with policy analyses, and monitor virtually every supervisors' committee hearing for her. "I am constantly looking for ways to make decisions in greater depth, to understand all the ramifications of the decisions on the people of the city and to put together legislation which reflects the interest of those I represent," she explained at the time. "The think tank helps me do that."

The think tank generated dozens of ideas for Feinstein, but its most important contribution was a noise-pollution-control ordinance for San Francisco that became a model for the nation after she pushed it through the board. Within a few years, however, many of the group's members had drifted away from their patroness and her demands. "It got to be almost like a second job," a Harvard Business School graduate who was an early leader of the group said at the time.

"Dianne was a very difficult person to work for," Haas recalled. "One of the things we learned was that she did not treat volunteers very well. A volunteer operation requires a lot of care and feeding and she treated people as staff: 'I need this by tomorrow,' she would say, and not thankful, let alone grateful."

If working for Dianne was frustrating for volunteers, it was more so for her paid staff. "I don't get ulcers, I give them," she was fond of boasting. At City Hall her first administrative assistant was Bruce Kennedy, who lasted only about eight months before he returned to a job in local television, worn down by Dianne's constant calls and obsession with detail. "She was hard to work for," he said. "She would do and redo every letter, redo it and redo it and redo it. She was smart and impatient with people who weren't. She believed she could handle a lot more than the rest of us could."

Another former aide, who now holds a prominent position in city government, recalled a time when the supervisors' aides were agitating for a pay raise and all signed a petition supporting it. After Dianne's aide signed the petition, he was summoned to her office and ordered to remove his name. "You don't sign anything without talking to me first," she told him coldly. "Everything you do reflects on me."

"Staff decisions have to be based on 'what kind of decision on this problem would the boss want me to make?'" Feinstein said. "When people act independently of the head figure, it causes conflicts. You can't let staff run you. The person in charge has got to be the guiding post."

Peter Nardoza, who worked longer for Feinstein at City Hall than any other aide, said that she

> is a true workaholic. She is very demanding and very difficult to work for. There were days you simply wanted to go for her throat. She feels most comfortable when she's most tough. But there's also something there that continually attracted me, another side that is very maternal and communicates great personal warmth.

Although Feinstein's temperament was common knowledge at City Hall, it was her charming side that was more reflected in the newspapers. Throughout her local career she enjoyed highly favorable news coverage, which did not include personal matters such as her divorce and legal battles with Jack Berman.

Berman sued her several times in the late 1960s, once when he discovered that Dianne and Bert were using "Feinstein" as his daughter's last name at school in violation of the divorce settlement, and again when he was refused permission to take Kathy on a Christmas vacation as allowed under the joint-custody agreement. Things between them grew so tense that Bert handled the family's dealings with Jack, while Dianne stopped talking to him.

But Feinstein's private life stayed private, and any coverage of her and her family was glowing, if not idealized. Typical was a profile of the couple that ran in the Sunday *Examiner* not long after her inauguration. Called "The Big Man in Dianne's Life," it also demonstrates the problems of perception faced by Bert Feinstein as a pioneering political spouse.

When Mama is in politics, there's many an unkind query heard about who wears the pants in the family. Such is the fearsome image of a lady politico. The husband of San Francisco's most prominent political mama allows as how that's true.

"But they put it more nicely to me," chuckled the spouse of Dianne Feinstein, the city's beautiful new supervisor and president of the board of supervisors. "They just ask, 'Why did you let your wife go into politics?'"

Amazingly enough, Dr. Bertram Feinstein, 55, likes seeing his 36-year-old wife of seven years in public service. As he puts it, "I didn't marry a housekeeper."

Does Bert Feinstein feel humbled or intimidated now that the little woman is occupying the limelight? Not this husband.

"What kind of companion would she be," he asks hypothetically, "if I insisted she stay home with her pots and pans and housework?"

To which Dianne added, "Anyway, I don't like to cook."

If Dianne and Bert joshed and joked about the unusual demands upon their political family, it was less easy for Kathy, who at this time began to use the name Katherine. Then twelve, she had left public school to enroll at the

Hamlin School, an exclusive academy just down the block from Sacred Heart. She had grown extremely close to Bert but felt the frequent absence of her mother, who she said was "around about half the time."

"She never had time," Katherine recalled. "Yes, I think I was deprived of time—although I don't think it matters much in the long run. I would do it differently. But I'd rather have that kind of mother than an overweight housewife."

Katherine also always thought that she was treated differently because she was the daughter of a prominent politician. "After my mother was elected, people were paying attention to me and making judgments about me—'if your mother is on the board of supervisors, you must be stuck up,'" she said. "When your parents are in political life, you aren't normal. Everybody talks about the benefits, but I don't know what the benefits are."

AMONG THOSE MOST ANNOYED with all the positive news coverage of Feinstein was John Barbagelata.

Even before meeting her, he had formed a bad opinion of Feinstein from a neighborhood friend who attended Sacred Heart with her. This woman confided to John that Dianne was so exceedingly ambitious that she had declared her intention to be mayor of San Francisco as far back as high school.

Barbagelata had run for supervisor against his better judgment and all the odds. He finished fourth as a nonincumbent, but his triumph was always overshadowed by Dianne's.

A salty, plainspoken man, Barbagelata was what native San Franciscans, perhaps the most parochial people in the world, call "born and raised." In the 1960s, his real estate business was booming on the west side of Twin Peaks. The highest points in San Francisco, "the peaks" are the demarcation line between the city's fog belt and its sunnier neighborhoods—and, in political terms, between its conservative and liberal citizens. Life was good for him, his wife, and eight children except for one thing: he saw his town going to the dogs.

There was the massive busing plan to ship kids out of their neighborhoods and into schools miles away, which Barbagelata and his neighbors fought. Then came the homosexuals, holding hands and kissing right out on the street, and liberal politicians like Willie Brown and George Moscone wooing their votes. The worst was the invasion of long-haired hippies with their free sex and free drugs in the Haight-Ashbury district. Barbagelata had been to Calcutta but "this was worse," he said, especially with the embarrassment of seeing his town portrayed on national TV as a mecca of deviant social revolution.

A lot of people in San Francisco shared his belief in traditional families and moral values, so he ran for supervisor to give them a voice at City Hall. He spent $800 for an old web printing press, bought reams of paper, and taught his oldest son how to run it. Before long, he had papered the neighborhoods west of the peaks with pamphlets, like a cross between George Babbitt and Tom Paine, calling on the citizens to save their city from ruin. "Haven't you had enough? Our city is in sad shape," his flyer declared. "A vote for Barbagelata is a vote for change. Let's start cleaning house."

In the campaign, the pundits and the insiders paid even less attention to Barbagelata than they did to Feinstein. But as he would do time and again over the next ten years, he showed how well he understood the often forgotten people of the city, shocking the political establishment by winning a seat on the board of supervisors. When he won, the papers promptly pointed out that his name meant "frozen beard" in Italian, which seemed very fitting after he promised he would be "a real tough supervisor—the meanest one you ever saw."

Barbagelata had run a business long enough to know that you couldn't cut costs without cutting the payroll. So it seemed clear to him that all the annual fuss about City Hall budget problems boiled down to rapacious wages, fringe benefits, and sweetheart deals that the city workers' unions had made with the supervisors in exchange for campaign contributions and election support. The only solution was holding the line on city employees, and he waged a lonely battle for years to do that.

But Dianne and her allies on the board took a different tack to balance the budget. In her first year she backed a package of new taxes on business, arguing that it was the best alternative to higher property taxes. Over Barbagelata's objections, Dianne and five allies approved a new employer payroll tax, a new parking tax, a new utilities tax, a doubling of the existing business tax on gross receipts, and, later, a new ticket tax on events at Candlestick Park. Soon after, she pressed unsuccessfully for a municipal income tax for San Francisco.

"All of these antibusiness taxes are forcing many businesses to leave San Francisco," Barbagelata said at the time. The 1970 fight over taxes was the first of many the two supervisors would have over budget issues, which dominated City Hall debate for the next decade. "Dianne Feinstein did more damage to San Francisco than any politician in history," said Barbagelata, still thundering twenty years later.

The two clashed on less weighty matters than public finance. At one point during their first year, Barbagelata fought bitterly against Feinstein's wish to fly the flag of the United Nations over the Opera House to celebrate an anniversary of the founding of the UN in San Francisco. This mundane matter deteriorated into a nasty name-calling session that illustrated the personal nature of their feud and ended with Barbagelata angrily accusing Dianne of "tongue-lashing" him in front of his colleagues.

On a more substantive issue, Feinstein and Barbagelata also differed over the city's court-ordered school-busing integration plan. Like other big cities, San Francisco at the time was being torn apart by the emotions over busing. Amid a series of teacher strikes, some parents held their children out of school rather than put them on crosstown buses in accordance with a federal judge's order. Chinese Americans tried to stop the plan while blacks took legal action to enforce it.

Dianne became a favorite of the busing-for-integration forces while Barbagelata opposed the plan. He was not the city's most visible foe of busing, however. That was Mayor Alioto, whose disagreements with Feinstein over this and other issues would build into a political showdown a year later.

Antibusing efforts lost in court and before the school board. So the mayor and Barbagelata pressed the attack in the spring of 1970 with a proposed amendment to the city charter to make the school board, which was then appointed, an elective body. This would have given a boost to the antibusing forces, who were well organized politically and probably could have elected a majority that supported their stand. But when Alioto's plan came up before a supervisors' committee for a hearing, Dianne produced a competing proposal. It called for expanding the size of the school board and making it elected, but with members chosen within nine districts rather than at large, a feature that would have watered down the strength of the antibusing forces.

Dianne, who as a Stanford student leader had focused on the intricacies of nuts-and-bolts debate, set off a round of mind-numbing discussion over the arcane election processes involved in each school board plan. The net effect of Feinstein's measure was to muddy the waters, and delay consideration of Alioto's plan until it was too late to get it on the upcoming ballot. Russ Cone wrote that since the mayor's election in 1967, this marked "the first major Alioto defeat on the [supervisors'] side of City Hall." It would not be the last, however.

The most controversial aspect of Alioto's reign in the mayor's office was his downtown development policy, derided by critics as "Manhattanization." For twenty years, debate raged over the economic, social, and aesthetic costs and benefits of this policy, whose purpose was to attract corporate headquarters, banks, insurance, and other white-collar service companies to San Francisco, transforming its economy and making it the financial gateway to Asia. Opponents, led by the liberal, slow-growth neighborhood movement that had helped elect Feinstein, argued that Manhattanization cost the city more in services than it returned in taxes, that it benefited commuters instead of residents in the types of jobs created, that it destroyed small and blue-collar businesses, and that it generated waves of density outward from downtown.

The physical effects of Alioto's policy, which was supported by a strong coalition of business and labor interests, was easy to see: during his first term of office, thirty-one high rises representing millions of square feet of office space had been built or approved, changing the skyline of San Francisco forever.

Dianne had come to office as a staunch opponent of Manhattanization. During the campaign she said:

> Much of the special feeling of San Francisco comes because we are graced with hills and a certain subtle view made possible by the dimension of our building. But this will vanish if we continue to surround the city with tall buildings.
>
> There is a necessity that we come up with the type of environmental controls that will protect that beauty of San Francisco in an unmarred and unpolluted condition.

A flash point of the development debate came in her first year in office. United States Steel Corporation had proposed to build a 550-foot skyscraper on the San Francisco waterfront, far bigger than anything allowed under existing planning codes. Alioto and his coalition pushed the project and the planning commission, appointed by the mayor, approved variances needed for the massive structure. But the supervisors had to affirm the decision, and their discussion of the proposal set off a monumental debate on the other side of City Hall.

The neighborhood-environmentalist forces organized a petition drive and unprecedented thousands of telegrams, coupons, letters, cards, and telephone calls poured into the supervisors' offices. In late October, residents packed a hearing of the board's Planning Committee, where one speaker charged that Alioto "has achieved more destruction of an American city than King Kong himself."

The key vote was scheduled for November 15, 1970. Supporters of the project now counterattacked, organizing the largest City Hall rally in history. Hundreds of building-trades workers, many wearing hardhats, packed into the chambers while another two thousand rallied across from City Hall in Civic Center Plaza.

Dianne declared her outright opposition to the U.S. Steel project. During hours of heated and emotional debate, she left her seat presiding on the dais to address the issue from the floor. Arguing that, despite its economic benefits, the project was overwhelmingly out of scale for the city and its waterfront, among the most valuable real estate on the West Coast, she was booed and jeered by the probuilding crowd.

She did not wither before them. "I am surprised at how easily these gentlemen are led," she said with contempt. "I suggest you go home and talk to your wives about this."

In the end, Dianne and her allies would win the war when a state regional planning agency blocked construction of the U.S. Steel building. But that day in late 1970 she lost a tactical victory, as the Alioto forces won a ninety-day delay to give them time to lobby wavering supervisors. In a prescient analysis, Russ Cone reported the next day that the delay "booted the issue into the 1971 mayor's race."

7

A BOXING LESSON

Be loyal.

—*Dianne Feinstein's Rules for Getting Ahead*

ONE AUTUMN NIGHT IN 1970, Dianne and a few friends covertly visited a pornographic theater in San Francisco. With Merla Zellerbach and her husband, Fred Goerner, in tow, Supervisor Feinstein went to get a first-hand look at porno films, which had suddenly become one of the fastest-growing industries in a city with a tradition of wide-open morals dating back to the Barbary Coast.

What she saw truly shocked her. "We have become a kind of smut capital of the United States," the board of supervisors' president told reporters a few days later. "I didn't quite believe the real low this kind of activity had reached until I went to one of these theaters and witnessed firsthand some of the activities there. As a woman, I feel very strongly about it, because part of what is happening, what is shown on the screens, works to the basic denigration and humiliation of the female."

Feinstein then launched a crusade against the smut industry that helped to put her into the top rank of San Francisco celebrity politicians. In a city that thrives on political and sexual gossip, her campaign became the talk of the town. Libertines and libertarians assailed her as a bluenose matron while conservatives on the west side of the city backed what she was trying to do.

As it happened, Feinstein's new burst of publicity coincided with the declining fortunes of Mayor Joseph Alioto. Hailed just a few years before as a rising star among national Democrats, Alioto was aggressively pursuing an ultimately successful libel suit against *Look* magazine, which had charged that he was a key figure in the Mafia. Alioto also was under federal indictment in the state of Washington in a case alleging his law firm had engaged in illegal fee splitting. In San Francisco, his national political ambitions rankled some, while his staunch opposition to busing stirred the angry integration contro-versy and his high-rise development binge and hard-line police tactics against hippies, gays, and anti–Vietnam War demonstrators infuriated liberals.

As he looked ahead to his 1971 reelection campaign, it added up to polit-ical trouble for Alioto. Soon gossip was buzzing about the possibility of the young supervisor Feinstein taking on the embattled mayor. As Feinstein's new crusade raised her public profile ever higher, environmentalists, minori-ties, and powerful people with axes to grind and agendas to push kept whis-pering the idea in her ear. Puffed up with her stunning victory of 1969, she kept listening.

After extended indecision, Feinstein at the very last moment decided to run against Alioto. It was the first and greatest political miscalculation of her career. "I should have known better and I didn't," she would reflect twenty years later. "But it brought a whole adage to me—I'll make a mistake once, but by God, I'm not going to make the same mistake twice."

DIANNE WAS AT A DINNER PARTY with Merla and Fred, among others, when conversation turned to the recent expansion of the pornographic film industry in San Francisco, led by the success of Jim and Artie Mitchell. Mak-ers of hits like *Behind the Green Door,* the Mitchell brothers introduced a new genre of feature-length sex films with attractive actors, elaborate costumes, and pretensions of plot wrapped around the mandatory hard-core scenes. On July 4, 1969, they opened what quickly became a popular theater just a few blocks from City Hall, an open commercial atmosphere far different from the dimly lit Tenderloin porno dens that customers had skulked into for years. Patrons at the new theater included judges, political figures, and City Hall reporters, some of whom routinely visited on their lunch hours.

The Mitchells were the most prominent among scores of would-be im-presarios, as the number of porno movie theaters grew from six to thirty in just eighteen months, amid City Hall whispers that organized crime money was behind some of them. But at the dinner party, one liberal guest ap-plauded the boom, arguing that "pornography is in the eye of the beholder, and that anyone who thought sex films were harmful had a hang-up of their own," another guest recalled.

In the same way that she conducted up-close-and-personal inspection tours of the jails, Feinstein decided to see for herself what was going on. A few nights later she led a small group to one of the theaters and was "appalled" by what she saw. With characteristic energy, and not much thought to the political consequences, she then opened an all-out attack on the industry.

She sponsored legislation to restrict the spread of such theaters and the content of what they could show and commissioned Goerner to research the industry in San Francisco. She secretly contacted the FBI to discuss allegations of organized crime influence and visited several newspaper publishers to demand that they stop carrying ads for porno movies; one of them angrily swept the page of movie ads she brought with her off his desk, telling her his advertising policies were none of her business.

On November 11 Zellerbach wrote a newspaper column in support of Feinstein's crusade. Headlined "Human Beings at Their Worst," the article began, "A door to hell has swung wide open in San Francisco, but only a few citizens are aware of it." Describing Dianne's visit to the porno theater, Zellerbach wrote:

> What we found was total degradation of the human spirit, a terrifying look into the darkest recesses of the sick mind.
>
> Later investigation revealed a still more horrible range of violence and debasement, including bestiality, whipping, torture, stabbings and gang rapes, photographed in living color and detail and presented to audiences of male voyeurs who furtively masturbated themselves or others during the show.
>
> The total degradation of the female in these films, the low cost, high profit lure to organized crime, the growing damage to our city's reputation should concern every resident.

The journalistic call to arms ignited the simmering controversy. One of Dianne's more articulate foes was Charles McCabe, an erudite and iconoclastic columnist for the *Chronicle*. He wrote a series of columns attacking Feinstein's anti-smut offensive as censorship and Big Motherism, the first headlined "Dianne Faces Life."

"And just how did a nice girl like Dianne Feinstein end up in one of those dirty movie houses in the Mission District?" a McCabe column began soon afterward. Echoing First Amendment arguments that divided communities across America, McCabe accused Feinstein of pursuing her crusade for crass political purposes. He portrayed her as a prudish busybody—a critique based primarily on gender that reinforced her image as an uptight do-gooder.

What really moved Mrs. Feinstein to her little adventure, and her later demand that right mindedness be enacted on all of us is something you don't have to be a big brain to figure out. The real reason lies in the hearts and minds of a segment of elderly Irish biddies and Jewish mothers and Italian mama mias and German hausfraus. These ladies, most of whom are mothers, are threatened by porno and take an awfully strong line on the subject. This they communicate one way or another, and often through priests and rabbis who have a vested interest in sin, to their duly elected representatives of whom Mrs. Feinstein is one. And conscientious.

The way to prevent the men from indulging their brutish natures is to pass laws, and more laws, and still more laws, to keep their pants firmly zipped at all times, except when the population explosion is to be assisted.

McCabe was not alone in his withering commentary. "She took a lot of flack over this issue, which really contributed to her white-glove image," Goerner remembered. "She very early on realized there were political negatives with this."

Some of the heaviest political fallout came in the gay community. Dianne had been the first major politician openly to court homosexual voters. But now she was hit with a backlash from gays leery of her moralizing and angry about some of her comments and actions. One of her early key supporters was an activist named Jim Foster who founded several of the city's gay political clubs, including the Society for Individual Rights, many of whose members backed Dianne in 1969. As the pornography debate intensified, she made a damage-control appearance before SIR that drew three hundred gays in May 1971.

At one point in her crusade Feinstein declared that among its other evils, pornography "promoted homosexual cruising," which some gays charged was a slander on their community. Confronted with the statement, Sacred Heart's Dianne told the group that she was as adamantly opposed to heterosexual cruising as to homosexual cruising. "The gay community has provided a tremendous richness to San Francisco," she told the raucous meeting. "I'm proud to be your representative and to help bring your community more into the mainstream of life here. But this kind of [porno-graphic] material makes a mockery of your community and your contributions as a constructive part of this city."

Feinstein placated her gay audience with specific promises to promote their agenda. She would back qualified, out-front homosexuals for elective office, push for a gay to be appointed to the city's Criminal Justice Council, permit "legitimate gay groups" to use public buildings for meetings, and sponsor an ordinance outlawing job discrimination based on sexual orientation. Her remarks mollified many of those who had challenged her antipornography effort, including George Mendenhall, editor of the organization's newsletter. "I think after tonight, she's got the homosexual vote behind her 100 percent, just like she did in the last election," he said. "We gave her the board of supervisors presidency. Her 3,000 vote margin [of victory] was gay."

Feinstein was true to her word, playing a leading role in making gay rights a major, mainstream issue in San Francisco. As far back as 1965, when she was still on the women's parole board, Dianne cast a dissenting vote against a new regulation which stated that the board "will not countenance homosexual relationships" and expressly prohibited parolees from having such associations. In July 1971, amid great controversy, she cast a deciding vote to put San Francisco on record in favor of landmark state legislation by assemblyman Willie Brown to legalize all private sex acts between consenting adults. The law was seen by the still-nascent gay-rights movement as a way to combat the harassment of homosexuals by police using antisodomy and public morality statutes.

More important, Feinstein authored and obtained passage of a measure to ban job and hiring discrimination against homosexuals in San Francisco. Her ordinance, the first of its kind in the nation, added sex and sexual orientation to race, creed, color, and place of national origin as forms of illegal discrimination. "It's about time we moved into the 1970s," she testified at an emotional committee hearing on the issue in August. "Driving homosexuality underground does not encourage the maturation process."

In his testimony, her gay ally Jim Foster made a personal appeal to conservative supervisors Barbagelata and Michael Driscoll, the latter a funeral director and Alioto ally whom the mayor had appointed to the board. "We are the same people you sell houses to, you eventually bury," Foster said. "In short, gentlemen, we are all around you."

Despite her substantive actions, however, Feinstein's anti-smut crusade planted seeds of doubt among some liberal gay activists about her commitment to and understanding of their cause. Those doubts would grow and eventually damage her politically at several key points in her career.

Despite the criticism from gays, Dianne pressed on with her campaign against pornography, a prime example of her sometimes paradoxical politics. She wrote to Republican governor Ronald Reagan, urging his support for state legislation to give local communities more power to regulate "obscene matter and obscene live conduct."

"Films devoted to bestiality, necrophilia and acts of sado-masochism such as torture and gang rape have become commonplace," she told Reagan. "From a theatrical viewpoint, it is recognized that most of these films lack plot, make no effort to distinguish right from wrong and present the most abnormal acts as acceptable and desirable."

She also introduced a sweeping antipornography ordinance, using the report she had commissioned by Goerner as evidence of the need for strict regulation. Amid extremely graphic descriptions of what was on the screens, Goerner's report noted that "at least 6,000 men" visited dirty movie houses each day. In its original form, Dianne's ordinance would have banned presentations of any sexual conduct, defined as "acts of masturbation, homosexuality, sexual intercourse or physical contact with a person's clothed or unclothed genitals, pubic area, buttocks, or, if such person be a female, breasts."

So broad and far-reaching was this attempt to regulate that even some allies did not support her. At one committee hearing, Supervisors Francois and Robert Gonzales, both attorneys, expressed concern about the constitutionality of her proposal after an attorney for legitimate movie houses testified that it would damage his clients. Dianne, sitting in the audience, grew so passionate about the subject that she twice interrupted the lawyer's testimony—"Can't you see what he's doing? He's going to fight anything," she yelled at one point—and had to be gaveled to order by Gonzales.

She amended her ordinance and relentlessly pursued her battle for several years. Eventually she succeeded in changing local zoning laws to restrict porno theaters and also helped to pass state legislation toughening child pornography laws. "It was, and is, I believe, a legitimate issue in the sense that at some point it ceases to be a freedom of expression issue," she said recently. "And that point is where children are involved or a real defamation of the integrity of an individual is done. It became very clear that the only way to really reasonably control the spread was through zoning, and that took care of that."

THE NEWSPAPERS had a field day with the porn issue, but Feinstein in her first term pressed a full agenda of other programs that drew less attention but, in the months of political drama that followed, would have greater impact. In 1970 Barbagelata suffered the first of several heart attacks, which he blamed on politics at City Hall. With her chief nemesis out of commission as 1971 began, Dianne continued to "dominate the initiative in city affairs," as Russ Cone wrote at the time.

Positioning herself as a champion of the burgeoning conservation movement, she pushed for new government regulation of many aspects of the environment. She drafted legislation to close loopholes in existing height limit laws and establish controls on the bulk and color of buildings permitted in all areas of the city. She also passed the noise-pollution-control ordinance drafted by her think tank and cast a key vote against construction of a long-debated new bridge into San Francisco. In February 1971 the slow-growth forces won a major victory when the state Bay Conservation and Development Commission stopped plans for the controversial U.S. Steel tower by imposing permanent height limits on the waterfront.

"We're a city struggling to keep alive," she said in a speech reflecting her apocalyptic views of the time. "I'm convinced the world has only ten years in which to come up with controls—on population, the automobile, residential use—with which to manage the environment, or it will be too late."

So formidable and visible did Feinstein become that concern about her ambitions began to grow within the mayor's office. In the spring a top aide to Alioto met privately with her and reported back that he obtained a promise she would not challenge the mayor. The aide even sent Feinstein a dozen red roses to memorialize the alleged deal. Within months, the roses would become a standing joke in Alioto's office.

In 1968 Alioto had nearly been chosen as the running mate of Hubert Humphrey, whom he nominated at the violence-plagued national convention in Chicago. But then came the damaging *Look* magazine article, based on anonymous federal law enforcement sources, and the $2.3 million fee-splitting case brought by the government, in which he was later acquitted. Alioto was convinced that Richard Nixon's Justice Department, under attorney general John Mitchell, was behind both. Preoccupied with clearing his name nationally, he had become damaged goods locally.

By April, persistent rumors that Feinstein would seek to unseat him in November were so rampant that the *Oakland Tribune* published a story stating flatly that she had decided to run. "That's not so," Feinstein said the next day. "I am not a candidate. I do not plan to become a candidate. I have even turned down attendance at some meetings where I felt the effort might be made to promote me as a candidate. With [the] problems facing the city, I want to be free to work with the mayor in helping resolve these matters."

But as spring turned into summer in 1971, the rumors would not die. Francois, unhappy with Alioto's stand on busing and controversies involving police department actions in the black community, privately urged her to run. So did William Brinton, a prominent attorney and former planning commissioner who was feuding with the mayor over the massive Yerba Buena Center redevelopment project. And so did some neighborhood leaders opposed to Alioto's development policies, including attorney Jim Haas who led the think tank. "A number of us kept lobbying her to do it," Haas recalled. "It was largely a reaction to Alioto—that he was not providing leadership, that he was a bully on the wrong side of too many issues."

The deadline for declaring a candidacy was Friday, September 19. As the date approached, Alioto foes kept trying to persuade Feinstein, appealing to her ambition and arguing that the mayor was mortally wounded. Dianne kept making firm statements of noncandidacy in public while actively considering the matter in private. Only a few days before the close of filing, she insisted to the press that reports of her imminent candidacy were "just rumors." "I don't want to run for mayor," she said, adding that it would be "foolish" for her to get in a mere seven weeks before the election.

At least the latter statement was true.

Still agonizing about whether to run forty-eight hours before the deadline, an indecisive Feinstein convened a meeting at Lyon Street with about a dozen close friends and supporters. "It went back and forth, back and forth," said Haas, who left early in the evening after urging Dianne to run. Fred Goerner argued strenuously that it would be a mistake to challenge the mayor, then also left as the meeting dragged on past midnight. Bruce Kennedy, who recalled that "we had had a lot to drink," and Lynn, who thought running was a mistake, both stayed late. By the time they left, both were convinced that Dianne would not run. Among the last to leave was Terry Francois, whose advice carried the day.

Early in the morning Dianne started calling supporters and telling them she would run against Alioto—and seek to make history by becoming the first woman mayor of a major American city. "You left too early," she told Goerner. "I've decided to do it."

Three hours before filing closed on Friday, Dianne appeared at the registrar's office with two hundred supporters who spelled out her name like cheerleaders and then sang "For she's a jolly good fellow" as she signed her candidacy papers. It was the high point of her campaign.

FEINSTEIN'S FORMAL ANNOUNCEMENT was made at her Pacific Heights home. The "slim matron with flashing blue eyes," the press noted, "selected a powder blue outfit with white buttons" for the occasion.

In a mild shot at Alioto's ethical troubles, she pledged "a leadership of total dedication, total integrity, and total truth." Reporters, burned by her earlier strong denials, were more interested in her credibility. In response to questions, she insisted that she was running not because of personal ambition but for selfless public purposes. "I'm running for mayor because I'm not a political animal," she declared with a straight face. "After a lot of analysis, I really do feel I'm a better executive and a better administrator" than Alioto.

Whatever analysis went into Dianne's decision in the bleary early morning hours of debate at Lyon Street was skewed by the late entry into the race of yet another major candidate, attorney Harold Dobbs. A Republican and former supervisor, Dobbs had lost to Alioto in 1967 but, like Feinstein, now was willing to bet that the politically injured mayor was unelectable. Dobbs had scheduled his announcement press conference at the same time as hers, before he knew she was running, and only a few reporters attended his event. The *Chronicle* reported the next day that he provided a truck to haul everyone to Lyon Street and piggyback onto Feinstein's press conference.

In Alioto's camp, reaction to the last-minute entrants was lighthearted—at least in public. "Anyone can enter the mayor's race and Harold usually does," the mayor said of Dobbs. As for Feinstein, he merely said, "The more the merrier."

Behind the scenes, the mayor and his men were not merry. "The Alioto folks were very unhappy with her," recalled John Monaghan, the saloon keeper who had introduced Dianne to campaigns and now served Alioto as a City Hall political aide. "They figured they'd been double-crossed." Monaghan had a lot of fun regaling people with the tale of the dozen red roses sent to seal the alleged bargain with Feinstein. Alioto, who also had received assurance that Dianne would not run from several top labor leaders who talked to her, was not all that amused. "Did I resent the fact she ran against me? Yes," he recalled. "I am Sicilian. I think there is a certain loyalty in politics. I had supported her and given her her first job in city government and she went after me when I was vulnerable."

Feinstein almost instantly regretted getting into the campaign. "I shouldn't have been in that race, I didn't belong in it," she said. "It was too soon. I should have stayed where I was, earned my reputation, earned my spurs, become a good legislator. But you get someplace and you allow yourself to be seduced by people who, for their own reasons, want you in a race. There's only one reason to be in a race, and that's your own, not others'."

Within the Alioto camp, among those most outraged was Sandy Weiner, the brash campaign consultant who had engineered Dianne's 1969 upset. He had discussed a possible mayoral bid with Dianne in 1971 and later told friends she assured him she would not run. Then he signed up to run Alioto's reelection campaign. After she announced, Weiner had an angry phone conversation with her. "We're going teach you a lesson—you better keep your promises in politics," he yelled. "I'm going to make sure that you finish third."

Weiner was not the only key former supporter now against Dianne. Fund-raiser Ann Alanson, hotelman Mel Swig, community activist Eloise Westbrook, and other members of the impressive coalition Dianne had forged in 1969 now lined up with the incumbent. "Mrs. Feinstein has been a good supervisor but she is way over her head in running for a job in which she has no legal, business, or administrative experience," said Agar Jaicks, the Democratic county committee leader who had been one of Dianne's chief sponsors in 1969.

Assemblyman Willie Brown, who had been the only elected official to support her in her first run, called Dianne "a female Joe Alioto. If you have two Aliotos, why not pick Joe?" he said. "I just don't think she's offered the breath of fresh air to move away from the incumbent."

Feinstein did keep some loyalists, beginning with her family. Bert and Leon again led the fund-raising effort, pitching in $15,000 apiece, as did Bert's father. Lynn and Bruce, despite their reservations, worked full time on the campaign. Even Jack Berman, disregarding his icy relationship with Dianne, made a campaign contribution after Katherine called and asked him to do it.

But she won only a smattering of institutional support. The Black Leadership Forum, a liberal group founded by Francois, narrowly endorsed her, as did several key gay organizations. At one point Merla Zellerbach and Fred

Goerner were dispatched to represent her at a transvestite ball, where an annual "Empress of San Francisco" contest was held. The two were paraded down a runway and received an enthusiastic response ("Fred got asked to dance," his wife recalled) in recognition of the respect that Feinstein was showing the gay community.

"You know my stand on the homophile community—my door is open," she told members of the politically active, gay-oriented Tavern Guild. "I'm all for people to live their individual lifestyles without undue harassment."

The 1971 campaign also brought in some new people who would become important in her career and personal life. One was attorney Gene Gartland, who was brought to Lyon Street by Mendelsohn. They talked about politics for a while and, as he got up to leave, Gartland looked at Dianne and asked, "Get stuck out on the bay lately?"

"You're him," she said with surprise, suddenly recognizing the man who had towed her in from the Golden Gate during her brief stint as a sailor. Gartland became a trusted adviser and, with his wife, a close friend of the Feinsteins.

The campaign also attracted an energetic young operative named Marcia Smolens. Newly arrived from New Jersey, where she had taught public school in the ghetto, she was unemployed when she wandered into Dianne's headquarters wearing blue jeans and an Army jacket, intrigued by the idea of a woman running for mayor. She was put to work answering phones. Among her first callers was Dianne's mother, who phoned several times with various demands. Smolens, who knew nothing of the family secrets, chatted amiably with Betty. When she left that day, she told Lynn she wouldn't be back because she needed a paying job. "Please come back," Lynn told her. "You're the only one who's been able to handle our mother." Before long, Smolens was one of the few paid staff members, working twelve hours a day on the campaign.

One day late in the campaign, she was hitchhiking to work and a black limousine stopped for her. When the door opened she saw Joe Alioto inside, with several members of his family. Finding discretion the better part of valor, she didn't mention she was working for Dianne and had the driver drop her a few blocks from headquarters.

The rest of the Feinstein organization, which had impressed professionals in 1969 with its proficiency, was thrown together on the run, and performed like it. With Weiner working against her, Dianne hired as her manager Ken Macker,

a sports promoter and public relations man whom Goerner recalled as "a conge-
nial guy who let the campaign staff run wild while he drank white wine and
tended to other accounts." Dianne's TV spots, which had been the key to her
victory two years earlier, were a disaster.

Rick Seifert, a local writer who worked in the campaign, later recounted
Macker's less-than-inspirational opening to the address to the troops: "At the
first meeting with volunteers the day after filing, Macker, when introduced
as the new campaign manager and asked to run the meeting, declined to
take charge, saying that he felt he could learn more by listening to others,"
Seifert wrote. "None of us realized then how right he was."

Feinstein hired *Chronicle* City Hall reporter Maitland Zane as press secretary. It was his first, and last, venture onto the other side of politics. He
found that the smiling, friendly person he had covered as a supervisor was
different from the woman he now encountered as a boss. "I found myself in
a whirlpool," he recalled. "Everything was improvised. The candidate was a
tyrant who was trying to do everything but lick the stamps and mail the flyers. She thought she could run the campaign and be the candidate."

As Macker floundered, Bert quietly went to Bruce Kennedy and asked
him to start running the show.

At times the energy of Dianne's hard-core supporters created a sense of
momentum, especially when she would breeze into the headquarters and
thrill the faithful, decked out in their "I love Dianne" buttons. "Whenever
Dianne came to the headquarters, it was electric," Smolens said. "But it was
a very insular campaign. We had no idea that in the world out there, we
were very small in number." The harsh political reality was that San Francisco voters simply did not see Feinstein as equal to the job of mayor. That
was clear in a poll that Kennedy commissioned and then refused to show
even to Lynn, so bad were the numbers.

"I didn't belong in the race," Feinstein said recently. "I wasn't clear why I
was running, nor did I have the experience or the base. If there was any race
I wish I could have undone, it was that one, because I got out there and got
creamed."

BESIDES DRUBBING HER on organization, Alioto pummeled Dianne on
issues. For months she had criticized the mayor for playing politics with the
sweeping busing plan, ordered by a federal judge in April 1971, that had
divided the city. After the mayor endorsed a boycott of the busing program,

she accused him of "acting irresponsibly" and "fanning the potential for violence." But her position was untenable, for both political and personal reasons.

In June San Franciscans had voted on a policy resolution on public school busing, opposing the court-ordered plan by a more than three-to-one margin. Despite such sentiment, Feinstein saw Alioto's actions in the controversy as a key reason for taking on the mayor. "It is inconvenient, costly, and tiring on our children," she said of the busing plan. "But busing to achieve integration is the law of the land, and we must abide by the law." Her lofty statements might at least have won her points for standing on principle—until the Alioto camp spread the word that the advocate of busing other people's children sent her own daughter to an exclusive private school.

"She was a double-standard hypocrite" on busing, recalled Quentin Kopp. Kopp, who years before had had a dead-end date with Dianne, was the lawyer representing a group of Chinese American parents who had intervened in the court case in an effort to stop the forced busing plan for their children. In 1971, as Dianne ran for mayor, Kopp campaigned successfully for supervisor as an antibusing candidate, doing so well that Alioto invited him to ride in the mayoral limousine to events in the final weeks of the campaign.

Another costly issue for Dianne was her support of tax increases. Besides the package of new business taxes she backed as a freshman supervisor, she also had promoted the idea of a city income tax. The proposal was studiously researched by the think tank, whose members calculated that a local tax of 1 to 1.5 percent of adjusted gross income would bring an additional $38 to $53 million a year into the treasury. In the campaign, Dianne tried to cast the idea as a way to capture revenue from commuters, to avoid property-tax increases on city homeowners:

> We have been exploring a form of municipal income tax on income earned in San Francisco, which would bring in new revenue from those who earn their living in San Francisco . . . but who live elsewhere. Without such a tax . . . significant reductions in property tax are impossible.

But the tax was fraught with problems, not the least of which was that it was illegal, because the state banned local governments from collecting taxes on earned income. One night at a candidates' forum held at a savings and loan office west of Twin Peaks, where Kopp had quickly built a loyal follow-ing among conservative voters, Dianne proposed it once again. In a scene that would soon be frequently repeated at City Hall, Kopp angrily re-sponded, accusing Feinstein of "intellectual dishonesty" in proposing such a tax. "It infuriated me," he recalled. "I was so offended intellectually and of-fended by her bullshit."

Dobbs, the Republican mayoral entry who challenged Dianne for the role of chief foil to Alioto, hung the income tax proposal around her neck like a stone. "With no previous employment prior to her election as a super-visor," he thundered in one speech, "with no savvy on how a city must live within its means, she has already helped saddle all of you with a payroll tax, a gross receipts tax, a garage tax, a utility tax, and a sewer tax. Now she has the nerve to announce . . . that the way to solve our crushing tax burden is add just one more tax—a city tax on every penny you earn, just like the state and federal income taxers."

Goerner, among others, warned Dianne of the problems inherent in the tax proposal. But, characteristically, she felt that the idea represented sound public policy and that its merits would overcome the political costs. "I warned her about the coming tax revolt, but she didn't believe it," he said. "It was part of being privileged and not having to worry about paying taxes."

As a political matter, the net effect of the drumbeat of attacks on busing and taxes was to underscore Dianne's image as a Pacific Heights matron out of touch with ordinary working people, someone who did not have to push a shopping cart or worry about making ends meet. It didn't help when she pointed out that, "I have a housekeeper who does everything—the market-ing, the preparing and serving of meals. But I've always felt that the impor-tant thing was the kind of time you spend with your family, not the amount."

If there was one wedge issue that Feinstein might have been expected to use against Alioto, it was the boiling debate about downtown development. With the pro-business Dobbs running on the right of the mayor, Dianne seemed to have the very active, liberal environmental movement to herself. "I am opposed to Manhattanization of San Francisco by high-rise developers and I insist that they shift the emphasis to rebuilding deteriorating neighbor-hoods," she said at one event. But while cloaking herself in anti-Manhat-tanization rhetoric, her actions were more cautious.

Besides the mayor's race, there was avid interest in 1971 in a simultaneous campaign over a ballot measure seeking to impose strict and permanent height limits on buildings in San Francisco. The neighborhood movement, which had crystallized when city residents staged the antifreeway revolt in the 1960s—leaving stubs of unfinished freeways as testament to its power— gained even more momentum in the high-rise battle and the U.S. Steel victory. Now, the slow-growth forces had qualified for the ballot a measure, called Proposition T, to limit all new buildings to six stories. It was a radical idea and Dianne characteristically tried to steer a middle-of-the-road course that satisfied its supporters, whom Monaghan derisively called "the bird-watcher vote," while not alienating its staunch business and labor opponents.

Her hesitation in taking a clear stand on the hottest measure on the ballot made her look indecisive and cost her volunteers she sorely needed. In late October, she finally announced her opposition to the ballot measure, saying it was "neither wise nor possible to arrive at a rigid yardstick" on building height. Typically, she tried to soften the blow with her own compromise plan for an eighteen-month moratorium on high rises while a new urban design plan for the city was finished.

It was too little, too late. Although Proposition T was defeated, it won many thousands more votes than Feinstein, who did not obtain the environmental support she had hoped. Her decision not to back the measure stirred distrust of her within the slow-growth movement, as her antipornography crusade had done with some gays.

Dianne also did not capitalize on another of Alioto's perceived weaknesses, his much publicized ethical problems. Within her campaign there was an ongoing debate about whether she should attack the mayor head on over the fee-splitting case. Her reluctance to do so struck some insiders as based on a naive sense that hardball politics was played by Queensberry rules. "Joe and his wife were once quite kind to me," Zane recalled Dianne telling him at one point. "He's innocent until proven guilty."

A month before the election, Dianne got a clear opening for an ethical attack on ethics when police chief Al Nelder abruptly resigned amid reports that he had been pressured to endorse the mayor. Nelder, a career cop who would later be elected a supervisor and become one of Feinstein's close advisers and allies, felt that he was being undermined by Alioto. Despite urgings by several advisers that she accuse Alioto of "strong-arm tactics" and "back-room politics," Dianne refused to jump on the issue. "It's not my style," she told them. "They'll accuse me of playing politics with the police." After hesitating for several days, she finally rebuked Alioto on the issue, but he quickly performed political jujitsu on crime, one of Dianne's best issues.

A few weeks before the election, a white police officer shot and killed a black burglary suspect in Hunters Point, setting off an angry reaction in the black community. Dianne criticized the "hands-off" approach of Alioto's police commission to the shooting and promised to appoint a new commission with new, independent powers to investigate such incidents. Alioto swiftly charged that Feinstein was advocating a "civilian review board," portraying her as a liberal on crime despite the fact that since her days on the prison board she had grown more conservative on criminal justice issues and was a dependable vote for the police department.

"I'm going to have to take a heavy scurrilous attack from the mayor," she said at a debate after Alioto had assailed her as soft on crime. "Well, Joe Alioto, I can take it as much as you can dish it out." On that score, as on so many others in 1971, she was badly mistaken. For while Dianne ran a Queensberry challenge to Alioto, he gave her what Monaghan called "a little boxing lesson."

At a time when the women's movement was still emerging, and when political correctness was unheard of, the 1971 election was a sexist milestone. "It takes a *strong* man to run a big city," Alioto proclaimed in his campaign brochure. At every opportunity Alioto or his surrogates reminded voters that he was a "tough man" doing a "tough job," a double-edged message that both highlighted Alioto's greatest political asset and underscored Dianne's biggest weakness—widespread doubts that a woman could handle the job.

Dobbs was even less subtle, and more sarcastic. After Feinstein complained about the rough campaign tactics of her opponents, the Republican called for her to "go back to the kitchen."

She says "men are picking on poor little me." Old Harry Truman uttered more than one political truth. But the one that applies the most forcefully to Mrs. Feinstein is, "if you can't stand the heat, get out of the kitchen." Of course, in her case, it might be altered to advise that if she can't stand the heat of a campaign, the office of mayor might prove a bit too wearing and perhaps she should go back to the kitchen.

In sheer numbers, Dianne's bid to make history as the nation's first major woman mayor might have benefited from the fact that registered women voters outnumbered their male counterparts by 178,000 to 162,000. But the tricky crosscurrents of gender politics jolted her throughout the campaign. At headquarters, Lynn constantly fended off questions from female callers who doubted a woman could be a chief executive. "They'd say, 'She's a nice lady, but should she really be our mayor?'" Lynn recalled. At the same time, feminists complained that Dianne did not make gender a big enough issue. Among them was a Feinstein volunteer who wrote a critical analysis of the campaign in the *San Francisco Fault,* an alternative newspaper. "More people at the headquarters today, specifically more men," it began. "Six or eight of them, a little self-consciously think tank types, segregated in a conference room. But no women. Why is that, Dianne?"

Her ground-breaking campaign, plus Alioto's much-publicized legal problems, drew national attention to the race. A *Washington Post* reporter summed up Dianne's image problems and the cultural conflicts inherent in her struggle to demonstrate executive ability for a traditional man's job without forsaking the traditional femininity that had been such an important part of her success:

> Most observers agree that Mrs. Feinstein's Junior League starchiness (she good naturedly accepts the title "Mrs. Clean") and civic league programs (her latest proposal: neighborhood meetings for community input on budget matters), have made it difficult for her to emerge as a sharply etched personality with tough minded ideas.

A female political reporter for the Associated Press described her as "no strident crusader, very much of a woman." She also wrote that

> Mrs. Feinstein herself says that while she agrees with many of the goals of women's liberation, such as economic and political equality, she feels no identification with the bra burners.
>
> "I am not a threat to [my husband]," Mrs. Feinstein said. "I have worked all through our marriage and he still brings me breakfast in bed every Sunday morning."

Feinstein herself reflected that, at the time, she felt women looked at her and thought, "What's wrong with her? If she's so young and pretty, why isn't she at home?"

"Women have petty jealousies against each other," she said then. "They suspect and mistrust one another. This is one of our greatest detriments as females." At a local chapter meeting of the National Organization for Women, where she was endorsed, Dianne spoke about how difficult it was to run for high public office. "Most women can't accept a woman running a city," she said. "They feel as threatened as men do."

Crushed by local political issues and national cultural mores, Feinstein limped to the finish line, while Alioto got a second wind to take full advantage of his incumbency and finish strong. Feinstein desperately tried to seize the initiative, challenging him to "come out and fight like a man" by debating her one-on-one. The mayor responded with a condescending offer to take her along on his excursions since she was "having trouble raising an audience" and to draw her a map of the city since she "might have difficulty finding the way."

"Joe was unforgiving and unforgetting," said Hadley Roff, Dianne's old acquaintance from Stanford who would become her top adviser but at the time was Alioto's campaign spokesman. When Feinstein complained bitterly that Alioto volunteers were tearing down her campaign signs, Roff with mock solemnity vowed to investigate her claim, adding that "maybe this is an indication that her campaign is failing and people don't want her signs up anymore."

Her most humiliating moment came when a press conference was interrupted by the owner of a topless nightclub called the Garden of Eden who tried to present her with a $500 contribution. Mindful of her anti-smut campaign, he brought along three scantily clad dancers who shed their fur coats on cue to reveal bare bellies painted in Day-Glo to spell out, "Dianne for mayor." "It was about the only time we got her on TV the whole campaign," recalled press secretary Zane.

Her emotional rock, as always, was Bert, who did double duty for some of the distraught staff. After Jim Haas lost his temper at headquarters, he recalled, Bert asked him to come to his office at the hospital for a private chat. "You need to relax," he told Haas there. "Here's some Valium."

Long before the polls closed election day, Dianne knew her bold gambit had failed badly. When the votes were counted, Alioto was easily reelected on the strength of his big business–big labor coalition, winning by twenty-seven thousand votes, nearly double his margin of victory four years before.

Sandy Weiner was good to his word: Dianne finished an embarrassing third, behind Harold Dobbs, capturing less than one-quarter of the total vote.

The next day, after a postmortem press conference, Dianne was asked by a female TV reporter if she thought the lack of support from women had been crucial to her defeat. Dianne answered no. As she walked away, the reporter smirked at her cameraman, "She still doesn't get it," ironically presaging by twenty years a rallying cry of the Year of the Woman in politics. Dianne's sister Yvonne, who had come to town to help on the campaign, overheard the comment. "She was absolutely right about women not backing Dianne," Yvonne recalled thinking. "It was like a punch in the stomach."

8

Squeezed in the Middle

Be a team player.

—Dianne Feinstein's Rules for Getting Ahead

In February 1973 Dianne opened the door at Lyon Street to Ron Smith, a well-dressed and well-mannered young political consultant who in a short time in the business had achieved a reputation as a winner. The thirty-something Smith had worked since his graduation from Stanford for Republican candidates. Now, through mutual friend Marcia Smolens, he had an interview appointment with Democrat Feinstein, who was facing a campaign that could make or break her political career.

Looking around, impressed at the well-appointed living room, Smith set down his briefcase, accidentally knocking over and scattering a delicate arrangement of porcelain Tiffany flowers on the table. It was an inauspicious start to a political relationship that would first blossom with victory—but ultimately wither in defeat.

Chastened by her 1971 collapse, Feinstein worked patiently to rebuild her political fortunes. Over the years she would repeat a pattern of defeat and comeback, persevering in political wars and invoking San Francisco's symbol—the mythic phoenix rising from the ashes.

Back at City Hall she was forced, after two years as board president, to give up her spotlight seat on the dais and join her colleagues on the floor of the chambers. Although she again threw herself into work and adjusted to the hardball political lessons she had learned, by 1973 she was worried. Nearing the end of the four-year term that began with such promise, she faced a reelection battle she thought might end her career as quickly as it began. With the antibusing sweep of 1971, voters clearly were in a more conservative mood and she now faced a rematch with her archnemesis, John Barbagelata, that would highlight issues of city spending and crime.

Although she would triumph over him again, it would be a short-lived victory. In 1975 Feinstein reached a second time for the biggest political prize in San Francisco, now as the front-runner for mayor. But she would blunder into yet another disastrous campaign finish. Even more painfully, death and disease would soon take a new emotional toll.

When it was over, a friend recalled, "Dianne felt that she wouldn't have the future she always thought she was going to have."

AFTER THE 1971 LOSS, Dianne and Bert nursed her political wounds at Pajaro Dunes as they gazed out at the ocean through big windows streaked with rain. But returning to City Hall gave her a rude awakening, because the "unforgiving and unforgetting" Alioto wasted little time in punishing his upstart rival.

As a full-time supervisor, Feinstein had served as the city's representative to a host of regional government agencies that combined politics and policy. For several years she had held a seat on the Bay Area Air Pollution Control District board, a multicounty agency that drew yawns from most politicians but dealt with technical planning issues that fascinated her. On the board she had set about the thankless task of learning the intricacies of air basin emissions management and CO_2 and lead standards. Now her tenure gave her the right to become chairman of the board, a modest honor that would boost her political profile at an opportune time.

But Alioto snatched it away. It was the mayor's prerogative to appoint San Francisco's representative and he now declared that the air-pollution problem had grown so serious, it would be necessary for him personally to take the seat. When Feinstein complained to the press, Alioto publicly responded in high-handed fashion: "I appointed her originally and I think she should express her gratitude for that, rather than this kind of spite. It would have been more gracious of her to acknowledge the fact that I maintained her as my personal representative up to this very moment."

In private, according to Dianne, Alioto delivered the message in starker terms: "You don't cash loser's tickets at the winner's window." The epithet haunted her for several years. "I was," she said, remembering the times, "banished to Siberia."

As Feinstein took her new seat in the ornate board chambers, a new political dynamic was emerging among the supervisors. Quentin Kopp, the lanky and aggressive antibusing lawyer, had won a seat, as had John Molinari, the Republican son of a local judge. Together they formed a new conservative coalition with Barbagelata on fiscal issues.

As Feinstein had done two years before, Kopp became an instant standout at City Hall. Dubbed "the town grouch" by Herb Caen, Kopp turned the cross-examination skills he'd acquired prosecuting waterfront thugs in New York onto the labyrinth of unaccountability that was city government in San Francisco. Casting himself as the fleeced taxpayers' best friend, he challenged everyone from the mayor to the medical examiner. He churned out a flurry of cost-cutting measures, proposed numerous amendments to a byzantine city charter that is longer than the U.S. Constitution, and constantly demanded written opinions from the city attorney about the propriety of official actions.

Kopp's abiding interest, shared with Barbagelata, was the sweetheart pay-and-fringe-benefit deals that compliant supervisors for years had provided public employee unions. Chairing the committee with jurisdiction over union contracts, Kopp and his two allies mounted an unprecedented offensive against the unions. Triggering a period of intense public labor strife in San Francisco, Kopp's committee in March 1972 drafted a wage package that for the first time in years included no annual raises for many city employees. "We fully expect to be criticized, pressured, even vilified" for the action, Kopp said. "But we refuse to surrender our responsibility." The unions managed to defeat the proposal, but five supervisors voted for it. Feinstein voted with the six-member liberal majority to approve small raises. It was a hint of things to come, as the city grew more polarized on labor matters.

While siding with the liberals on the wage issue, Feinstein burnished her conservative law-and-order credentials. She pushed a plan for promotions to be based more on merit than on politics and pressed for more beat patrolmen and better equipment for cops. "She was always on top of the department. She was a reliable vote for the police," said Al Nelder, who had quit as chief under Alioto and was about to enter politics himself.

Feinstein also quietly abandoned her staunch opposition to the death penalty, the morality of which she had vehemently challenged in her writings while a member of the women's prison board. It was the beginning of a transformation that would shape an important part of her political identity as a national political figure. "I began to look differently at the streets," she recalled, reciting grisly details of the brutal robbery-murders of a neighborhood grocer and his wife during her 1970s tenure on the board. "I began to see that there are people who have no regard for other people's lives—and over time came to forge the view that by your acts you can abrogate your own right to life."

After years of debate following the Supreme Court decision that halted executions, Californians in 1972 voted two-to-one to reinstate the death penalty. San Francisco bucked the conservative tide, however, voting solidly against the ballot measure. Soon afterward, a resolution came before the supervisors, seeking their endorsement of a state bill that would address the courts' concerns while imposing the death penalty for certain crimes, including the killing of a police officer or fireman. With little notice, a majority of the board, including Dianne, voted in favor of the bill.

When the local Democratic committee learned of the vote, it reacted with outrage and demanded that the supervisors who were Democrats retract their votes. "It's a gut issue for liberals in San Francisco," said committee chairman Agar Jaicks. "Emotions run very high on the death penalty."

Several supervisors pleaded that they were unaware of the implications of what they were voting on in the advisory resolution—but not Dianne. "I have sat through the funerals of seven policemen," she declared. "And I know that this kind of deterrent is necessary. I don't believe in the death penalty generally, but for this exception."

In an insightful profile that year, San Francisco writer Mary Jean Haley captured Feinstein's brand of politics in an examination of her record to that point titled "Paradoxical Liberal." She noted Dianne's opposition to height limits, coupled with her demand for down-zoning; her push for more police and statements at the time in support of decriminalization of marijuana; her crusade against sex theaters and embrace of homosexual rights. "[She is] a popular but paradoxical liberal with a tendency to waffle or reverse on traditionally liberal issues which leaves some of her supporters baffled and outraged," Haley wrote, describing Dianne as "conscientious and hardworking, but not agile."

But even as Feinstein grappled with weighty issues, she also generated the kind of "only Dianne" headlines that endeared her to generations of local news editors. On July 25, 1972, she marched into the supervisors' executive bathroom, just off the chambers, which at the time was an exclusively male province. "It's a liberated bathroom now," she declared when she came out, noting the unfairness of the women's room being located far from the board's offices.

Unfortunately for her, the saga did not end there. Her action offended some of her more macho colleagues, who refused to lock the door while using the facility despite her frequent requests, embarrassing the modest Feinstein. "I believe in equality, come on in," Gonzales, who took particular relish in discomfiting her, would say when she walked in on him.

Dianne at one point made a political statement by having a Venus's-flytrap placed in the men's marble urinal. Molinari claimed to have watered it at one late-night meeting, after repeated warnings to Feinstein. The offending plant soon was removed.

Not long afterward, Feinstein accidentally locked herself into the liberated bathroom when the much-debated sixty-year-old brass lock on the door jammed. She drew attention by banging on the door. A slender-hipped city carpenter crawled out a window and, braced by a rope, made his way thirty feet along the outside of City Hall's second story, wiggled into the tiny window of the rest room, and removed the door hinges as other city workers battered down the door. "I'm mortified," she said as she came out to face a gauntlet of cackling newsmen.

WHEN DIANNE AND RON SMITH first discussed her 1973 reelection, he was struck by the fact that she sincerely seemed to fear she might lose her seat, when all his information and political instincts told him it couldn't happen. "She viewed it as whether she could resurrect her career, whether she was viable," Smith said. "It was not looked at as a prelude to the 1975 mayor's race or anything else—it was looked at strictly as salvation."

A gentle man in a business full of sharks, Smith felt "an immediate closeness" to Dianne. Despite their rocky introduction, he soon became devoted to her career, captured by the personal warmth and concern that softened her temper and admiring her earnest commitment to public service. Before long he was a frequent guest at Lyon Street, eating meals prepared by Dianne's housekeeper off TV tables, or driving down to Pajaro for a weekend visit when Dianne in her blue jeans would make eggs and coffee and they would discuss the latest poll.

"With Dianne, everything is always incredibly intense," Smith said.

Assembling a campaign team, he hired Smolens to manage day-to-day affairs and a Republican pollster named Joe Shumate, who would later work for governor Pete Wilson, to do his survey research. Shumate's first poll showed her a "clear number one" in the field for five seats, which included Barbagelata and three other incumbents. But "she didn't believe it," the pollster recalled. "It seemed a combination of personal insecurity and the conventional wisdom that she was damaged goods."

Feinstein had outspent the field in 1969 but could not count on a financial advantage this time. Determined that Barbagelata would beat her in their second race, Barbagelata and Kopp had pushed through a campaign-spending-limit law. "The purpose was to stop her," Kopp said of the spending limit.

Barbagelata again cranked up his printing press and focused his flyers on the neighborhoods populated by homeowners and conservatives who shared his views. But Barbagelata was always a reluctant, awkward campaigner who hated what he called "the phoniness" of politics. On a personal appearance level in San Francisco's face-to-face campaigning, he was no match for Dianne with her telegenic smile, her Sacred Heart breeding, and her friendly, if formal, manner.

As in 1969, Feinstein's campaign again outclassed the field. Ann Alanson, whose first husband had died, had remarried a physician named Dr. Maurice Eliaser and once again contributed her contacts and skills to Dianne. One early fund-raising event was a St. Patrick's Day bash at an Irish bar that Eliaser planned with a simple menu—Irish stew. But Feinstein, ever watchful of the smallest details, called and asked Ann what kind of salad dressing was on the menu. When Eliaser told her there would not be a salad, Dianne insisted that "you have to have a first course." "She was really unhappy about the salad, so I loaded up the place with green carnations," Eliaser recalled. "Working with Dianne, you had to get used to this thing that she couldn't delegate."

On June 22 Feinstein celebrated her fortieth birthday with a big fund-raiser at the Swigs' Fairmont Hotel. Guests included Senator Alan Cranston, Assembly Speaker Leo McCarthy, Assemblyman Willie Brown, and power broker Cyril Magnin—a clear sign that, after 1971, the establishment was back behind her.

That summer, Dianne was surprised when an old friend took a very anti-establishment action that recalled her "social responsibility" training. Sister Mary Mardel, her Sacred Heart headmistress, was jailed with several compatriots in Fresno for joining a nonviolent protest on behalf of farm workers led by Cesar Chavez. When Feinstein found out, she called the jail to speak with her old teacher.

"Sister, what are you doing in jail? What about all the white gloves?" Mardel recalled her former pupil asking. "In her mind, I was still mother superior. She was shocked. This was the most surprising thing to her."

AMONG THE STRONGEST MESSAGES of Feinstein's campaign was her law-and-order stance. In one mailer she was photographed with the head of the Police Officers Association. Many of her campaign materials featured pictures of her and her daughter, with tough vows by the candidate to make the city safe for families. "We used Katherine with Dianne a lot to send a message that she was concerned about the protection and safety of children," Smith said.

Despite such tactics, Dianne again found that women still had a hard time being perceived as tough. At one forum Feinstein showed up in her typical smart Magnin suit and shoes. As she spoke, a female supporter, with her own curly hair sticking out at odd angles, one stocking up and one down, and a hemline two inches below her coat, rushed up to Smith, standing in the back of the hall. "Dianne is wearing the wrong shade of hose with that dress," Smith recalled the woman complaining. "That's all you needed to know about being a woman candidate at that time."

But by autumn the Feinstein campaign was running on all cylinders. Her slogan, "First on your ballot," seemed to her campaign team to presage that she would again win the presidency and reestablish herself politically. Dianne remained insecure, however. Late in the campaign she demanded a new brochure that Smith considered a waste of money. But she badgered him and, a few days before the election, he had it printed.

Copies of it arrived at her house shortly before she and Bert left to campaign at the long-awaited opening of the Bay Area Rapid Transit system. When she got to the event, she stalked to a phone booth, called the headquarters, and bellowed at Smolens, who had the bad luck to answer the phone. Dianne's trademark red campaign color had bled an awful pink and there were several misspellings, including the designation of the "Alice B. Toklas" gay Democratic club as the "Alice B. Tokens" club. "She was screaming unbelievably," recalled Smolens, who held the phone inches from her ear. "Bert said later the whole phone booth was shaking."

A preelection news analysis by Jerry Burns, the *Chronicle's* City Hall reporter, captured her political strengths and weaknesses at the time: "Mrs. Feinstein has been patiently cleaning up the wreckage, broadening her constituency and planning for the future," he wrote. "Nobody puts in longer hours, is more accessible and has a greater zest" for government.

Sounding less than zestful, however, the supervisor complained in the article that she was unappreciated: "People evaluate others' records as a whole. Me, they find one issue they don't agree with and jump on it. I'm not perfect but I hope to God I'm growing in the process."

Noting her "grim application" to her job, the article also quoted several anonymous opinions of Feinstein by fellow supervisors. "If she had more of a sense of humor she'd be happier, but then she'd do less," said one. "She doesn't have the common touch and she never will," said another.

Just before election day, Bernard Orsi, a top Alioto aide, spied Dianne at City Hall and told her, "I got a new poll out" on the supervisors' race.

"Bernie, how am I doing?" she eagerly asked him.

"Well, Dianne you're out of the money, but you're not doing so badly. You know you may get number six even."

Given that only five seats were up, she feared anew that she would lose. On election night, though, her insecurities once more proved groundless. She again finished first, ahead of Barbagelata, who came in second. As an added bonus, her new ally and mentor, former police chief Al Nelder, also was elected.

After the campaign, Feinstein hosted a celebration luncheon for campaign workers and friends at the elegant restaurant L'Etoile. Those who had borne the brunt of her unstinting demands now saw the warm side of her personality on full display. She was "the most gracious, the most perfect hostess," said Marcia Smolens, who recalled Dianne going around the room to pay touching personal thanks to each person. She presented some with wonderful gifts, including a jade necklace with an eighteen-karat gold chain she gave to Smolens.

Soon after, she gave Ron Smith a $500 suit and took him to lunch to savor her victory yet again. "All those people thought I was finished and I wasn't," he recalled her saying.

ON THE DAY AFTER her 1973 reelection, Feinstein said she did not plan to run for mayor again, a promise she would break within a year. "I have absolutely no thoughts of running for mayor," she said. "I'm going to be a full-time supervisor and concentrate on our legislative programs."

Topping her agenda was a fight against the spread of violent crime, which was on the rise. Muggings on public transit by teenage gangs were commonplace and several highly publicized brutal murders had horrified San Franciscans. By the end of 1974, a string of racially motivated, random killings of whites by blacks known as the "Zebra" murders and the incredible saga of the kidnapping of newspaper heiress Patricia Hearst made international headlines and frightened the town. Before long, Dianne herself would become a victim of terrorist violence.

Such gruesome matters, however, were far away from the political love fest that began her second term as board president in early January. Her allies delivered predictable encomiums ("We find you very beautiful and charming and we'd like to see you presiding over the board," Francois said), but it was the vanquished Barbagelata who shocked the crowd. Four years ago he had been the only dissenter against Dianne for president. Today, he ceremoniously rose to present her with a 1916 Brunswick record of the Regent Club Orchestra performing "I'm in Heaven When I See You Smile."

"John," she said girlishly, "this is the nicest thing you've ever done."

Their honeymoon did not last long. Taking a page from Alioto's book of hardball politics, Feinstein removed both Barbagelata and Kopp from positions on influential committees and banished them to a panel overseeing advisory resolutions on state and national affairs. "She gave it to us doggy style," Kopp recalled.

So he and Barbagelata began a guerrilla war against Feinstein. First, they launched a filibuster to protest the new committee assignments. At one point, Barbagelata rose to complain about Mendelsohn replacing him on the Finance Committee and began a personal attack on Feinstein's close ally.

"I'll ask you to sit down," she ordered, in her schoolmarm voice.

"I don't need a mommy, I've got a mommy at home," he snarled back, just before she cut off his microphone.

Petty bickering over perquisites spilled over into more substantive matters, as the annual package of city workers' wages and benefits came before the board. Because employees' salaries represented 70 percent of the city budget, the kind of reforms that Barbagelata and Kopp kept unsuccessfully proposing gained more credence as property taxes kept climbing. The board had begun to stiffen its stance against the unions, which strongly backed Alioto and held sway in the self-proclaimed "labor town."

In early 1974 the full board passed a conservative pay package that had small or no wage increases for thousands of nurses, janitors, clerks, and other workers represented by the Service Employees International Union. A resultant strike, the most destructive in years, lasted nine days. Bus drivers and operators from the Municipal Railway and from regional lines like BART honored the picket lines, snarling the city's traffic and stranding 350,000 commuters. Public hospitals closed and raw sewage emptied into the bay.

The supervisors, led by Feinstein, finally settled the strike with $4.5 million in additional wage increases, over objections by Barbagelata and Kopp. "I would like to compliment you on the way you mounted your picket lines," AFL-CIO chief Jack Crowley told the strikers after it was over, "in the way you kept this city in turmoil until your demands were met."

But if the unions had won the battle, they were about to lose the war. The strike, coupled with skyrocketing property taxes, ignited grass-roots anger at the deals many city employees were getting at City Hall. Jackson Rannells, labor reporter for the *Chronicle,* fueled the controversy with a series of well-researched articles detailing the scope of the giveaways. Among other things, he revealed that 230 city street sweepers would make $17,000 that year, a more-than-comfortable income for the time and nearly $4,000 more than a police officer with four years' experience would earn.

The "$17,000 street sweepers" became a national story and a local symbol of scandal that created a backlash at city workers. The strike and Rannells's revelations set off a stampede among the supervisors to reform and rein in runaway city wages and fringe benefits—and to try to head off the brewing taxpayers' revolt.

Feinstein and Barbagelata competed to take the lead. The Republican real estate man put forth a thirty-four-page plan to peg public employees' pay to an annual survey of private-industry wages and to restructure civil service to save millions of dollars. Feinstein's less sweeping plan linked pay raises in San Francisco to those in other large California cities and counties but allowed the supervisors to negotiate special fringe benefits—such as a dental plan the unions were demanding—banned by Barbagelata's measure.

With her superior ability to "count to six," Feinstein succeeded in getting her colleagues to put her more modest plan on the November ballot, while Barbagelata could not muster the necessary votes for his. As had happened in the Manhattanization debate, however, Feinstein's bid for centrist compromise did not please either side in the polarized debate.

Labor vilified her measure, known as Proposition L, as a union-busting tool. On the other side, Barbagelata and the angry homeowners he spoke for assailed it as a "phony sell-out" disguised as reform. The campaign over

Feinstein's Proposition L became the biggest political fight of 1974, and established battle lines for the 1975 mayoral campaign.

Emotions ran high. Unions organized a "female only picket line" in front of Feinstein's home, to protest both Proposition L and her action in crossing a picket line in the strike to help patients at San Francisco General. Union leader Maxine Jenkins sharply attacked Feinstein with a statement that mocked her Pacific Heights matron image.

> While Dianne casts herself as the representative for women's issues in the city and rides on the back of the women's movement, she is unworthy of support from women, as she works against the basic survival needs of the city's poorest working women and represents instead wealthy members of the Chamber of Commerce. The lowest paid city workers are women. They make barely enough to survive and will be immeasurably hurt by Feinstein's proposal.
>
> Contrary to popular belief, women do not work for pin money or luxuries for themselves and their families.

Feinstein reacted with a rare public outburst of emotion at a board meeting where she said she had received telephoned threats. "I consider a demonstration at my home outrageous," she said. "The only person who must cross that line is my sixteen-year-old daughter. If any harm comes to my family, I will come at you like a tiger."

Although Dianne had never cast herself or campaigned as a feminist crusader, her success and high visibility still were seen as an important symbol of political advances for women. But the bitterness of the Proposition L fight undercut her standing among liberal women. Soon afterward, Gloria Steinem, the charismatic women's movement leader, was to appear at a fund-raiser for Feinstein. Dianne diplomatically withdrew the invitation. "Gloria does a great deal of fund-raising for candidates, but when there is an issue dividing local women we feel it is unfair for someone to come in from the outside and take sides," a spokeswoman for Steinem said at the time.

On election night, Feinstein suffered another loss when Proposition L was narrowly defeated by a combination of those who saw it as a blow against labor and those who thought it did not go far enough. That night, a union leader who had a city consulting contract proclaimed that the defeat of the measure spelled the end of her mayoral ambitions. "Goody two shoes is out," he cackled to reporters, using the Alioto inner circle's derisive nickname for Dianne.

The next morning, the *Chronicle* and the *Examiner* later reported, Feinstein phoned the city budget analyst, seeking information about the pay and duties of the consultant who had made the comment. It was a questionable act for a supervisor, whose charter duties did not include monitoring individual employees, and several colleagues criticized her.

Feinstein told reporters later that she had not seen the "Goody Two Shoes" quote in the paper but was only checking out a tip that the consultant had done political work on city time. "I'm not out to get his job, but I do want to know if he was getting paid by the city while he was working on the anti–Proposition L campaign," she said then. "I think I have the right, even the mandate, to find out if the taxpayers' money is being spent properly."

Jerry Burns followed up in the *Chronicle* with a feature story about the real "Goody Two Shoes," a character in an eighteenth-century story by Oliver Goldsmith. Goody's real name was Margery Meanwell, and she happened to be "the village's finest student as well as its nicest person by far."

Dianne was not amused. "Goody Two Shoes," she snapped, "is long since gone."

FEINSTEIN'S DEFIANCE in challenging the claim that she was "out of the running" for the mayor's race clearly signaled that she was in. Despite her expressed lack of interest the winter before, Ron Smith by autumn was laying plans for her campaign. The political terrain was much different than in 1971 and this would be no eleventh-hour amateurish effort. The biggest difference was that Alioto legally was prohibited from seeking a third term, so there would be no incumbent. Also, voters had recently passed a measure requiring the mayor to win a majority vote; since no one would likely do so in a crowded field, the top two finishers in November would proceed to a December runoff, meaning that Dianne had only to finish second in the primary to be in a position to win.

And, as the close Proposition L vote had shown, San Francisco in 1975 was a very polarized city. No one would really know until November 1978 how polarized it was, but the constant push and pull of liberals and conservatives, developers and environmentalists, taxpayers and unions, minorities and whites, gays and families were building explosive tensions into local politics. San Francisco by then was almost two distinct cities separated by gulfs of geography, economics, ethnicity, and political values. The neighborhoods on the bay, or east side, were populated largely by nonwhite, younger, single renters in nontraditional-family households; on the west, or ocean side, were white, older, married, and traditional-family homeowners.

Amid these sharp divisions, Dianne would run as the only candidate who could unify the city. The self-proclaimed "centrist" would campaign as a healer, a moderate technocrat, a professional woman who could bring together warring factions and whose nuts-and-bolts knowledge of City Hall would bring the kind of pragmatic, "effective and efficient" ideas that had marked her politics since Stanford.

The lineup of mayoral rivals gave sustenance to the strategy. Her chief foe on the left was state senator George Moscone, an easygoing but savvy former supervisor who had led the 1960s "freeway revolt" before becoming a legislative leader in Sacramento. An unabashed liberal lawyer, he had represented civil rights workers in Mississippi, fought for gay rights, and led the statewide anti-death-penalty campaign in 1972. Moscone would be the champion of the "Burton machine," the coalition of labor, minorities, environmentalists, and liberal gays led by Phil Burton and Willie Brown.

While formidable, Moscone had been out of the city for nearly eight years, and his standing as senate majority leader was more impressive in Sacramento than in parochial San Francisco. Also, there were constant rumors about his personal indiscretions ("George Moscone has two drinks and thinks he's invisible," one close friend said at the time), but such stories never made the papers. The Feinstein campaign received police reports embarrassing to Moscone, but she personally ordered that the material not be used.

To Moscone's right was his senate colleague Milton Marks. An affable, moderate Republican, Marks had won some tough races in a Democratic town, less by legislative accomplishment than by a mastery of retail politics summed up in the joke that "Milton would attend the opening of an envelope."

The conservative favorite was Jack Ertola, Feinstein's predecessor as board president in 1969, who was then a judge. Although appreciated by old-time San Franciscans, Ertola had been out of the limelight for several years and was unknown to many of the newcomers who had flocked to the city in the 1970s.

There were also rumors that Kopp or Barbagelata might run. But Kopp was unwilling to risk his board seat, up in 1975, and Barbagelata, despite his intensely loyal flock of vocal followers, was not taken very seriously.

Against this field, Feinstein's major assets clearly were experience and the highest public profile among the contenders, despite the "paradoxical" stands that concerned some of her erstwhile supporters. "She had her own base, which was built on personality and good government," said political reporter Rollin Post.

Similar conclusions were reached in the camps of her chief foes. Harvey Hukari, an Ertola operative who prepared background research on all the candidates, wrote in a confidential report that Dianne "poses a real threat to all the other candidates. Not only will she be able to match the others in the ability to run a high-powered, well-financed campaign, but she will take Democratic votes from Moscone, Jewish and liberal Republican votes from Marks and moderate votes away from Ertola" or other conservatives.

In Moscone's law office a young lawyer named Duane Garrett, who years later would become one of Dianne's closest advisers, was in charge of "opposition research"—and hard-pressed to find much that was damaging on Feinstein. "I had a very hard time getting a handle on who Dianne was," Garrett recalled. "There was nothing in her career about which you could say 'ah ha' on a vote. She was a raging moderate."

Corey Busch, a senate aide to Moscone, recalled that within their campaign, "basically it was Dianne who was the opponent." But Don Bradley, Moscone's manager and a Democratic war-horse who had worked for the Kennedys, Lyndon Johnson, and Pat Brown, also saw weakness in that "it was hard to identify her ideology in an ideological town," Busch said.

Ron Smith realized that Dianne's greatest strength might be her greatest weakness: she was neither liberal enough for liberals nor conservative enough for conservatives. Despite her experience before getting into politics, she also was perceived as a woman who had never sullied her hands in the real world. Her Sacred Heart style and intense desire for privacy served to hide the personal pain she had endured but never discussed in public. "Everyone always pictures her as the way they want her to be and, when she isn't, they become disappointed," said Smith. "Because she was probusing, liberals figured she was liberal on everything and got mad when she became pro–death penalty."

Despite such concerns, Feinstein entered 1975 as the front-runner. She enjoyed consistently favorable coverage from the two major dailies, both of which backed her. The *Examiner* published a very early and gushing endorsement:

She is that rare person, a citizen who deliberately chose public
affairs as a career and trained for it from the beginning of her college
years at Stanford. She is that even rarer person, a political leader who
has been toughened, but not hardened by experience in the political
arena. The slim and lovely young woman who astonished the town six
years ago . . . in her maiden political race has grown into the mature
and still lovely leader in municipal affairs.

Al Nelder was her campaign chairman while Ron Smith again installed
Smolens as the day-to-day manager and she recruited a young gay man
named Peter Nardoza, then new to San Francisco, who would become one
of Feinstein's most loyal, longtime aides.

Shumate's first poll showed her running first in the crowded field, and he
and Smith both urged her to press the advantage with an early formal announcement to create momentum and a bandwagon effect. But after the
poll, the candidate, Smith, and Shumate had a meeting at City Hall in which
she said that "this might not be the best time for me to run." "It was
strange," Shumate recalled. "It was in part a question of tactics and in part an
indication that she still was not sure of herself."

Smith told her, "There's no question in my mind that we'll be in the
runoff."

Then Dr. Goldman died.

DR. GOLDMAN'S HOUSEKEEPER found him unconscious in his apartment.
Leon did not want his colleagues at UC to see him in his weakened condition, Dianne said, so he was taken by ambulance to another hospital, gravely
ill. He was diagnosed with cancer, a condition he was apparently aware of
but had not confided to anyone. The day before he had performed surgery
for fourteen hours. "He never gave in to his physical condition, never,
never, never," said Dianne.

For six weeks Dr. Goldman suffered in intensive care, insisting that all the
technology was futile. "He was, in effect, terminal. We didn't tell him,"
Dianne recalled. "He was on dialysis, and he had a tracheotomy. He kept
saying, 'Leave me alone. Don't do this.' And I said, 'Why dad?' And he said,
'My symptoms are those of a terminal cancer patient. Don't do it to me.' So
he knew all along, and then we knew that he knew. So then we finally just
pulled out everything. That's what he wanted."

Yvonne and her husband, Walter Banks, came down from Seattle and the sisters and their spouses took turns keeping vigil at the bedside of the man they idolized. On March 3, Dianne and Bert, Lynn and Bruce, Yvonne and Walter, and Leon's old friend Dr. Norman Sweet stood around his bedside, held hands, and said the Lord's Prayer. A moment later a nurse said, "He's gone."

Dianne's father and most influential mentor, who taught her that she could accomplish anything she wanted, was dead at age seventy-one. "He was just an amazing human being. He always had this thing, 'Mind over matter,'" said Dianne. "He was there all the way through for me, active in every campaign. He wanted so badly to see me win."

Tributes came from the worlds of medicine and politics, including one from Mayor Alioto, who declared that "San Francisco has lost one of its leading citizens." For a time, the mayor's race was forgotten. "Everything stopped when Leon died," said Smith.

Characteristically, Dianne "got into her 'keep going' mode and set about organizing the funeral," Lynn recalled. "She threw herself into that." In a moving service at Temple Sherith Israel, Dianne delivered a eulogy and UC interns and residents attended in white medical coats and stethoscopes. Both of his former wives came to the service.

Six weeks after her father's death, Dianne formally declared her candidacy before two hundred supporters at the St. Francis Hotel. In her speech she promised to create more jobs and put more police officers on the street. Reminding the crowd that "people said I was all washed up" in 1971, she promised now to "end once and for all the nonsense that a woman is not capable of providing the strength and toughness necessary to lead our city." She pledged to free citizens from "the tyranny of crime." The erstwhile liberal who had to come to office and promptly backed a host of tax increases said that as mayor she would concentrate on "cutting expenditures" and impose no new taxes.

Two months later, archrival Barbagelata, whose record as a fiscal conservative was more consistent than Dianne's, walked into the registrar's office and, without fanfare, took out papers to run for mayor. No one thought much of it at the time. "We never took him seriously," confessed Smith. "We couldn't believe people in San Francisco would take him seriously."

Barbagelata said he ran largely in an effort to head off a Feinstein victory. But it was one of her key supporters who played a secret, crucial role in helping him decide to enter the race. Mo Bernstein, the City Hall fixer who was one of Feinstein's mentors, quietly slipped a poll to Barbagelata that showed him placing second in the crowded mayoral field. Monaghan, among other pros, scoffed at the survey as "the poll that Mo conducted in the bathroom" and saw through Bernstein's ruse: Barbagelata's entry would put three Italians into the campaign, dividing that substantial vote even further with Moscone and Ertola, and helping Dianne's chances.

But Barbagelata had a cordial relationship with Bernstein and thought the poll was accurate, he said. For reasons no one could foresee, it turned out to be.

Ignoring her nemesis, Feinstein pressed her familiar case of full-time effectiveness: "I'm the only candidate who doesn't have a law practice or a business to worry about," she said. "I don't have the responsibility of earning a livelihood and I think that's a good thing" because it left her free to work on city problems. In late summer Dianne was still the strong front-runner. Then the police went on strike.

THE FOUR-DAY STRIKE in August 1975 of uniformed patrolmen, later joined by San Francisco firefighters, was the most momentous labor action since the general strike of 1934. Locally, it transformed the political landscape; nationally, it signaled the start of a sharp decline in the power of public employee unions.

The strike began on Monday, August 18, shortly after the supervisors rejected the Police Officers Association's demand for a 13 percent annual raise, in line with traditional practice of pegging their wages to their highest-paid colleagues in other jurisdictions. Amid the burgeoning resentment against city employees that began with the ugly strike of 1974, the supervisors had another reason to oppose the cops: a few weeks before, the assessor had announced huge hikes in property assessments that zoomed as much as 100 percent for some homeowners. With two of the eleven supervisors running for mayor, and six others seeking reelection, there was a lot of political motivation to hold the line.

Complaining that they were scapegoats for the city's fiscal problems, the police packed the chambers and, after an emotional hearing, immediately struck. For the next four days, San Franciscans witnessed a chaotic spectacle. Some officers arrogantly stalked picket lines with service revolvers strapped to their hips, while others got drunk and shot out streetlights. A few among the nineteen hundred officers defied the strike and several of them were assaulted. Patrol cars' tires were slashed and their keys stolen. A rifleman fired on a group of pickets and an angry motorist ran down two strikers.

With only forty-five officers working shifts ordinarily staffed by three hundred, there were fears of a massive crime wave. It did not happen, although some criminals took advantage of the strike. On one night, thieves calmly walked into three restaurants and a hotel and systematically robbed the patrons, while other thugs looted stores in the Mission district.

The supervisors had legal authority for labor contracts, but Alioto maintained a high profile as he, board members, and representatives of the police holed up in separate rooms at the Jack Tar Hotel. No real negotiating took place, however, because each side held firm. The city obtained a court order declaring the strike illegal, but the process server who tried to deliver it to the head of the police union was hustled out by burly officers guarding him.

On the second day of the strike, seventeen hundred firefighters also walked out in a wage dispute. That night, with Alioto at the hotel, a bomb exploded at his Presidio Terrace house, shattering windows and blowing in the four-inch-thick front door. No one was hurt, but a sign was left in the front yard of the mayor who had vowed earlier to fire the strikers. The sign said, Don't Threaten Us.

Alioto, who said in a recent interview that he had back-channel assurances from labor allies that "the cops would be there if they're needed," told reporters at the time that he did not believe the bomb was strike-related. He took a postmidnight stroll through the Tenderloin, with TV cameras in tow, to demonstrate that the city was safe.

As board president, Dianne spoke publicly for the supervisors and condemned the cops for "setting back the cause of law and order for a decade. Everybody is watching us," she said. "Every major city in the U.S. is facing a severe fiscal situation and every city is going to have to learn to say no and make it stick."

But privately, she was "very anxious to get it settled," one colleague recalled, and some campaign advisers worried about her appearing too moderate. At one point she left the hotel for a campaign event scheduled in a North Beach restaurant. Smith, fretting about the political impact of the strike, demanded that she start "showing she was really standing up to the police," he recalled. She told him her position in the negotiations was too sensitive.

"Look, you can't win unless you come across as strong and fighting the police," Smith argued. "But she always perceived that if she did the right thing, the moderate thing, she would win."

Late Wednesday night, Dianne had gone home when Alioto called to urge her to reconvene the board to try to reach a settlement. "It became the most polarized situation I have ever seen," she said. "I felt there was nothing to be gained by convening the board." When she refused, the mayor acted unilaterally. Invoking seldom-used powers, he declared a public emergency and personally settled the strike. Overriding the board's unanimous opposition, at 3:00 A.M. he gave the police a substantial portion of the raise they had sought and granted amnesty to strikers he had only days earlier threatened to fire. Publicly, Alioto said he had acted out of "reason"; privately, he told some allies on the board that the police "were the ones with the guns."

The reaction was fierce and instantaneous. Taxpayers flooded City Hall with angry calls, lawsuits were filed to stop the settlement, and supervisors denounced Alioto's move as "an outlaw action." With restraint, Dianne primly called it "a deep issue of morality and principle." Barbagelata cut right to the bone: "It's a sad day for San Francisco when the mayor is becoming the first dictator in the U.S. The men out there on the streets violating the law are hypocrites," he thundered.

Giving voice to public outrage, Barbagelata ignited his campaign like wildfire. He promptly introduced a raft of ballot measures, many of which he had tried and failed to put before voters previously, to rein in the salary-setting formulas for police and firefighters and to make public strikes illegal. The colleagues who had long scoffed at him now rushed these measures onto the ballot.

Feinstein had her own ideas for reform in the wake of the strike. She blamed the incumbent police chief for not collecting the weapons of strikers and vowed that, as mayor, she would hire a new chief. She also offered a detailed plan for compulsory arbitration in future labor disputes. But her "policy-speak" sounded mealymouthed next to Barbagelata.

"Dianne is always talking out of both sides of her mouth," he charged.

FROM THEN ON, Barbagelata pursued a very simple and effective campaign strategy: he ran directly at Dianne Feinstein. Conceding the left to Moscone, he consolidated his base among conservatives and wooed more moderate, swing voters who might have been Dianne's but for their fury over the police strike. "I kept saying 'her or me, her or me,' " said Barbagelata, who printed up thousands of leaflets featuring a side-by-side comparison of votes by Feinstein and him on eight key budget issues. "Feinstein controls the budget and finance committee of the board of supervisors," it read. "Her proposals have needlessly cost the taxpayers of San Francisco millions upon millions of dollars and driven thousands of jobs out of the city."

Suddenly, the crank that no one took seriously was rolling. "The strike kick-started Barbagelata's campaign and ruined the effectiveness rationale for Dianne's candidacy," said Shumate, "because she was supposed to be the technocrat who could run the city." In Moscone's camp there was glee. They were sure Barbagelata would not make the runoff but delighted to see him softening up the woman they would face.

Despite the attacks, Dianne was still running first in early October. She and Smith stuck to their game plan. With a spending limit imposed on the race, they would squirrel away money for the runoff. But Barbagelata's relentless assault took its toll in the stretch. Dianne increasingly grew irritable. Smith and Smolens gave orders that she was not to be driven on Nineteenth Avenue, a main traffic artery on the west side of the city, because she got so mad at all the Barbagelata signs displayed in the middle-class homes there.

Around Columbus Day, she got in a "don't want to do it mode" about the schedule, an adviser recalled, and refused to ride in the annual parade that was a major cultural event for Italians. Dianne had always hated riding in parades, but with Bert's help, the ever-patient Smith coaxed and cajoled her into attending. "If there's a drop of rain I'm not going," she finally announced after hours of argument over the trivial matter. The next day, as she took her place on the back of an open car where the parade assembled, it started raining, hard. Others ran for cover, but Dianne sat on the car beneath an umbrella, "smiling as if it was the thing she wanted most in the world," the adviser said.

With acute instinct, Dianne was reacting personally to what was happening politically: she was getting elbowed out at the finish, caught between leftist Moscone and right-wing Barbagelata. The strategy of running as a unifier of a polarized city was turning out to be fatal in the ideological, interest-group politics of San Francisco. "I'm a centrist, basically," she said, reflecting on 1975. "And what happened was, I got squeezed very clearly between the left and right."

Angry antitax homeowners who backed Barbagelata found Feinstein as wishy-washy as did the hard-line environmentalists who lined up with Moscone. Liberal women broke for Moscone; the housewives who backed Barbagelata still did not approve of a woman being mayor. In the increasingly vocal gay-rights movement, Dianne's genteel sensibilities rankled; even her old ally Jim Foster endorsed Moscone. As Smith put it, "The middle-class gays and drag-queen decorators were for her, but the emerging activists were not."

And while Feinstein won a share of blacks and other minorities, Moscone piled up the big numbers in those precincts, as the network of unions, churches, and patronage employees stitched together by Burton and Brown came through.

A few days before the election, Dianne, Gene Gartland, and Smith met in the living room at Lyon Street. The young operative told them that while "we had slipped," Dianne was still ahead. "Can Barbagelata catch us in a week?" she remembered asking Smith, wondering if the $80,000 set aside for the runoff should be spent now.

"No, I don't think he can," Smith answered.

"Ron, if you're wrong, I'm going to hang you from that chandelier," she told him.

"And I'm going to push the trapdoor," Gartland added. They all shared a good laugh.

Nearly twenty years later, Ron Smith still replays the 1975 mayor's race in his mind and remembers that "Our polling did not show the bottom dropping out. If I felt we were sinking, I would have done something. Dianne had a great sinking feeling about it all weekend. But she always did."

On election night, Dianne waited for results in a suite at the Miyako Hotel in San Francisco's Japantown. From the first reports, it became clear that something was terribly wrong. Moscone was winning, Barbagelata was second. As the bad news piled up, she slumped deeper and deeper into the stuffed chair from which she was gazing numbly at the TV. Smith walked back and forth to an adjoining suite, muttering "I just don't understand it."

"Ron was unbelieving and Bert was devastated," Smolens recalled. "Dianne was stunned and stricken."

Bowing out early, she put on her brave public smile for the crowd that had gathered in a downstairs ballroom for a big celebration. Behind her, Bert was grim-faced and Katherine glumly slumped, flowers drooping in her hand.

"I'd like you to go home tonight and get a good night's sleep," Dianne said. "And I hope your *Chronicle* newsboy will be on time with some good news. We are not going to concede at this time. We'll get together tomorrow morning."

The next few hours did not change the result. Moscone finished first with more than 40 percent; Barbagelata beat Feinstein for second place, 28 percent to 27 percent. Once again, she had finished a dismal third for mayor, this time humiliated by her political archenemy. It was a truly crushing defeat, but not as crushing as the news that came next.

9

DEATH

Never use your family as an excuse.

—Dianne Feinstein's Rules for Getting Ahead

ON JUNE 22, 1976, WHEN DIANNE was getting ready to go out to celebrate her forty-third birthday, Bert came home and told her he had cancer. A few days before, her husband had had his annual checkup and his doctor had found a small polyp in his abdomen. A biopsy was done and now the pathology slides had come back with the grim news that it was malignant.

It was one of those events that changes everything in an instant, and it set in motion a two-year odyssey of pain, false hopes, and crushing loss. Through it all, Dianne did what she had always done in the face of personal adversity: suffered her anguish in private while performing her duties in public, "compartmentalizing" the fear and grief that gnawed at her.

"I used to cry in the shower," she recalled. "I'd turn on the shower and just cry and cry and cry until I couldn't cry anymore. And then go on."

Ministering to Bert as he endured the torments of his cancer and a catalogue of failed tries at a cure, Feinstein was resolute in maintaining her composure and self-control in her work at City Hall. Even without the added burden of his illness, it was an extraordinarily difficult time in San Francisco, a bizarre period of political tumult, disorder, terror, and violence.

During this period, the city's mainstream politics also were transformed by a group of liberal activists who pushed through a populist reform that sought to open up City Hall to political voices of increasingly diverse neighborhoods and ethnic groups. Feinstein fought the liberal reformers, but when they won, she skillfully adapted and resiliently maintained her leadership role in San Francisco despite her personal anguish and string of political losses.

Then San Francisco was shaken to its foundations by two cataclysmic events in November of 1978, one perpetrated by a madman minister who preached a catechism of fundamentalist Christianity and revolutionary communism, the other by a law-and-order policeman turned politician who seethed beneath a surface of all-American normality with a murderous fury.

When the explosions came, Dianne's life again was changed in an instant, and she played the role of her lifetime to perfection. "It was," recalled the Reverend Cecil Williams, who through the period of violence became a confidante of Dianne's, "a time of very strong insanity."

THE MORNING AFTER her 1975 defeat, Feinstein summoned her campaign staff to Lyon Street for a painful postmortem. "Everyone was in great pain," Shumate said. "She just kept going over and over everything—what could we have done, was it her, was it some tactic? I remember thinking, maybe we'll get out of here at lunchtime, then one, then two, and then three o'clock. I was never so relieved to get out of a meeting."

Smith was so stunned he spent the next three days, unshaven, going to one movie after another, from morning to night. Eighteen years after the campaign, he said, "There isn't a day that goes by that I don't think about the 1975 mayor's race" and compared himself to a pediatrician who lost a sick child of close friends.

"Ron always blamed himself, but it was not his fault," Dianne said, looking back. "But I learned a lesson, and the lesson was, you go flat out in a campaign. You don't hold back, because you may not win the primary."

The Feinsteins retreated to Pajaro, where Dianne relived the campaign in her head.

> I had to replay it in my mind as a way of living with the result, of purging it out of myself. The disappointment was more profound this time. I'd wake up in the middle of the night thinking that we should have done this or done that to get a few thousand more votes.
>
> We thought people would see through the attacks on me but we were wrong. We made a mistake.

At Pajaro Dianne buried herself in *Shogun*, James Clavell's epic novel of feudal Japan. "It opened to me, at a time when I was rubbed raw with defeat, some philosophical concepts that have been very important to me since," she said. After a lifetime of constant striving for success, she was taken with the fatalistic philosophy of patience and acceptance expounded in its pages. "I remember one, that 'you have to watch a rock grow,' you have to have that kind of patience. The other was about a flower, 'a perfect flower with a single drop of water,' and the symbolism of doing one thing right," she said.

While she tried briefly to escape from politics, George Moscone, facing a runoff against a wild-card opponent for whom he had not prepared, actively sought her endorsement. He drove down to see her and spent a day discussing her views of city government. A few days later a top Moscone aide visited her at Lyon Street for a briefing she requested before delivering an endorsement.

"She wanted me to jump through a lot of hoops," the aide recalled. "She sat there imperiously and wanted to know about appointments and what her role would be and other things. But it was clear she was crushed and devastated by her defeat. And she was curious about what we thought she had done wrong."

Feinstein did endorse Moscone and, in one of the wildest and most bizarre elections in city history, the liberal lawmaker narrowly beat the conservative maverick. The win came amid widespread charges, and considerable evidence, of vote fraud—and controversy over the decisive role played by a politically ambitious minister named Jim Jones.

At a postelection press conference, Moscone answered questions on a host of tough issues. He turned his head from one reporter to another, then asked in a plaintive voice, "Isn't anybody going to wish me good luck?"

The mayor elect left with his wife for a brief Hawaiian vacation, while Feinstein returned to her tiny supervisor's office at City Hall. For the first time she believed that, as a woman, she would never be elected mayor. "I became convinced in that one," she said. "All of the political images were macho, tough, male. I felt for that reason I was unelectable as mayor."

At the time an *Examiner* writer asked Dianne to describe her "hidden dreams or ambitions." Uncharacteristically, she revealed her fantasies in vivid detail:

> One is to be the female parallel of the Scarlet Pimpernel or Horatio Hornblower—adventure and swashbuckling in the France and England of a past century. Another is to be a fine ballerina or stage actress. Shakespeare, O'Neill, even Ibsen. Evening soirees, pleasant encounters. Disciplined work and stimulating people.

Another is to sail the Pacific on a three-masted schooner and find that island. Live, love and laugh. No worry about trying to help someone, mountains of paperwork, the pain of failure or the so-short flush of victory. Just the wind of the sea, the sunset and a new dawn.

"And one was to be mayor of San Francisco," she added poignantly.

"She was crushed by that defeat," said Fred Goerner. "But it proved her resiliency. That would have crushed the spirit of another person."

SEVEN MONTHS AFTER THE DEFEAT, Bert came home with his devastating diagnosis. That night, the couple went ahead with their plans for a birthday celebration at a restaurant with friends, who provided an elaborate cake and a tarot card reader. They didn't share the bad news with the friends or the fortune-teller.

Bert soon after had surgery to remove the tumor and, at first, the news was good. The cancer seemed not to have spread and the prognosis was excellent, Dianne recalled.

The prognosis was wrong. The next year, in 1977, when Dianne was again running for the board, Bert performed surgery in the morning, then went out in the afternoon in his jeans and wool cap to hang campaign house signs. Suddenly he felt an excruciating, stabbing pain. He came home doubled over, clutching his side, she said.

At his doctor's office, he heard the words that, as a physician, he knew spelled his death sentence: the cancer had spread to his liver. His friend, Gene Gartland, picked him up from the doctor. "He got in the car and just said, 'That's it,'" Gartland recalled.

Outwardly at least, Bert seemed at peace, at times even nonchalant. He took Merla Zellerbach out to lunch, where he described the surgery he had undergone as having "a 95 percent success rate. Unfortunately, I'm in the other 5 percent," he wryly added.

"He said it matter-of-factly, not wanting sympathy, and quickly changed the subject," Zellerbach said. "Self-pity was not his way."

Katherine recalled that the illness was "totally unexpected. He was incredibly healthy—he swam three times a week, he played tennis, never smoked, drank in moderation, did Royal Canadian Air Force exercises before everybody started doing it."

Dianne was devastated by the news. A friend recalled that

She didn't believe it at first. She was in denial. Then she showed
fear, which she always camouflaged so well, about losing someone she
truly loved.

She always had this ability to treat things clinically, rationally, step
back, but she couldn't do it with this. She became frantic about trying
to save her husband's life. Those were the only times I saw her lose her
composure, when she was not in control.

Compounding the crisis, Dianne's mother's behavior had grown more
bizarre than ever. After she began wandering on the roof of her Nob Hill
apartment, Dianne arranged for a live-in nurse, but she could not deal with
Betty. Her mother received a CAT-scan examination that revealed the
chronic brain syndrome that had destroyed her ability to reason. "The part
of the brain that controls judgment and reason had effectively atrophied,"
Feinstein said she was told. "You couldn't reason with her because she had
no insight. She didn't know why she did what she did."

Dianne and her sisters found a facility where Betty had her own apartment, but again the staff could not handle her. They put her in a nursing
home, where she wandered off and tried to take a child from a neighboring
home, apparently believing it to be one of her daughters. Finally they placed
her in a secure facility in San Jose, where Dianne and Bert would visit her
once a week, although she rarely recognized them.

Although she could not control the metastasizing cells that were killing
her husband, Dianne with characteristic energy threw herself into trying.
She called Bert's doctor and said, "'Just tell me—once you have liver cancer,
what is it? I mean, do we have a chance?' And he said, 'If you do nothing,
it's six months. If we treat it, we may get two or three years.'"

"So we decided to treat it," she said. "And from that point on, it was just
terrible, it was just terrible." Bert got chemotherapy treatments, with their
sickening injections, which left him weak and exhausted with vomiting and
nausea. Then he had a small pump implanted in a blood vessel, to provide
direct infusion of the toxic chemicals to kill the killer cells.

By now, Dianne was "reading everything, consulting everyone, seeking
every kind of experimental treatment" that might buy more time for Bert.
Gus and Rosemary Lee, two of Dianne's strong and early supporters in

Chinatown, spent hours with her as she sat or knelt at Bert's bedside. They arranged to have him seen by an acupuncturist, at a time when the medical establishment still viewed such practice as akin to voodoo. It gave him some relief from the pain, but only for a time.

One of the roommates, Barbara Corneille, was interested in spiritualism and the psychology of illness, and she brought a hypnotist to see Bert, she said. Dianne, the daughter of a rigorous academic practitioner who considered even psychotherapy to be a pseudoscience, at first was openly skeptical. "Dianne, if it gives him only five minutes of relief, it's worth it," Barbara told her, and when it did, Dianne had the hypnotist return.

Katherine had enrolled at UC Berkeley and legally changed her last name to Feinstein. As Bert's condition worsened, she dropped out of school for a time to be with the man she considered her father.

The full measure of the family's desperation came in January 1978 when the three of them flew, on what Katherine would later call "a mad search," to a clinic in New Mexico for an experimental treatment that was claimed to kill cancer cells. In the treatment, Dianne recalled, Bert was put under general anesthesia and his body heated to a high temperature, which was maintained for about an hour. The procedure was to be repeated over several days. The first time Bert came out of the anesthesia, he was hallucinating and flailing about, but was released with Dianne and Katherine to return to their hotel.

"We went back to this hotel and he was in terrible pain, he was asking for morphine," Dianne said. "I was trying to get it from the doctor and the doctor wouldn't pay attention to me. I was begging the doctor to come see him and I couldn't move him but he [the doctor] wouldn't.

"So I said, 'Then I'm going to go out to the hospital and steal it if I have to.' And it was snowing and sleeting and Katherine and I went and they finally gave us the drug. And Bert was supposed to go through the treatment again and he just couldn't go through it."

Her husband by now was too weak and wracked with pain to move by himself. A thousand miles from home, in the dead of winter, Dianne and Katherine could not get him on a plane to San Francisco by themselves. Early the next morning, she called Gartland at home and begged for help. "It was one of the few times I heard her truly distraught," Gartland said. "'I don't know what to do, I can't get Bert on the plane. He doesn't have the strength.' That was the only time I ever heard her not able to hack it."

Their friend flew to New Mexico at once and half-carried Bert onto the plane. He rallied a bit on the flight home, but Dianne took him directly to Mt. Zion, his home hospital, where he remained for a month. The end was near.

IF THEY HAD BEEN EQUALLY DESPERATE but from quite another world—poor not rich, black not white, unimportant not influential—the Feinsteins might have turned in their despair to someone else who offered cures for cancer in mid-1970s San Francisco. Not far from City Hall, the Reverend Jim Jones, a black-haired white man from Indiana who got his start selling monkeys on the street, was drawing thousands of mostly black parishioners from poor neighborhoods to his "People's Temple" with a blend of idealistic socialism and pure snake-oil hokum.

Soon after his arrival in San Francisco in the early 1970s, Jones started aggressively courting politicians—and put on a good public show for his many friends in the media and the liberal establishment, like George Moscone, Willie Brown, and Rosalyn Carter, wife of the president of the United States.

The politicians were duly impressed with Jones's guided-tour spiels about his health clinic, preschool breakfast program, senior center, and rehabilitation work with hard-core delinquents. They were also enamored of the bus loads of warm bodies that Jim Jones could produce on short notice to build crowds, pack demonstrations, walk precincts, and vote as they were told to do—as they did for Moscone, who owed his narrow win over Barbagelata in part to People's Temple.

But in the very secret world behind the locked doors of the temple, Jones put on a different kind of show: endless diatribes about his incarnation as Jesus Christ; beatings of church members whose lives, property, bodies, and families he totally controlled; and faked cancer cures, in which he would remove "tumors" made of rotting chicken guts to prove his healing powers.

In November 1978 Jones would lead his flock into the greatest mass murder-suicide in history, following the assassination of a Bay Area congressman and four others, in a ritual of death and madness in the jungles of "Jonestown" near Port Kaituma, Guyana.

But in 1976 the Temple's secrets had not yet been exposed and Jones was a prominent and respected member of San Francisco's liberal power structure. So in Jones's debt was Moscone that Jones rejected an appointment to the Human Rights Commission as beneath him. The mayor responded by handing him a more important post on the board overseeing public housing, where many of Jones's faithful lived, and then twisting the arms of other commissioners to elect Jones their chairman.

Perhaps more than anything, the specter of an insane minister who managed to dupe the political establishment and rise swiftly to the highest political councils of the community symbolized the surreal civic psychosis that gripped and convulsed much of San Francisco in the 1970s. The violence of striking city employees and the spectacle of lawless cops toting guns on picket lines seemed at times to reflect a breaking of the social contract, as citizens witnessed increasingly bizarre, pseudopolitical terrorism, including an assassination attempt on President Gerald Ford during a visit to San Francisco in 1975.

The violent period began in 1973 with a spree of random killings and shootings of white people by what would prove to be a gang of murderous black Muslims. The "Zebra" killings, so-called after the police radio code for such incidents, eventually claimed fifteen victims and inflamed racial passions in the city.

Then, in February 1974, three gun-toting people wearing ski masks burst into the Berkeley apartment of Patricia Hearst, beat her boyfriend, and kidnapped the heiress to the publishing fortune. The fantastic tale of Patty Hearst and the Symbionese Liberation Army captured headlines and occupied the FBI and San Francisco police department for more than a year with a crime spree of bank robbery, rape, the assassination of Oakland's school superintendent, and other acts of terror, all rationalized and celebrated in "communiqués" from the "revolutionary soldiers" that were widely disseminated by the media.

At one point the Reverend Cecil Williams, who ministered to the down-and-out at Glide Memorial Church in the seedy Tenderloin district, became an intermediary between the SLA and the Hearst family. Not long afterward he was surprised to get a phone call from Supervisor Feinstein, offering to help him in any way she could. His image of her was of an uptight, upscale woman out of touch with the people he served, but the sincerity and genuine concern in her offer touched him.

"She was the only politician who called," Williams said. "She said, 'You don't know who I am, but I want you to know that I want to be with you.' She was a very sophisticated woman who at that point had not connected with the poor. But, unlike many politicians, she was capable of growth and she became much more sympathetic, much more empathetic, much more humane."

Feinstein always had a special political interest in crime issues. But the terror now unfolding in San Francisco had personal impacts on her life. After Patty Hearst was kidnapped, the police assigned a full-time bodyguard to Katherine, fearing she might become the next kidnap victim of the SLA.

Dianne and other supervisors became targets of an "underground" terrorist group calling itself the New World Liberation Front, which investigators connected to at least seventy bombings, mostly in northern California. At the time, an FBI agent referred to San Francisco as the "Belfast of North America." According to a 1977 investigation of the incidents published in *Human Events* magazine:

> The NWLF campaign is not something to be scoffed at or smiled away. It is a terrorist campaign aimed, for the first time, at hijacking an American city by subjugating its legislature. Bombs and bullets and communiqués are the weapons in the war of nerves, and the targets are the city's elected legislators.

The NWLF campaign of intimidation and terror against Feinstein and other supervisors began in 1975 when the mysterious group demanded more spending on city jails and public health programs. Between frequent bombings—the Opera House, the exclusive Pacific Union Club, the Presidio army base, homes of prominent corporate executives, and Pacific Gas and Electric Company's facilities all were targeted within a few months—the group used an "aboveground" courier named Jacques Rogier to deliver its frequent threats to City Hall.

"The following dogs will be put on a death warrant: John Barbagelata, Dianne Feinstein, Quentin Kopp," warned one such "communiqué."

"Dianne," began another, delivered to her office from the "Central Command, People's Forces" of the NWLF, "As you fear what will happen to you and your family, so do poor people fear for our families . . . Just what sort of understanding and compassion do you expect us to show you buzzards? We are giving you ten times more justice than we have ever received from the rich and their lackeys. If we dealt out justice as it's dealt us, we would have shot you long ago for your horrible crimes against the people."

Amid the violence and threats, Feinstein requested an intelligence briefing from police department brass. Among those dispatched was a young officer working on the terrorist cases named Jim Molinari, who was bright, political, and clearly on his way up in the department. "Go talk to her but don't tell her anything," Molinari recalled that his boss told him.

As Dianne sat with her feet on the table, closely questioning the officers, it quickly became evident to Molinari that this genteel lady supervisor had her own, very good sources in law enforcement who had provided solid background on the NWLF. But after listening in silence to her sharp questions for a while, he snapped at her.

"So what do you want us to do about it, dear?" he asked sarcastically.

"How dare you speak to me like that?" she snarled at Molinari.

The NWLF grew ever more active, and in 1976 Dianne and several colleagues narrowly escaped death. On January 10, one of Kopp's aides noticed a layer of foil under the outer wrapping of a box that had been delivered to him, and that he had carried around in his car all day. Suspicious, she called the bomb squad, who found that it was a candy box packed with dynamite.

When Kopp called Barbagelata to tell him, his political ally discovered that a similar package had been delivered to his home. Two of his young daughters had tossed it back and forth while bringing it into the house. The brown-paper-wrapped package was addressed to "The people's choice, John Barbagelata." Inside, police found two sticks of dynamite the size of toothpaste tubes, with a mousetrap wired to trigger the explosive when the box was opened. A step-by-step diagram for assembling such a bomb was conveniently contained in one of the NWLF communiqués freely distributed by Jacques Rogier.

Barbagelata's caricature as a "Deranged Buzzard" was put on NWLF "Wanted for Murder" posters hung on light poles around the city. His windows were shot at, his children were threatened, and his real estate office was vandalized on a regular basis. He started packing a .38 pistol and keeping a shotgun under the seat of his car. He, Dianne, and other supervisors were given "executive security," a police bodyguard who traveled with them.

Even that wasn't enough. In the cold, predawn hours of Tuesday, December 14, nineteen-year-old Katherine, home for Christmas vacation, was sleeping in her street-side, second-story room in the Feinstein home. She was awakened by a "popping sound" shortly after 2:00 A.M. Thinking perhaps a car had backfired, she went back to sleep.

But when she looked out at the window box the next morning, she saw a green gelatin substance in a plastic wrapper on which she could read the letters "E-X-P-L." At that hour Dianne was on her way to City Hall and saw police surrounding Mt. Zion hospital. She called the department to find what was going on and learned they were investigating a bomb threat; at the same moment, Katherine was calling police to come for the bomb at Lyon Street.

The police chief said the bomb planted at Dianne's home "would have been lethal" but did not explode because the detonator misfired after the explosive gel got too cold as the temperature fell during the night. A communiqué soon followed. It said that Dianne's house was targeted to draw attention to the problems at the city prisons and warned that the supervisors had only forty-eight hours to respond to the NWLF demand for more money for the jails.

"The time has come," Feinstein defiantly answered, "when the fear and intimidation that everyone feels has got to stop."

A few months later, another attack was carried out when windows were shot out at the Feinsteins' shoreline vacation home in Pajaro Dunes overlooking Monterey Bay. "I don't intend to give in to a threat in any way, shape, or form," she said after this incident. She was serious about it, too. She got a permit and learned to shoot at the police academy. Then, she started packing a .38 caliber pistol in her purse.

WHILE TINY BANDS OF TERRORISTS and radical crazies waged campaigns of violence, large numbers of grass-roots activists labored to transform San Francisco's political system by peaceful and responsible means. In November 1976 the liberal coalition that had elected Moscone—environmental and neighborhood groups, ethnic minorities, gays, and much of labor—surprised the establishment by passing a ballot measure that changed the at-large method of electing supervisors in place since 1900.

Arguing that Feinstein, Barbagelata, Kopp, and their colleagues represented the same basic constituency of business and development interests that fueled their expensive citywide campaigns, the liberal activists passed a plan to elect supervisors from eleven districts. This, they argued, would make the board responsible to voters instead of to campaign contributors and special interests.

Earlier initiatives for district elections had been rejected by voters, so the Chamber of Commerce and other foes of the plan had paid little attention to the latest liberal bid to pass it. Though taken by surprise by its passage, they responded swiftly. Before district elections even took effect, two separate measures to repeal the system were qualified for a special election in August 1977.

The loud and fervent campaigns over the repeal measures reflected anew the push-and-pull polarization of the two San Franciscos—one passing into history, one struggling to be born—that had clashed so bitterly in the 1975 mayoral race and squeezed out Feinstein's moderate views. Feinstein opposed district election of supervisors and led the campaign for one of the two measures, known as Proposition A, which called for a simple repeal of the 1976 vote putting the plan into effect. "A district board will be much more easily controlled by any given organization or any given politically potent leader. That doesn't make for brave independence," she argued, clearly referring to Moscone and the liberal "Burton machine."

The second measure, Proposition B, was sponsored by Barbagelata. It proposed a complex system in which supervisors would live in different districts but all run at large. Its true intent, however, had little to do with the board: it also would recall the mayor, district attorney, and sheriff elected in the liberal sweep of 1975 that defeated Barbagelata.

The columnist Charles McCabe clearly stated the historic stakes of the special election, as San Francisco stood at a crossroads.

> John Barbagelata represents what is left of what used to be San Francisco . . . the San Francisco that in a generation has gone down the tube, largely because of the minority groups that have come in since 1940 and sent scurrying to the suburbs the Irish and the Germans and the Italians that were the traditional power base here.
>
> He represents the San Francisco that is no more, a coalition of the dying. This coalition has the desperate strength of the moribund, of a group that is conscious that this probably represents their Last Hurrah as a social force in San Francisco.

The August special election proved the strength of the new San Francisco. Both the measure backed by Feinstein and that of Barbagelata were routed. The district-elections plan remained, as pent-up political energy of community activists was released in an unprecedented rush for the ballot box: 115 candidates went on the ballot to run in the eleven new districts that had carved up the city by geography, ethnicity, and political interest.

Many of the incumbents were concentrated in a few high-wealth neighborhoods. Five of them, including Barbagelata, Francois, and Nelder, decided not to run, while two others moved to better their political chances in new districts. Dianne was the only incumbent in District 2, an enclave of wealthy and middle-class neighborhoods, including her base in Pacific Heights.

It was during this campaign that the Feinsteins learned that Bert's cancer had spread. Even before that blow, she had hesitated about running for the board again, given her distaste for district elections, her twin defeats for mayor, the frustrations of eight years as a supervisor, and her desire to experience life beyond City Hall.

She had been an enthusiastic supporter of Jimmy Carter in the 1976 election and, early in his term, made a half-hearted effort to win a subcabinet appointment in his new administration. She also experimented anew with her media skills, filling in impressively as hostess of a local TV talk show. "She's excellent," the station's general manager said of her performance. "I told her she certainly had a good possibility of having a second career if things didn't work out in politics."

In the end, however, Feinstein decided to seek a third term on the board, if for no other reason than a good-government commitment to help ease a rough transition from a citywide to a district board.

Although heavily favored in the district race, she found herself in the familiar position of being attacked from both sides. Caryl Mezey, a liberal activist, campaigned by saying she had "the ability to work well in coalitions, while Dianne sets herself apart from a group." Republican businessman Lester O'Shea meanwhile assailed her from the right, citing her past support of tax increases as evidence of an antibusiness bent.

Night after night, Feinstein would go before neighborhood groups and deliver her earnest speeches about experience in office, fighting crime, "opposing any new taxes, such as a city income tax," and her hopes for a "new, moderate, mainstream coalition" at City Hall. But her heart wasn't in it. With Bert's condition driving her to despair, it took all her well-practiced self-discipline to keep going.

Peter Nardoza, the aide who had joined her at City Hall after the 1975 campaign, would pick her up early in the evening at Lyon Street. She would emerge with her red lipstick shining as bright as ever, then break down when she got into the car. "She had come to realize that Bert was going to die,"

Nardoza recalled. As he drove her to campaign coffees and other stops, "she would sit in the car next to me and just cry, cry, cry. Then we'd pull up to the next event and just like that," he said, snapping his fingers, "she'd be very cool and calm. It was amazing how she could bring herself into control."

Feinstein won the election easily, capturing more than half the vote and becoming part of the city's first district board in a century. Among her colleagues on the new board, which reflected much of the diversity of the new San Francisco, was a Chinese American, an Hispanic, a black woman, a single mother, and the city's first openly homosexual officeholder.

Harvey Milk, a camera store owner and community activist, had been elected in a colorful and wide-open battle in a district that included both the liberal Haight-Ashbury and the gay Castro neighborhoods.

Receiving far less notice was a married, white fireman named Dan White who won election from District 8, a collection of almost forgotten neighborhoods on the south-central rim of the city, home to many ethnic Catholics and other born-and-raised members of old San Francisco. Before he joined the fire department, White had been a police officer. Decrying the massive social changes that swept the city in the 1970s, he had proclaimed in his campaign that he was "not going to be forced out of San Francisco by splinter groups of radicals and social deviates [sic]." His slogan was simple if sophomoric: "Unite and Fight with Dan White."

DESPITE HER LACK OF ENTHUSIASM for being a district supervisor, Dianne adroitly maneuvered behind the scenes to become president of the new board. Under the old rules, the presidency went by tradition to the highest vote-getter in the election. In 1977 that would have been Kopp, who had run without any opposition in his district, a middle-class area on the west side of the city, and piled up twice as many votes as Dianne. But under the new system, all bets were off on tradition.

By chance, Kopp was stricken with appendicitis the Friday after the election. After his surgery he developed a serious infection and remained hospitalized for another week. Dianne called and said she'd like to visit him, but he told her not to bother. When he went home to recuperate a few days later, he discovered that she had been busy during his absence.

Newly elected supervisor Dan White, whose conservative views were closer to Kopp's than to Feinstein's, showed up on his doorstep one morning, he recalled, and told him that a deal was in the making for Dianne to be board president. "I don't want you to be left out, Quentin," White told Kopp. Kopp thought sourly to himself that Dianne had already got to White. He kept his own counsel, however, because he had some behind-the-scenes dealings of his own.

Shortly after the election, the soon-to-retire Barbagelata saw Feinstein alone in her office, crying, he recalled. The two old enemies had a heart-to-heart talk, he said; she spoke emotionally about Bert's illness and said she was fed up with City Hall. "Are you going to run for mayor again?" the suspicious Barbagelata asked her. When she told him no, he decided to broker a deal for his pal Kopp. He suggested that Kopp and several allies would support Feinstein for board president in her final term if she would back Kopp for mayor against Moscone in 1979.

No one knew at the time, but whoever the new board selected as its president would become mayor of San Francisco before the year was out.

Moscone, trying to make the difficult transition from legislator to executive, had had a shaky first two years in office. He had bumbled through another violent city workers' strike, he had consistently had trouble rounding up six votes on the board, and some of his key vetoes had been overridden. Kopp meanwhile had emerged as an effective chief critic of the rookie mayor, and many insiders were betting that the "Kosher Cowboy" would beat Moscone's reelection bid.

Now, Barbagelata told a skeptical Kopp that he had secured Feinstein's support for him. "I said, 'Dianne Feinstein is going to be a different person now,'" Barbagelata recalled. To "cement our new relationship," Barbagelata arranged a private lunch at Jack's, a movers and shakers' favorite, where Feinstein and allies Nelder and Francois broke bread with Barbagelata and Kopp.

More than a decade later, exactly what was said on January 5, 1978, remains a matter of sharp disagreement. Kopp and Barbagelata, before his death, insisted that Feinstein made a commitment to endorse Kopp for mayor. Dianne said there was some discussion at the lunch of "working together," but no agreement. Francois has died and Nelder did not recall much political conversation at all; he remembered that Dianne was very upset about Bert and was in no condition to talk about political deals.

"She agreed, there's no question about it," said Kopp. Said Feinstein: "There was no agreement to support him. I wasn't going to make any commitment. And if I had, it's possible to change one's mind, too."

In any case, other plots were being hatched. While Feinstein and Kopp talked, Harvey Milk simultaneously tried to organize the liberal members of the new board behind one of their own. Milk quietly set up a series of meetings that included Robert Gonzales, attorney Carol Ruth Silver, Chinese American lawyer Gordon Lau, and holdover Supervisor John Molinari, who had shifted his early conservative stance to become a close ally of the liberal Moscone.

"At the time, we assumed the other side would put up Quentin," Molinari recalled. But when Feinstein, whom Milk referred to as "the wicked witch of the west," emerged as the champion of the conservative wing, Milk was even more determined to elect a liberal.

"Dianne Feinstein was one of Harvey's archenemies," recalled Dick Pabich, a close friend and aide to Milk. "He thought she was moralistic, with her anti-smut campaign. She was pro-gay in some sense but homophobic in another."

With Kopp throwing his support to Feinstein, the key vote belonged to Ella Hutch, a labor union representative and close ally of Phil Burton, who seemed at first glance to belong in the liberal column. But when Milk approached Hutch with that argument, at a boisterous party at Pabich's house celebrating the election results, Hutch reacted with outrage. The two got into a shouting match behind closed doors, with Hutch charging that Milk took her vote for granted because she was a black woman.

Then "Mo got to Ella," recalled Molinari, referring to Feinstein's mentor, the power broker Mo Bernstein. After a chat with Bernstein, Hutch dropped out of sight for the final forty-eight hours before the vote.

By inauguration day, January 9, 1978, the politicking had reached a fever pitch. A beaming Dan White showed up for the ceremony with his pretty, pregnant wife, Mary Ann, bearing a fresh red rose for each of his new colleagues. But the star of the day was Milk, who proudly led a march from the Castro district to City Hall, his arm draped around his young male lover.

When Kopp entered the chambers, he rolled his eyes at the roses, and remembers hearing Gonzales snarl at him. "What the fuck did you get?" asked Gonzales, who had heard the rumors about Kopp's deal with Feinstein.

After the weeks of intrigue, Feinstein beat Lau, the liberal candidate, six-to-five, to become president of the board again. When she announced the new committee assignments, Kopp was named chairman of the powerful Finance Committee, along with his conservative ally, Supervisor Lee Dolson.

The third member was freshman Ella Hutch, who had nominated Feinstein for president and cast the decisive swing vote.

Following tradition, Supervisor Lau then asked that the vote for Feinstein be made unanimous. Milk and Silver, playing to their liberal supporters packing the audience, refused the courtesy and the final vote was nine-to-two.

"A true function of politics," said Milk, when he rose to speak, "is not just to pass laws and approve appropriations, but to give hope."

It was the kind of public slight Dianne despised. "Hope is fine, but you can't live on hope," she snapped, when she took the gavel a few minutes later. "The name of the game is six votes."

Feinstein's prediction that a district board would bring more self-interested posturing and petty bickering than ever to City Hall seemed on target. In the months that followed, virtually every issue, no matter how mundane, turned into a pitched battle, with the final tally on most votes ending up six-to-five one way or the other. Moscone's hope that district elections would provide him with a reliable liberal majority did not pan out, and the politics of the board were marked by back-stabbing, double-dealing, grandstanding, and pandering.

Everyone had a pet issue. Milk's was passage of a broad gay-rights ordinance that went beyond Feinstein's 1972 legislation to prohibit discrimination in employment and housing based on a person's sexual orientation. Dianne, of course, had a long history of support for gay rights. Besides her political actions, just a few months before she had offered the use of her backyard for a ceremony by two lesbian friends who wished to solemnize their long-term relationship. But when Milk's measure came before the board, she sharply criticized it—more because of her personal feelings than because of the issue.

Dianne said she could "see some problems coming down the pike, particularly in the field of housing," and wondered if landlords would be required to rent to gays who practiced sadomasochism:

> One of the uncomfortable parts of San Francisco's liberalism has been the encouragement of sadism and masochism . . . I don't want San Francisco to set up a backlash. If this city becomes an anything-goes city, a you-can-do-your-trip-in-the-street sort of place . . . it will be very, very hard.

After all that, she voted for the bill. Her gay ally Jim Foster later told friends that when he called to reprimand her for her speech, she said that "every time Harvey opens his mouth, I can't control myself."

Milk's election signaled the growing clout of the gay community, and the only vote against the gay-rights ordinance was cast by Dan White. Although he complained about its effect on his constituents, particularly Catholics, his vote, like Feinstein's comments, had more to do with pique than with policy. White had voted for Milk's bill in committee, speaking emotionally of how he had learned during his military service in Vietnam that "the sooner we leave discrimination in any form behind, the better off we'll all be." Then Milk crossed him.

White had been elected with a promise to block a city plan to move a psychiatric treatment center for teenagers to an empty convent in his district. He said it would put "arsonists, rapists, and other criminals" among the middle-class families of District 8. Feinstein supported his position. Dick Pabich, Milk's legislative aide, recalled that Harvey also "probably gave Dan the impression" that he would vote against the treatment center. But on the floor Harvey voted for the center, providing the one-vote margin by which the plan was approved—and White humiliated.

After that, White sulked and began to withdraw from the business of the board. Under financial pressure because he had been forced by city law to resign as a fireman when elected supervisor, he began to exhibit strange behavior that sometimes surprised his colleagues.

Molinari a few months later sponsored a routine street-closure permit so a bicycle race could be held in his largely Italian district on Columbus Day. White, asserting that people would be "trapped in their homes by police barricades" because of the bike race, vociferously argued against it. When Molinari easily prevailed on a ten-to-one vote for the mundane legislation, White stalked past him, slammed his fist on the back of Molinari's chair, and hissed, "I won't forget this."

From the time White came on the board, Feinstein had taken the young fireman, who clearly was not as sophisticated as his colleagues, under her wing. She was kind to his wife and sometimes had breakfast or lunch with Dan, counseling him about board business. Now, seeing White distraught over a trifling matter, she quietly motioned him to the dais, where she was presiding. "I said, 'Dan, what's going on, simmer down. This isn't a big deal, this is a routine small action,'" she recalled. "I looked at him and couldn't believe it. He was flushed, he was angry. There was a visceral response that, for the issue, should not have been there."

Later, she would think back to that moment many times.

ALL THE BACKBITING and bickering on the board seemed even more petty as Bert's illness and pain relentlessly consumed him. On his birthday, April 9, 1978, Dianne threw a big party for him. Confined to the hospital bed she had moved into their bedroom on the second floor, he rallied for the occasion. Dianne wore a long pink and white dress and filled the house with balloons, good cheer, and more than fifty friends. "It was a magnificent good-bye party," recalled Ron Smith. "Everybody was up when they were upstairs and everybody was down when they were downstairs."

Six days later, Bert was gone. With Dianne, Katherine, Lynn, and Bruce at his bedside, the courtly and urbane surgeon who had gently pushed, cajoled, and supported the young wife he worshiped, died at home on a Saturday night at the age of sixty-four, almost two years after he was diagnosed with cancer.

After his body was taken away, Lynn and Bruce left Lyon Street about 3:00 A.M. As they walked to their car, Lynn heard an awful wail come from the house. "Dianne never cried in public," she said. "I never heard anything like that."

10

THE WORLD GOES MAD

It was a very exciting trek.

—*Dianne Feinstein, November 26, 1978*

SHORTLY BEFORE MIDNIGHT on Saturday, November 18, 1978, Dianne slumped down into the car of Dick Blum, a close friend and investment banker with whom she had just returned from a trip to Nepal that left her sick and weak. Blum's Mercedes was parked at San Francisco International Airport and, as he turned on the ignition, the radio he kept tuned to all-news station KCBS came to life with an incredible story: local congressman Leo Ryan had reportedly been shot during a visit to Jim Jones's People's Temple commune in Guyana.

Riding into the city, they listened with horrified amazement to the first sketchy reports of what would soon erupt into a macabre tale of abomination and evil. Ryan, investigating complaints of abuse from concerned relatives of People's Temple members, had been assassinated, along with three newsmen and a temple defector, on a tiny airstrip in a godforsaken spot of coastal South American jungle called Port Kaituma. Within hours, more than nine hundred People's Temple members had died in a mass suicide-murder, bodies heaped upon each other, surrounding their crazed leader, Jones, who was dead of a gunshot wound to the head.

As the ghastly news unfolded the next week, Dianne, having contracted fever and dysentery in the Himalayas, read and watched from her sickbed. Unlike Moscone and other liberals, she had kept a cautious distance from Jones. She visited his church only once, and felt uneasy, although she looked with longing at the thousands of "volunteers" Jones provided for Moscone's 1975 campaign.

The worldwide shock of Jonestown, which underscored San Francisco's reputation as the kook capital of America, instantly pushed off the front page another story of considerable local political interest. While Dianne was away, her protégé, Dan White, had abruptly resigned his board of supervisors seat to Moscone, citing family and financial pressures. Then, just as abruptly, he had asked for reappointment from Moscone, who had vacillated about the decision.

At almost the same hour that Jones's flock was lining up obediently to kill themselves and murder their babies that fateful Saturday, White was meeting with Moscone in the mayor's office, making another plea to get back his seat.

At home on Lyon Street, Feinstein caught up on that situation too. She talked to White, who pleaded for her help, and then she asked Moscone to reappoint him. Dan, she recalled, "was desperate to get that job back."

BERT HAD DIED seven months before and, just a few days after the funeral, Dianne had returned to City Hall and become incensed at a Finance Committee hearing about Moscone's plan to delete money for 170 new police officers from the upcoming budget. "It's an act of perfidy," she declared, charging she had been "betrayed" by police chief Charles Gain.

Some City Hall denizens found it strange to see Feinstein engrossed in budget hearings so soon. But she was doing as she had done since childhood in the face of emotional pain: pushing it into a separate space and, with practiced self-discipline, following her father's dictum to "bury yourself in work."

Despite her brave front at City Hall, she was in despair. Katherine had returned to school at Berkeley and Dianne, now living alone, would crawl into bed when she got home, eat little, and seldom go out. Katherine and Dianne's friends tried to cheer her up, and her aide, Peter Nardoza, coaxed her out for a forty-fifth birthday celebration. But she was miserable. "Then along came Dick Blum," Nardoza recalled.

One day in June 1978 she got a call from investor Blum, a friend of Moscone's whom the mayor had picked to head a business-oriented Fiscal Advisory Committee to help straighten out the city's budget mess, which had suddenly become a true crisis a few weeks after Californians overwhelmingly passed the Proposition 13 property-tax-cut initiative. Feinstein and Blum had met before, in 1977, when she had called him to discuss a study comparing San Francisco's finances to those of other cities. They had met at Jack's and, with her police guard joining them for lunch, discussed public works bond ratings and long-term municipal investment strategies. "It was sort of a boring lunch," Blum remembered.

Blum, having recently gone through a divorce and opened his own company, now invited the widowed Feinstein out to discuss an update of his committee's work. They arranged to meet for dinner in Sausalito and did so during a break in a Monday board meeting. This time, there was little talk about municipal bonds; uncharacteristically, Dianne did not return to the board meeting. Soon, they were an item in the society pages and Herb Caen's column.

Tall, athletic, and smart, Blum provided both a spark of companionship and sound financial advice for Dianne, at a time when she was struggling with Bert's estate and some sour investments they had made during his illness. At first, some old friends of Dianne and Bert's were not happy about the new courtship. Merla Zellerbach and Fred Goerner had been on a long cruise when Bert died. When they returned several months later, they invited Dianne out to dinner; she asked if she could bring a date. She showed up with Blum and, "as the evening progressed, it became obvious something was going on across the table," Merla said. Fred, protective of Dianne's emotional vulnerability, looked increasingly askance. Finally he folded his arms and demanded of Blum, "What exactly are your intentions?"

"Strictly dishonorable," Blum answered with a straight face. They all laughed.

Feinstein's brightening mood was reflected in an appearance she made in October at the opening of a new retail attraction for tourists on the waterfront called Pier 39. It was an extremely controversial project and, during lengthy City Hall hearings, she had warned developer Warren Simmons that it would never open on his deadline. If it did, she promised, she would show up for the ceremonies in a bikini. Simmons won and, ever the modest Sacred Heart girl, Dianne paid off the bet by wearing an old-fashioned, man's wool bathing suit that Blum had bought from a collection of memorabilia from the long-closed Sutro Baths.

The same month, Dianne and Dick spent a weekend at Lake Tahoe. Over dinner he spoke of his passion for Tibetan Buddhism, the Himalayas, and his plans for an imminent return to Nepal for a long trekking trip in the spectacular, rugged mountains. She had told him she was restless for a change, so he offered her a halfhearted invitation to come along. "Frankly, I was more inclined to go by myself," Blum recalled. "I definitely wasn't selling it. I said, 'You're welcome to come if you want, but. . . ' "

She gulped a glass of wine and, to his shock, said, "I'll go with you." "Katherine was appalled," he said. "She thought her mother had gone bonkers."

The Friday before they left in late fall, Nardoza organized a little good-bye party for Feinstein at City Hall. Amid cake, champagne, and conversation, Dianne stood by the duplicating machine in the aides' office and had a long chat with Dick Pabich, the young assistant to Harvey Milk. Pabich, amazed that Dianne would pay so much attention to the lowly aide of a political foe, was even more surprised by what she said. "She said she had come to realize there was more to life than politics," he said. "She got very philosophical and spiritual and talked about going to see the Dalai Lama. It was a surprising conversation. I had the unmistakable impression that she was through with politics."

THEY WENT FIRST TO INDIA, where Blum was amused at Dianne's appalled reaction to the baksheesh men and the pungent smells at the Delhi railway station. They met the Dalai Lama in Dharamsala, and later flew to Kathmandu and on to a remote airstrip where they began their trek with a party of Sherpas, walking from early morning to night. But Dianne suffered from the start of the trek with a stomach ailment and, at a base camp of Mt. Everest, became dehydrated and feverish. Blum decided to take her out. After walking part of the way, she was carried down the mountain by a yak.

Back in civilization, she saw a doctor who prescribed antibiotics. A few days later they were in Rome, where she had an allergic reaction to the medicine on top of the dysentery she had contracted. In Rome she called Katherine, who told her about Dan White's sudden resignation from the board of supervisors. "I've always regretted that I wasn't there that month, always regretted it," she said years later, "because I think I would have sensed that something was going on."

THE SUNDAY THAT DIANNE was in her sickbed back in San Francisco, Moscone was in his City Hall office dealing with a bizarre juxtaposition of two problems. Jim Molinari, the ambitious young cop who had crossed Dianne in a meeting about terrorism several years before, had since been assigned to Moscone's personal security detail. When he picked up the mayor that Sunday morning, November 19, Moscone told him he had just gotten off the phone with the FBI about the nightmare unfolding in Jonestown— and a horrible rumor that Jones's remaining followers in San Francisco would soon repeat the mass suicide ritual, known by church code name as "White Night." "George was screaming, 'You won't fucking believe this,'" Molinari recalled.

By coincidence, Moscone had scheduled Sunday to have his photograph taken with his wife and four children for the Christmas card the mayor annually sent to thousands of friends and political supporters. Looking for a way to change the picture from the year before, Moscone wanted to include the family dog in the photo for Christmas 1978. Except the dog kept making messes all over the rug in the mayor's ceremonial office every time they were set to take the picture. While his son, Christopher, kept cleaning behind the dog with paper towels, Moscone's personal secretary, Cyr Copertini, kept ferrying in slips of paper, after getting off the phone with the latest confirmed news from Guyana. The press meanwhile had assembled and was in full bay in the mayor's outer office, demanding answers that no one had about Jonestown.

"It was surreal," Copertini recalled, of the scene in the inner office. "They kept trying to take the picture and George was in there gritting his teeth, saying, 'Let's get this over with.'"

As the photographer made yet another effort, Copertini carried in yet another a slip of paper that she quietly handed to the mayor. It said, "Leo Ryan is dead."

INSIDE THE MAYOR'S OFFICE, the uproar over Jonestown temporarily pushed the Dan White situation into the background. On Friday, November 10, White had walked out of his office and bumped into Bob Gonzales, who was quartered next to him on supervisors' row. "Bob, I just can't take it anymore," he told him. Then he walked out of the supervisors' office, Room 237, and over to the east side of City Hall, down a long marble-floored corridor to Room 200, the mayor's office.

Jim Molinari, whom White had known since they were kids, sat at his post in the outer office. When White told Molinari that he was quitting the board, the bodyguard invited him into the "John Monaghan Memorial Office," a small City Hall balcony where Monaghan in the Alioto years used to smoke and have confidential political conversations. "What's going on?" Molinari asked him. "Are you sure you're doing the right thing?" White said that he couldn't handle the hours or make it on his supervisor's pay—even with the lease he'd obtained, amid much political criticism, for a fast-food operation called the Hot Potato at Pier 39.

Besides his unhappy experience with politics as the art of compromise, White and his wife since the day of his inauguration less than a year before had gone from an income of $39,000 and no major financial obligations to a $9,600 salary, a mortgage, a baby, and the burdens of starting a small business, reporter Russ Cone would point out later.

Overwhelmed by his problems, Dan went in to the mayor and simply quit. After he left, Cyr Copertini remembered a sympathetic Moscone shaking his head and telling her, "Poor kid, he's got all this stuff on his shoulders."

Back at supervisors' row, Dan ran into supervisor John Molinari, no relation to Jim, and told him what he had just done. "He seemed like the weight of the world was lifted from his shoulders," recalled Molinari, who went home thinking that, in putting family ahead of politics, Dan White really had his priorities straight.

BY THE NEXT WEEK, however, White had changed his mind. After his surprise resignation hit the papers, allies and lobbyists flocked to see him, pressuring him to get back on the board. The largely white Police Officers Association, facing a showdown on settlement of an antidiscrimination lawsuit brought by minority officers, needed his vote. So did the real estate industry, trying to head off rent control in San Francisco. Family members had offered financial assistance.

So on Wednesday, November 15, five days after his resignation, White went back to Moscone and told him he wished to withdraw it. The mayor gave him back his resignation letter and told reporters, "A man has the right to change his mind." "That was George from the heart," Copertini recalled.

Then political and legal reality set in. The city attorney's office ruled that, because the board's clerk had already processed the resignation, White could not simply withdraw it. To get his seat back he would have to be formally reappointed by Moscone.

Now it was the mayor who felt the pressure. Much of it came from Harvey Milk and other liberals, who urged him to take advantage of the rare opportunity he had to name one of his own to the board—and to ensure that those six-to-five votes started going his way.

As the intrigue mounted, the next week, Feinstein, ill at home, spoke with White on the phone and he asked her to intercede with Moscone. She told Nardoza, who brought work over to Lyon Street, to prepare "a pro-Dan kind of letter, stressing continuity and the will of the people," he said. She called the mayor with the same message. Moscone, who one ally recalled privately considered Dianne "a big pain in the ass," was noncommittal. At the end of their conversation she recalled asking that, regardless of what he decided to do about White, Moscone give her a call before announcing his decision in public. On Monday morning, November 27, he did.

HAVING LOST CONSIDERABLE WEIGHT during her illness, Dianne had been going through her wardrobe, looking for something that fit. She finally settled on a camel-colored suit and turtleneck just before the mayor called at 9:00 A.M.

Moscone said he appreciated Dianne's advice but had decided not to reappoint White. Instead he had chosen Don Horanzy, a businessman and community activist from the district. Moscone was sure Dianne would like him. One more thing, the mayor added: White might start some trouble at the board meeting that day, maybe try to claim his old seat or something crazy like that. He'd appreciate it if Dianne could help smooth things over.

Feinstein tried to call White at home to talk to him before he heard the news from someone else. There was no answer.

MOSCONE WAS HAPPY that morning. After two years of on-the-job training and frustration, he was finally getting a handle on the mayor's office and, now, on the board of supervisors. Milk had been right—White's precipitous resignation was a splendid chance to tilt the balance of power on the board in his favor.

About 10:00 A.M., as the mayor worked on his remarks for the 11:30 press conference where he would announce Horanzy's appointment, Assemblyman Willie Brown dropped in for a chat. A lawyer, Brown had just delivered his closing argument on behalf of a defendant in a drunk-driving case that was being tried in a courtroom two floors above the mayor's office. While Brown waited for his verdict, he and Moscone adjourned to the private sitting room off the mayor's big ceremonial office. Over a cup of coffee, they "bullshitted for fifteen or twenty minutes" Brown said, had a couple of laughs and gossiped about the Dan White situation.

As Brown left, he recalled, the two made plans to go Christmas shopping the next week at the Wolf's Den, a lingerie shop at one of the city's department stores where male customers could sip champagne while pretty women modeled the merchandise of silk and satin.

HARVEY MILK COULD BARELY contain his glee. Gale Kaufman, Quentin Kopp's legislative aide, had walked into Room 237, where the supervisors' offices were located, to join Harvey for a sweet roll and coffee. In his tiny cubicle, Milk cackled to Kaufman how Moscone had just told him White would not be reappointed. He had lobbied Moscone feverishly not to reappoint White and the mayor had seen the light.

Milk's influence as a power broker was growing. After his historic election he became increasingly visible as a national spokesman for the gay-rights movement and, a few weeks before, had been instrumental in defeating a right-wing-sponsored state ballot initiative to prohibit homosexuals from being teachers. If things kept going, he might be positioned to run for mayor himself before long.

Ever eager to spread a secret, Milk rushed out to tell Dick Pabich the news that White would not be reappointed. Kaufman walked out the door behind him. "You're not leaving, are you?" she asked, behind Harvey.

"Are you kidding?" he answered. "I wouldn't miss this for the world."

WHILE WILLIE BROWN was chatting with Moscone, Dan White was getting ready to go to City Hall. He was seething. After Moscone had led him to believe he'd be reappointed, the mayor hadn't even called to tell him he was picking somebody else. Instead, White had heard it from a radio reporter who called the night before after getting tipped off by Moscone's press secretary.

After the Sunday night call, he talked to Kopp, who told him he would make a motion at the board to block anyone but White from claiming the District 8 seat, at least until Dan's lawsuit seeking reinstatement had been settled. White "made it clear he would show up at City Hall and there would be a confrontation" at the board, Kopp recalled.

Descending into a self-absorbed spiral of anger, depression, humiliation, self-pity, and rage, White did not sleep that night. About 9:15 on Monday morning, his legislative aide called to say that Moscone had ducked a group of White supporters bearing petitions for his reappointment when the mayor had arrived at City Hall. Not long afterward, White called her back and told her to come and get him.

Dan dressed in his best suit, tan and three-piece. To finish getting ready, he went to the closet in his basement den and got his .38 revolver from his days on the police force. He loaded the chamber with five bullets and dropped ten more into his pocket.

BLUM DROVE DIANNE from Lyon Street to City Hall and dropped her off about 9:30 A.M. before heading to his office downtown. She bounded up the steps and smiled at the newspaper hawker who always perched just inside the door and now chirped, "Hi Dianne, welcome home."

A few minutes later, she walked into the second-floor pressroom, directly across the hall from supervisors' row. She was greeted by K. Connie Kang, the *Examiner's* court reporter, and by Ralph Craib, filling in for the *Chronicle's* regular beat man. She gave a peck on the cheek to Maitland Zane, the press secretary in her ill-fated 1971 mayoral campaign, who had promptly returned to daily journalism after the race.

They gossiped about the White situation, and Kang was "impressed with her because she was kind of sticking up for White. I thought that was very humane." Then Craib mentioned the incredible stories still emerging about the bizarre practices inside the People's Temple. He asked her with a grin if she was one of the politicians for whom Jim Jones had procured sexual favors. "Oh Ralph," she smiled, "I wouldn't tell."

Then Kang asked her if she would run for mayor again. Feinstein, who had privately decided to get out of politics, said no, not this time.

IN HER OFFICE, DIANNE BUZZED for Nardoza and told him to keep looking for White. The board's president also summoned board clerk Gil Boreman and Jim Lazarus, the deputy city attorney who advised the board and had been the point man in the legal tussle surrounding White's resignation. The week before, White had been sitting in Lazarus's office discussing the case when Harvey Milk called to check on the situation. Lazarus tried to be as diplomatic as possible, but he could tell White knew who was on the other end of the line and exactly why he was calling.

This morning, Feinstein wanted counsel about what to do at that afternoon's meeting if White showed up and tried to claim the District 8 seat after Moscone had sworn in Horanzy. They agreed on the proper procedure:

Boreman simply would call Horanzy's name, not White's, when he called the roll. Legally, that would make it a done deal; if Dan tried to vote, Dianne would rule him out of order.

Tongue in cheek, Feinstein suggested that if Dan tried to sit down in the supervisor's chair, they would have Frankie Aiello, the board's beloved but squat and aging sergeant at arms, affectionately known as "Frongie," simply roll Dan White out the door in the chair.

They had a good laugh over that.

WHEN HE GOT IN THE CAR, White was "all fired up" and "wanted some action," his aide, Denise Apcar, would say later. He said he wanted Moscone to "tell him to his face" that he would not be reappointed and also wanted to see Milk, to ask him, "What have I done to you?"

"He didn't look at me at all" in the car, Apcar recalled. "He was squinting hard. He was very nervous and agitated, blowing on his hands and rubbing them a lot, like he was cold . . . He looked like he was going to cry."

She dropped White at the main entrance to City Hall, then went to park the car in a reserved space on the north side of the building. White went up the steps to the door, then remembered the metal detectors that had been installed during the NWLF bombing spree. Carrying a gun, he "didn't want to embarrass" the cop on duty, he said later. That was why, he said, he went back down the steps and walked a block to a side, basement entrance that adjoined the supervisors' parking spots.

But Apcar had the key to the side door, and she had decided to go for gas. White paced back and forth for several moments, then climbed through a large unlocked window into a room adjoining the office of a city civil engineer. White jumped down from the ledge and started to run out the door. "Hey, wait a second," the engineer called to him.

White stopped and turned around. "I had to get in. My aide was supposed to come down and let me in the side door but never showed up," he said. "And you are?" asked the man. "I'm Dan White, the city supervisor," he answered. "Say, I've got to go." Then he turned and ran out.

JIM MOLINARI SAT in the outer, public waiting room of Room 200 and wondered if White would cause a scene today, now that George was replacing him. If Dan came in the mayor's office, he thought, he'd see him first. Smooth and easygoing, he could talk Dan out of embarrassing himself.

In the wake of Jonestown, Molinari had written a memo to the mayor's staff ordering them not to use the several side entrances to the office that opened onto an inner hallway. Lined with pictures of San Francisco mayors, the hallway connected the public waiting room to Moscone's inner office. As long as those doors weren't used, any suspicious visitors would have to go past Molinari or his partner, Gary Womack, first.

CYR COPERTINI LOOKED UP from her desk and was surprised to see Dan White standing in front of her, decked out in a nice-looking, three-piece suit in a "good warm bright color." She assumed he had come in through the outer office, past the mayor's security detail. In fact, White had slipped through one of the side doors that Molinari had said were not to be used, behind a mail clerk who had unlocked the private entrance with her key and, at White's request, let him in behind her.

Copertini, the daughter of a Mission district workingman who had advised her to "get a good civil service job," was both tactful and tough as nails. She had been Moscone's first and only choice as confidential secretary after she played a key role in the office of his campaign manager, Don Bradley. White asked to see the mayor. Feeling "embarrassed for him," she stalled by saying she thought someone was with Moscone, who was alone working on his remarks for the Horanzy press conference.

She slipped into Moscone's office and whispered, "He's out there. He wants to see you," she recalled.

The mayor grimaced. "Wait, wait, let me think about this . . . What would you do?" he asked Cyr.

"Well, you can't have him telling the press you wouldn't even see him," she remembered telling him. She quickly added that he should have press secretary Mel Wax sit in with the two, as he routinely did at sensitive meetings.

The mayor said no, he'd see Dan alone. "George took the view this was going to be embarrassing for Dan and he didn't want anybody to see him," she said.

Cyr came out, to where White waited by the desk. He seemed calm as he asked for a glass of water. She got it for him and offered him the paper. He declined, and she said there was nothing in it anyway, except a story about Caroline Kennedy turning twenty-one.

"Twenty-one? Is that right?" White said, adding that the assassination of John F. Kennedy was "all so long ago."

"It's even more amazing when you think that John-John is now eighteen," he said.

Moscone buzzed a few minutes later and said he was ready to see White. He walked into the mayor's office at about 10:40 A.M.

"Good girl, Cyr," White said.

SHE SAT BACK DOWN and, through the thick oak door, soon "heard Dan's voice, very high-pitched. Then it was quiet. I guess that's when they went into the back room." The small rectangular sitting room in back of his formal office, where Moscone had talked to Willie Brown that morning, got a lot of use. The mayor liked to do business in private meetings there and, after work, enjoyed sitting there and having a drink or two with cronies, aides, and friends.

He had finally told White flatly that he would not reappoint him. White got excited, so Moscone invited him into the back room for a drink. The mayor poured two drinks, White told police later, and offered him a seat on the couch before settling down himself into the easy chair by the window.

Moscone asked him how this would affect his family and what Dan thought he'd be doing now.

CYR HEARD deep, thudding noises.

She couldn't place the sound, which was like someone trying to slam a car door shut and finally succeeding. She went to the window to have a look.

It bothered her, that sound, and she decided it was important to remember the pattern it had made. Three sharp repeats, a pause, and then a final thud.

Boom, boom, boom.

Boom.

RUDY NOTHENBERG WAS WAITING impatiently to see the mayor. Brilliant and abrasive, Moscone's chief budget aide rubbed a lot of people at City Hall the wrong way, but he knew how to get things done. A veteran of local Democratic campaigns, he had become a top aide to Willie Brown when the brash assemblyman ran the powerful Ways and Means Committee in Sacramento.

On the mayor's staff, he quickly earned the nickname "Ruthless Rudy." Now he was waiting for an 11:00 A.M. meeting with the mayor and a health department executive about a dental plan for city employees, a piece of serious business before the 11:30 hoopla about the new supervisor got started.

Cyr told him the mayor was talking to White, so he figured his meeting would have to be rescheduled. He walked out of the mayor's office to return to his own across the hall. As he left, he saw Dan White running toward him.

Now that White was gone, Nothenberg returned to the mayor's office. George was not at his desk but his coat was still on the coat rack, so Rudy went to look in the back room. As he walked in, he saw smoke curling up from the rug. Then he saw the mayor stretched out on the floor, a burning cigarette still between his fingers. Perhaps the mayor had fainted, he thought.

Then he saw the blood and yelled for help.

MOSCONE WAS already dead.

As the mayor inhaled his last lungful of Marlboro smoke, White stood, pulled out his .38, and fired a bullet into Moscone's chest that sent him reeling to the floor. A second shot ripped into the back of his shoulder. White leaned over Moscone, disabled on the ground, and, at point-blank range, fired a bullet into his brain.

Then one more.

LESS THAN A MINUTE LATER, Dick Pabich was standing outside his office across the hall from Harvey Milk's when he saw White hurry to the door of Room 237, the entrance to the supervisors' quarters. What a jerk, thought Dick, acting like he's still a big-deal supervisor.

Peter Nardoza, whom Dianne had been pressing all morning to find Dan, saw White at the same time. "Dan, Dianne wants to see you," he said, standing in the hallway.

"Well, that will have to wait," White answered. Then he let himself in with a key to the oak and frosted-glass door.

Dianne's office was the first inside and she saw him right away. "Dan," she said, rising from behind her desk.

"I have something to do first," he replied, hurrying down the hall. He ducked his head into Milk's office, directly across the hall from his own. "Harv, can I see you a minute?" he said.

"Sure," Milk answered, crossing the narrow hallway to Dan's office, where White shut the door behind them. "I heard the door slam and I then heard 'Oh no,' " recalled Dianne.

Having reloaded after killing Moscone, White again had five bullets in his gun and, this time, he used them all. As he had with Moscone, he first disabled Milk with shots to the upper body, three of them now, then positioned himself to fire two rounds at close range into Harvey's skull.

Dianne had learned to use the pistol she carried after the NWLF tried to bomb her home. She knew the sounds and smell of gunfire. And gunpowder was heavy in the air.

Hearing the first shot, she thought that White had killed himself. But the firing didn't stop and, besides, there was Dan, coming out of his office, "whipping by and out the door."

Two minutes had passed since he shot the mayor.

Dianne rose as if in slow motion. She tried to compel her mind and body to work together, her head thick with dread and confusion as she forced herself up from her desk and looked down the hall and saw all the doors along the narrow hallway closed.

She pushed open the door of White's office, which was pinned shut by the body of Harvey Milk. She saw him splayed there on his stomach, blood and brain matter splattered on the wall.

The daughter and the widow of doctors, she instinctively reached to find a pulse. Her fingers slipped into a bullet hole.

AT 10:57 A.M. JIM MOLINARI called in a code 217 for the shooting at the mayor's office, which went out immediately on the police radio.

The dispatcher was Dan White's sister.

As officers from every district headed for City Hall with sirens blaring, a city paramedic entered Moscone's office three minutes after the call, extinguished the mayor's still-burning cigarette, and determined that he was dead.

On the west side of City Hall, Nardoza, who had heard nothing from across the hall, got a call on his intercom that there had been a shooting. He hurried into Room 237 and saw Dianne coming out of Dan's office, "white as a ghost."

Pabich too was called from across the hall. As he opened the door, "there stood Dianne Feinstein, her face completely drained and white, shrieking, 'Don't get excited, calm down.'"

Feinstein and Pabich both called police chief Charles Gain at the Hall of Justice. They didn't know that he was already responding to the shooting of the mayor.

Desperately waiting for the police, Nardoza stuck his head out the door and saw dozens of black-booted cops stomping up the stairs. Thank God, he thought, at last help is coming. But the cops kept running past him, heading for Room 200.

"No, you're going the wrong way," Nardoza yelled.

ALMOST LOST in the instant chaos was Don Horanzy, who had been waiting to be sworn in by George Moscone as the new supervisor from District 8. With him were his wife, a native of the Philippines, and daughters, all of them dressed in colorful costumes from her native land to celebrate the big day.

Amid the tumult, they wandered past Cyr's desk. "My God," she thought to herself, not recognizing them, "they're still letting tourists in."

CHIEF GAIN WENT FIRST to the mayor's office and then, under police escort, walked the block-long corridor from Room 200 to Feinstein's office. There he informed her that Moscone was dead and learned that Milk also had been killed.

Dianne's first call was to Dick Blum. "She came on the phone and said, 'The mayor's been shot and killed and Harvey Milk has been shot and killed and we think Dan did it. Come up here just as fast as you can.' It was just like the whole world changed," Blum said.

As he jumped in his car for the short drive to City Hall, a clamoring horde of reporters already was banging on the locked door to Room 237. Dianne tried to light a cigarette but was shaking too much. She saw that the camel-colored skirt she had carefully selected that morning was stained with the blood of Harvey Milk. She knew she had to make a formal announcement.

With Gain and Nardoza flanking her, she moved as if in a dream out the door and then forward a few paces to three marble steps in the same corridor that Dan White had crossed between two killings moments before. Gathering all her self-control, she took a few breaths. She focused on a single face in the crowd of reporters that looked at her with urgency and fear. Voice quavering, she spoke thirty-three words that were instantly transmitted across the nation and around the world.

"As president of the board of supervisors, it is my duty to inform you that both Mayor Moscone and Supervisor Harvey Milk have been shot and killed."

Hardened reporters recoiled in an almost visible wave of repulsion. "Oh my God," someone shouted.

"The suspect is Supervisor Dan White," Dianne added.

Twelve years later, she would make a political campaign advertisement from footage of that moment. A viewer looking closely at the ad could see Peter Nardoza behind her, his eyes shifting from side to side. Fearfully, he was looking for Dan White, who was still at large.

WILLIE BROWN HEARD from the bailiffs in the courtroom that there had been a shooting and raced downstairs. Nothenberg, coming out of Moscone's office, told him "the guy White killed the mayor," Brown remembered.

Then he went into the mayor's office and "immediately turned my attention to the legal question of succession" under the charter.

It was very clear. As president of the board, Dianne became acting mayor the instant Moscone died. But after the emergency succession, the board had the power to decide who would complete the slain mayor's unfinished term.

FEINSTEIN AND BLUM, Chief Gain and Supervisor John Molinari drove to George Moscone's house. The mayor's wife, Gina, and his mother, Lee, were headed to a family funeral in Napa County, north of the city, when a bulletin came on the radio that their husband and son had been killed. Scores of people were descending on the house, comforting the children, bringing food, getting in the way.

Sue Bierman, Dianne's old neighbor and a close friend and ally of Moscone, stood out front with the cops, acting as unofficial gatekeeper. At one point so many members of the Catholic clergy had arrived that she went inside to ask Gina "if there was a limit."

"Nobody but Susie would wonder if there was a limit on nuns," Mrs. Moscone said to the guests, with a laugh that briefly punctured the tears, Sue remembered.

Feinstein arrived and spoke quietly to Gina, one widow to another. "Dianne was comforting to all of us," Bierman said. "She knew we needed comforting."

AT 12:30 P.M., Dianne held a brief news conference.

"Today, San Francisco has experienced a double tragedy of incredible proportions," she said. "As acting mayor, I order an immediate state of mourning in our city.

"The city and county of San Francisco must and will pull itself together at this time. We will carry on as best as we possibly can."

She was determined that the board meeting would start on time. "From the very first, she was in control and concerned about the orderly procedures and wanted to make sure everything was done properly," said Supervisor Molinari. "She felt it important that the board get back for our meeting so people would understand that the government was not in disarray."

With two supervisors' chairs tragically empty, the meeting began on time at 2:00 P.M. It was brief.

"I think we all have to share the same sense of shame and the same sense of outrage," Feinstein said, before calling for a silent prayer. After a moment, she said, "With the prayer and in sorrow, this board is in recess until the call of the chair."

Then she banged her gavel and walked out.

DISTRICT ATTORNEY JOE FREITAS was in Washington, D.C., where he was conferring with State Department officials about Jonestown. After a meeting, he stopped at the National Geographic Society to renew his magazine subscription, then walked back to the Hay Adams Hotel, where a bellman came running through the lobby to say he had an "urgent, urgent" call from his office.

When he heard what had happened, Freitas got a police escort to Dulles Airport and flew back to San Francisco. That night he met at his apartment with top assistants, homicide inspectors, and prosecutors. They told him the case against White for two premeditated murders was airtight.

After all, they told Freitas, White had sneaked a weapon into City Hall, wounded then delivered the coup de grace to the mayor, reloaded, run to find Milk, and then demanded the car keys from his aide for his escape. He phoned his wife from a fast-food restaurant called the Doggie Diner, then walked to nearby St. Mary's Cathedral. She took a cab from Pier 39 and walked with him to Northern Station, a few blocks away, where he surrendered to an old friend from the Police Officers Association. Within two hours of the killings, he had given a full taped confession to the police.

"The evidence was overwhelming," Freitas said. "This was clearly a double murder."

BILL COBLENTZ, San Francisco's most politically influential attorney, was in Venice, Italy, for meetings with foreign clients with farming interests in

California when he got a call from Mo Bernstein. "He said George Moscone had been killed," Coblentz recalled. "I said, 'Don't joke about things like that, for God's sake.'

"He said, 'No, it's true.' Then, typical Mo, he shifted gears and said, 'We've got to get Dianne as mayor. Here's some people I need you to call.'"

Part Three

THE NATIONAL STAGE

11

WHITE NIGHT

Learn how to be a manager.

—*Dianne Feinstein's Rules for Getting Ahead*

ON NOVEMBER 29, 1978, DIANNE STOOD before a grieving crowd outside San Francisco City Hall and performed the role she had been preparing for all her life. "In our sorrow," she began, "this lovely jewel of a city seems a dark and saddened place." It was her formal eulogy to the murdered Mayor Moscone and Supervisor Harvey Milk, and it would be etched as the finest moment of her political career.

Following fast on the Jonestown massacre, the City Hall murders had heaped an almost unendurable burden of anguish and shock onto a shaken city. Now Feinstein spoke, in sensitive tones of caring, comfort, and condolence, of inspirational themes of survival and determination to persevere through pain. Her brief public speech reassured and resonated with personal experience, at a time when San Francisco was struggling to escape a nightmare.

"The people of San Francisco are indomitable even in the moments of greatest adversity," she said. "As we reconstructed the city after the physical damage done by the earthquake and fire, so, too, can we rebuild from the spiritual damage caused to the body politic."

Since the awful moment she announced the assassinations to the world, Dianne had been a ubiquitous and soothing figure of dignity and condolence, a black-suited, white-bowed civic widow who, eight months after burying her husband, now led a city through cathartic rituals of public mourning. "I hope I projected a calm stability," she reflected a decade later, "regardless of whether I felt it myself."

The night of the assassinations, a moving candlelight march of thousands proceeded from the Castro district to City Hall, where Dianne spoke and Joan Baez sang soothing ballads. In the days that followed, the public lined up to pay tribute at two closed coffins that lay in state beneath the splendid dome of City Hall, while Moscone and Milk were honored with majestic and touching memorial services.

Behind the scenes, a more prosaic drama played out. Within hours of Moscone's death, some of Feinstein's closest advisers and several of the slain mayor's allies began a quiet campaign to ensure that she would be elected by the supervisors to complete the one year and forty-one days that remained of his term. The speed with which the lobbying began reflected the political reality that a massive vacuum of power had suddenly opened in the polarized city.

Feinstein emerged successful in both the public and the private political arenas, not only winning the office that voters had twice denied her but also gaining an instant visibility on the national political scene. Although feeling uncertain, she moved quickly to put her personal stamp on an office that, despite constant conflicts and challenges, she would hold for the next nine years.

It would not be easy. Within six months of her taking over as mayor, the city was rocked by yet another violent aftershock of November 1978. The most destructive riot in San Francisco's history was triggered by a lenient verdict handed down by a jury sympathetic to Dan White. If Feinstein's handling of the sad aftermath of the City Hall killings was her finest moment, her failure of leadership before the violence of "White Night" would be her worst.

The incident left her politically vulnerable, open yet again to the charge that a woman could not be tough enough to be the city's chief executive. It led inevitably to an intense and bitter race against an old rival that revived memories of how she had wilted in two earlier campaigns for mayor. She still had to prove, to herself and to the city, that "toughness doesn't always come in a pinstripe suit."

ON THE NIGHT of the assassinations, a group of Feinstein's friends and advisers gathered at Lyon Street. Amid the coffee and shock over the events of the day, Mo Bernstein started talking about "who could get six votes" to become mayor. "No, Mo, not tonight," Dianne interrupted, Nardoza recalled.

But the next morning, Supervisor Robert Gonzales got a call soliciting his support of Feinstein. The day before, the liberal supervisor had stood at his law office window, on the fourteenth floor of a high rise near City Hall, and watched the mortal remains of George Moscone taken out of a side door in a black rubberized body bag. Now, less than twenty-four hours later, one of San Francisco's most politically wired businessmen was on the phone, urging Gonzales to vote for Dianne for mayor.

"The guy said there'd been a meeting and that he'd been asked to contact me on behalf of Dianne for mayor," Gonzales recalled. The man mentioned Mo Bernstein and Dick Blum. "The last thing on my mind was who the next mayor was. I said, 'Tell Mo and those guys I haven't decided.'"

Although Blum did not recall such a meeting, he said of the late Bernstein, "This was Mo's moment in the sun. He specialized in electing supervisors, basically, and he was trying to help Dianne." Feinstein said that she had given no approval for an effort on her behalf to put together the votes on the board that would decide who finished Moscone's term. "Mo was being Mo, and nobody controlled Mo," she said. "It became clear to me that it would be difficult to put together six votes, but we did nothing until the funeral was over."

Nevertheless, a behind-the-scenes campaign on Feinstein's behalf was under way by Tuesday morning, when Gonzales got the call. He decided to make some calls of his own. He arranged a meeting with Supervisors Lau, Molinari, and Silver, four-fifths of the liberal coalition that had tried to stop Feinstein's election as board president in another exercise in behind-the-scenes politicking just eleven months before. The ringleader of that group was no longer available.

The four liberals ended their meeting with a vague agreement that no one would make any quick commitments and they would "keep our powder dry," according to Gonzales. But "the smoke was not cleared" from the assassinations, Molinari recalled, before the politicking grew intense along supervisors' row.

Key factors in Feinstein's favor were quick endorsements by Willie Brown, Moscone's ally, and by Freitas, the liberal district attorney who had been mentioned as a possible mayoral contender himself. Another was the intermediary role played by Blum, who was trusted by the Moscone forces as a friend and appointee of the late mayor's, at the same time that he was dating Feinstein.

On Saturday, Gonzales was on page one of the *Chronicle,* declaring his interest in the job. But he was already too late. After Moscone's funeral on Thursday, Gonzales's erstwhile ally Molinari walked up to Feinstein and suggested lunch. They went to the Concordia Club, where she asked for his support. Although the two previously had not been close, Molinari soon publicly endorsed her for mayor, splitting the liberal bloc. A few weeks later, he enjoyed her support in his successful bid to replace her as board president. "The bandwagon for Dianne was rolling," Molinari recalled. "Dianne during that week had really pulled people together." By the weekend, Silver, who got a call from Bernstein, and Lau also were behind Feinstein.

By Monday, December 4, one week after the assassinations, the private lobbying, combined with Feinstein's overarching public performance, had eliminated all but rearguard opposition to her selection as mayor. With two seats vacant and Dianne ineligible to vote for herself, she won by the bare majority of the board votes needed, six-to-two. Kopp, complaining of private political deals, and Lee Dolson, who wanted more time to consider the matter, voted against her. A year before, Feinstein had made an alliance with conservatives to be elected board president; this time she won with liberals.

"I didn't see any point in prolonging the agony," recalled Gonzales, who signaled his retreat from consideration as mayor by nominating Feinstein, calling her "a person who will move us past this week of tragedy." For Molinari, "what it boiled down to was not whether we should elect Dianne, but what reasons we had to take it away from her. There weren't any."

Feinstein, who as a supervisor prided herself on her ability to "count to six," was so sure of victory that she had State Supreme Court Chief Justice Rose Bird standing by to administer the mayoral oath of office. About a hundred feet from where Harvey Milk was murdered the week before, Feinstein became the city's thirty-eighth mayor, the first woman to hold the job, and the ninth female chief executive of a major American city.

Mindful that, after two failed bids at election, she had assumed office only because of tragedy, Feinstein took the oath with "no sense of joy," she said, but in a "somber, reflective frame of mind."

AT FIRST, SHE COULDN'T walk into Moscone's office. On the day of the assassinations, Deputy Mayor Nothenberg, who had found the mayor's body, escorted her to Room 200 to address Moscone's staff. Outside the door, she started to break down, and Rudy took her into his office until she collected herself enough to say a few words of sympathy to his aides. After that, how-ever, she took charge, and hallmarks of what would become her long may-oralty soon became clear.

Feinstein brought Peter Nardoza with her from across the hall but tried to keep Moscone's staff intact. There was a rapid change in the personal style of the city's chief executive, however. Moscone had been a casual man who would wander with coffee in hand into staff offices to chat or exchange jokes; he delegated authority happily and was far more loved than feared by those who worked for him. Feinstein was anything but casual. She instituted a dress code: jackets and ties for men; skirts or dresses for women—no pantsuits in the office. She ordered all police officials, including the chief, to wear uni-forms. She wanted to see all the messages that came into the mayor's office. She worked long hours, going through a dozen or more appointments and appearances a day and calling staffers late into the night at home. And she began every week by presiding over a Monday morning meeting of more than fifty department heads in her office.

Within days of Feinstein's moving into the mayor's office, a friend of Cyr Copertini's told the confidential secretary, "You should look at yourself—you used to be so relaxed and now there's this constant tension on your face." "I certainly wanted to stay" in the job, Cyr recalled, "but I had to get used to a new, rigid style."

One of the first to learn a lesson was Nothenberg, who as deputy mayor was used to exercising broad decision-making control. But when Feinstein found out that he had recommended the firing of a city department head to a mayoral commission, she called him on the carpet. He was informed that decisions from the mayor's office henceforth would cross her desk.

"She wanted and insisted on getting an enormous amount of background information before she would take an action, whether it was a policy deci-sion or a personal appearance," said Nothenberg, who went on to prosper under Feinstein administrations. "She likes to get an incredible amount of detail and inordinate amounts of information."

Copertini recalled a staffer who wrote a report that Dianne at first praised highly; a short time later the woman got a second call from the mayor com-plaining that the report was on the wrong kind of paper. Another former Feinstein aide recalled drafting a speech that included the phrase, "As Thomas Jefferson wrote in the Declaration of Independence," and being asked by the mayor, "How do you know Thomas Jefferson wrote that?"

Copertini, who served four mayors as appointments secretary, including nine years with Feinstein, said that Dianne "always had one more question than you had the answer for."

Feinstein's desire for information and control extended to the smallest details. When she first took over, she had two police officers carry the several boxes of daily mail to her car at night so that she could read it at home. "She had been critical of other mayors and she was the mayor who was going to read every piece of correspondence," Cyr said.

"It's true that I demanded a level of performance from my staff," Feinstein said. "As I'd go around the city, people would say, 'I wrote to you and you didn't bother to answer.' And I said, 'But we did.' And under somebody's desk were two boxes of letters that had been written and nobody bothered to mail them. I just couldn't have that. The bureaucrats are here long after you. What I tried to do was to have the relationship with them directly."

On policy matters Feinstein moved more slowly, but also surely. She had vowed that assassination would not change the course of politics in San Francisco, but inevitably it did. Whatever Dan White's personal motives, his crimes politically pushed the city to the right in terms of development policies, a more pro-business orientation, and the type of people appointed to key commissions, the citizen bodies by which mayors seek to govern the city under its cumbersome charter.

In an interview nine days after the assassinations, Dianne criticized Moscone's political orientation. She praised his dedication to bringing more women and minorities into city government but complained that too many of these commissioners were liberal. "I heard complaints from the business community and from many ordinary, tax-paying small homeowners," she said of Moscone's appointments. Then she added a clear message to the late mayor's commissioners.

Moscone, like other San Francisco mayors before him, had invited his appointees to dissent and feel free to air their opinions. Feinstein, in polite, couched words that foretold swift actions she would take in years to come, made it clear that that was not her way. "I anticipate that a commission which is directly under my jurisdiction should share my goals," she said. "If someone wants to continue serving, we should discuss our goals and, if we disagree on basic principles, they probably wouldn't want to continue to serve."

Betty Goldman with her three daughters: from left, Yvonne, Lynn, and Dianne, early 1940s.

Dr. Leon Goldman in 1956.

The Goldman sisters at home in San Francisco. "We hated those pictures," said the senator's sister Lynn.

Queen of the Junior
Grand National Exposition,
1951.

Dianne and Bert Feinstein.
She said, "As a marriage, it was a ten."

With husband Bert Feinstein, announcing
her candidacy for San Francisco Board of
Supervisors, May 1969.

With new supervisor
Quentin Kopp, whose
1971 election happened at
the same time that Dianne
was humiliated in her first
race for mayor.

With Bert, at their home after a terrorist bomb was planted outside
their daughter's bedroom window, December 1976.

Dianne pledged to appear in a bikini if the Pier 39 tourist complex opened on time. She wore a vintage suit from the old Sutro Baths to fulfill her promise, August 1978.

Acting Mayor Feinstein just after the assassinations of Mayor George Moscone and Supervisor Harvey Milk. She opened the session with a silent prayer, November 27, 1978.

Outside City Hall an outraged mob protested the verdict in
the Dan White assassination case, May 21, 1979.

Mayor Feinstein brought a management style to City Hall that
matched the dignity of the mayor's formal office.

A rare moment of public emotion before the press at the announcement of a vote to recall Mayor Feinstein from office, January 1983.

Mayor Feinstein kept a firefighter's coat in the trunk of her car and often appeared at the scenes of major blazes.

With presidential candidate Walter Mondale at her interview for the vice-presidential spot on the 1984 ticket.

Mayor Feinstein and financier Richard Blum set a regal tone for her administration at their City Hall wedding, January 1980, just after she was sworn in for her new term.

As candidate for governor of California, 1990. Her theme, "tough and caring," was highlighted by a pro-death penalty stance and a call for early childhood education.

With daughter Katherine, 1990.

With Barbara Boxer the day
after both women won their
nominations to run for the
U.S. Senate, June 1992.

Senator Feinstein leads a
group of women senators
and feminist leaders down
the steps of the Capitol
to a press conference on
abortion funding,
July 1993.

Backed by Senators
Metzenbaum (D-OH)
and DeConcini (D-AZ)
at a press conference after
the Senate passed the
measure she authored
that banned a variety of
assault weapons.

On the most immediate political problem she faced—appointing three new supervisors—Feinstein's actions would have earned Moscone's approval. Don Horanzy, the businessman who had been waiting to be sworn in at the time of the killings, was quickly appointed to Dan White's old seat. For her own seat, Dianne asked a community screening committee in her district to review candidates and recommend a short list. She picked a forty-one-year-old state government attorney named Louise Renne. On the day of her appointment, a *Chronicle* reporter dubbed Renne a "clone" of Dianne. To Renne's lasting displeasure, the label stuck, despite the fact that she was far more active in the women's and environmental movements than Feinstein.

The toughest choice was Harvey Milk's seat. Milk's assassination had galvanized the gay community, which ironically became far more powerful now that its leader had been martyred. In a chilling twist to the tragedy of November 27, it was disclosed that Milk had made a tape a few days after being elected in which he named four people he would consider worthy successors in the event he was assassinated. At the time, Dick Pabich thought that it was one of Harvey's dramatic conceits. But now, amid the roiling crosscurrents of gay community politics, the tape loomed large as Dianne took weeks to contemplate the crucial choice.

Among politically active gays, there was a basic split between the followers of Milk, younger and more militant, and those represented by more mainstream figures such as Jim Foster, Feinstein's ally and an enemy of Harvey's. In delaying her decision, Feinstein upset virtually all factions in the splintered gay community, as she considered some twenty-five candidates, interviewed and reinterviewed contenders, and floated names, including that of a notorious drag queen whom she briefly considered as a "caretaker" appointment.

One of those on Harvey's list was Harry Britt, a former minister from Texas who was president of the progressive gay Democratic club started by Milk. Although active in grass-roots politics, he was not particularly interested in serving on the board of supervisors: "I knew what Harvey's life was like and I knew what my life was like and I liked my life a lot better." But on New Year's Eve, Dianne called Britt at home ("I was embarrassed because I didn't have a date and here was Dianne Feinstein calling me at home"), told him that her "file was empty" on him, and asked for more background information.

Convinced that if he did not take the job, Feinstein would give it to someone unacceptable to the Milk faction, Britt accepted her offer of appointment. Dianne regretted the move almost immediately, as the leftist Britt on the board came to oppose her on nearly every major issue.

"She said, 'If you're appointed, you're part of the team,'" Britt recalled. "I responded that 'I'll be loyal,' but she had to understand that she could expect me to honor my commitment to carry on for Harvey Milk."

FEINSTEIN ALSO CLOSELY associated herself with President Carter's administration, building on her early and enthusiastic support for him in 1976 to establish a strong personal relationship. In January 1979 she flew to Washington for a conference on mayors and met with Carter privately. Not long afterward, she was back in Washington to testify again on urban policy before a House budget committee and echoed the theme of renewal she often sounded after the assassinations.

"What I would like to do, if I may, is just talk to you briefly from the heart," she told the committee. "Because we rose once from an earthquake, we are once again arising from the stigma of assassination, to become like a phoenix and develop from our ashes a new rebirth."

Her connections to the highest councils of the federal government were aided by Blum, who had been an early financial supporter and policy adviser to Vice President Walter Mondale. The high visibility of Blum in the early days of Feinstein's mayoralty, which contrasted sharply with Bert's self-effacing role, soon became the focus of commentary in San Francisco, fueled by the perception that he wielded broad influence behind the scenes and that he was one of her top advisers.

The couple announced in March 1979 that they planned to marry, and in May Blum took over management of the Carlton Hotel, one of the investments in the tangle of finances left by Bert's illness and death. Herb Caen, whose column is the first thing many San Franciscans turn to with their morning coffee, quickly dubbed Blum "the prince consort," a nickname that stuck like glue, and also took to referring to "Dianne Feinblum," "Blumstein," and so on. Blum soon lowered his public profile.

With the goodwill of a shaken city behind her, Feinstein earned rave reviews in the early months after becoming mayor. She was seemingly everywhere in public, so visible that a hotel staged a fashion show featuring the

"Dianne look"—tailored suits and silk blouses with trademark big bows—while gay drag clubs held "Dianne Feinstein look-alike" contests. Nationally, she was the subject of a host of favorable profiles in the major media, from the *Washington Post* to *People* magazine.

In early May, Dianne's friend President Jimmy Carter came to San Francisco to speak at a tribute for George Moscone at the War Memorial Opera House. He described the death of the mayor as a "national tragedy" and went on to say that

> San Francisco has shown its ability to survive shocks, and this event tonight . . . what's gone on before, has helped us all to realize that San Francisco is still strong enough and united enough to survive this second major shock that came during the end of 1978.
>
> I appreciate Dianne Feinstein, who, with her calm and compassionate leadership, preserved the precious attributes of this city during those trying days . . . And you demonstrated again a special spirit by being able, during this event, to change grief and loss into love and hope.

Then the Dan White verdict came in.

IN THE FIRST MOMENTS of his opening statement to the jury, Dan White's lawyer conceded that his client had shot and killed George Moscone and Harvey Milk. But that was not the paramount issue in the trial, defense attorney Douglas Schmidt argued. "The issue in this trial is properly to understand why that happened," Schmidt told the jurors. "Good people, fine people with fine backgrounds, simply don't kill people in cold blood. It just doesn't happen."

That was how White's lawyer framed his defense in the fifteen-day trial, and in the end that was how the jury saw it. Eleven members of the jury that heard the case were white and working class, the kind of old-time San Franciscans whose views of what had been happening to their city were closer to White's than to those of Moscone and Milk.

Tom Norman, Freitas's top prosecutor, put on a straightforward case that proved what everyone already knew—that Dan White had shot and killed Mayor Moscone and Supervisor Milk. But the prosecution devoted less time to the key question of motive upon which White's attorney focused.

For the prosecution, it was clear that something was amiss when on the third day of the trial they played White's sobbing taped confession, taken ninety minutes after the killings, in which he described the "pressures" he was under but expressed no remorse for the killings. "At least four jurors had tears in their eyes," recalled prosecutor Norman.

White's attorney, Schmidt, skillfully used psychiatric and character testimony and surgical cross-examination to prove his basic thesis: though his client had killed, he was incapable of doing so "willfully . . . and with malice aforethought." Schmidt brought forth a parade of friends and family members who testified that White for years had exhibited symptoms of what they only later would learn was the mental illness of depression. And he put on the stand an array of expert psychiatric witnesses to provide a medical framework for the anecdotal evidence. He also presented testimony that White's depression was signaled by his consumption of large amounts of junk food, which led to Schmidt's legal tactics being called "the Twinkie defense."

A prime example of his trial skill came in his cross-examination of Feinstein, who was called as a prosecution witness. Wearing a cranberry skirt and sweater with a white blouse and bow, the new mayor described under direct examination how she had seen Dan come into the supervisors' chambers, heard the shots, saw him leave, and then discovered Harvey's body. Although dramatic, it did not advance the prosecution case.

Then Schmidt cross-examined. Dianne described her mentoring relationship to White, the "frustrating" experience of being a supervisor, and her attempts to reach him the morning of the assassinations to "soften the blow" of his not being reappointed to the board. Schmidt asked whether Dianne thought White was "idealistic." Norman objected, but the judge allowed the mayor to answer.

"I felt that Dan had very strong ideals. He had always worked very hard, and he took the process very seriously," she said.

"Given that you knew Dan White quite well," Schmidt next asked, "would it be your opinion that the man you knew was the type of man that would have shot two people?"

"No," Feinstein answered. "It would not be my opinion."

Good people, fine people with fine backgrounds, simply don't kill people in cold blood, Schmidt had told the jury. It just doesn't happen.

Throughout his trial, Dan White sat at the defense desk like a pale, lifeless statue, staring vacantly at the wall. During Dianne's testimony, he wept.

On May 21, 1979, at 5:28 P.M., the jury reported its verdict: White was guilty, not of murder, but of two counts of voluntary manslaughter, the lesser crime that Schmidt had argued his client had committed. The jury accepted Schmidt's argument that White killed with "diminished capacity."

He faced a maximum prison sentence of seven years, eight months.

TV REPORTERS STANDING BY at the Hall of Justice went live with bulletins about the verdict, incredulity in their faces and voices straining journalistic objectivity. The verdict seemed as unbelievable as the events that precipitated it.

White had strapped on a loaded gun and brought extra bullets to City Hall, sneaked in a window to avoid a metal detector, killed the mayor at point-blank range, reloaded, hurried across City Hall, found Harvey Milk, and done the same to him. Within two minutes, he had snuffed out the lives of both the city's highest elected official, a forty-nine-year-old father of four children, and the nation's most prominent gay-rights spokesman. For this, he would be sentenced as he would have been in a vehicular homicide case.

As word of the verdicts swept through the city, some TV stations switched to on-the-scene reports from the Castro district, where stunned and angry gays were interviewed and asked on camera if they thought violence might result.

The news was also announced over the police-band radio. Moscone had never been popular with rank-and-file cops, largely because of his position favoring quotas for minorities and women on the force and for bringing in Charles Gain, a liberal outsider, as chief. Some cops had raised money for a Dan White defense committee. Now someone sang "Danny Boy" on the communications channel.

At City Hall Dianne held a press conference at 6:30 P.M. Denouncing the verdict, she said, "As far as I'm concerned, these were two murders. I think it's important that this town pull itself together again. We've gone through a physical bloodbath and now we are going through a mental one." Then she went home for dinner.

By 7:00 P.M. a large crowd had gathered in the Castro, as often happened spontaneously during big political events, and it grew amid cries of "out of the bars and into the streets," the anthem chant of the gay-rights movement. But no one expected trouble from the gays. The night of the assassinations, tens of thousands had marched peacefully down Market Street to City Hall, holding candles aloft in an emotional and tender tribute to their martyred leader.

Tonight would be no candlelight march. Shortly after 8:00 P.M. several thousand marchers, reinforced by protesters from elsewhere in the city, had arrived at City Hall. Before long, some were hurling rocks, parking meter posts, street signs, trash cans, and newspaper racks at windows. They ripped fluted-iron grillwork from the building to wield as spears to smash the finely worked formal entrance doors of the building.

While many police officers were soon on the scene, they were under orders from Gain to stand their positions and not disperse the mob, because he believed doing so would lead to too many injuries and more widespread violence. More protesters, some having seen live TV reports of the riot, showed up, many of them nongay and militant. Riot-clad officers stood their ground, getting hit with bricks, bottles, and metal missiles.

District attorney Freitas, who had taken members of his failed prosecution team out for a commiserative North Beach dinner, arrived on the scene. He watched the growing frenzy in front of City Hall and thought to himself, "Charlie's being pretty fucking mild about this."

Feinstein, hearing radio reports of the early stages of the riot, returned with Blum to City Hall about 8:45 and spoke to Gain, stressing to him the importance of not allowing rioters inside, where they might destroy records. In her second-floor office, she listened to the sounds of shattering glass and roars of anger—"Kill Dan White"—and decided not to walk out on her balcony and try to address the crowd. "I had never seen a mob before," she recalled. "I had never seen the electricity, the inability to reason or speak to it. There was nothing that mob could listen to." At one point, Supervisor Silver went outside to address the crowd, which she recalled was "increasing in size and ugliness." As she spoke, someone hurled a rock that struck her in the face and she was helped back inside City Hall bleeding profusely.

At about 9:30, Dianne talked to Gain in her office and urged him to take some action. He emphasized his strategy of keeping the crowd in the plaza around City Hall, saying that widespread burning and looting might result if it was dispersed. Uncharacteristically, Feinstein deferred to his judgment.

For the next few hours, chaos reigned outside City Hall. The crowd kept growing larger, more violent, and, in the face of the passive police strategy, more daring. Officers became human targets and several were attacked while riot squads were held back or, in one case, ordered to retreat before the mob. "We should have prepared for this," a police officer overheard Feinstein say as the riot raged. "We should have had the streets blocked off."

Inside the mayor's office, Feinstein was "very distressed, very subdued, and very quiet," recalled Louise Renne, whom the mayor had appointed to her own seat on the board. A former top city official recalled that Feinstein looked "deep in shock" during the riot. Besieged inside her office—except when she, Blum, and several others fled briefly from a wafting cloud of tear gas to the other side of City Hall—Feinstein seemed "shell-shocked," said a supervisors' aide who watched her that night. "It was a very long night," she said, "and Dianne never gave the impression she was making decisions."

The mayor several times tried to reach the chief, but Gain, not wearing a radio as he roamed between the lobby of City Hall, Room 200, and a command post half a block away, proved hard to find. Shortly before 11:00 P.M., as she saw a police car start to burn, the mayor again urged Gain clear the mob; he said he would as soon as he had enough men.

About 11:00 P.M. the mob set fire to a long row of police cars double-parked near City Hall, torching them with flaming trash and flares, as the eerie wailing of dying sirens pierced through the acrid smoke that flashed with flames and the glare of television lights. Not long after, police were finally given the order to clear Civic Center Plaza and disperse the crowd. With only a few more officers on the scene than at the beginning of the riot, and facing a much larger crowd, they quickly accomplished the job.

With their pent-up fury finally unloosed, some officers turned to violence of their own. As vandals smashed windows on Market Street, protesters, bystanders, and newsmen alike were beaten with police batons. When the bars began to empty in the Castro district before the 2:00 A.M. closing, simmering police officers confronted crowds of taunting gays. Supervisor Harry Britt, later criticized for inflaming the situation, screamed, "The police don't belong here." A few minutes later, a squad of riot-clad cops invaded a saloon and beat fleeing patrons, igniting charges of police brutality.

Shortly after midnight Feinstein called department heads at home, ordering them to secure City Hall, get the streets cleaned up, and begin repairing the widespread damage to city property. At 2:30 A.M. she met with Gain, the fire chief, and other law enforcement officials for a briefing on the situation and to lay plans for possible new trouble the next night, which would have been Harvey Milk's forty-ninth birthday.

Reflecting on the lessons of what was called the White Night riot, she said:

> I had been mayor a very short period of time. I never as mayor
> again in a major incident let myself get separated from the command

structure. I was not at the command post, so I did not know what commands were being given and I kept asking "Where is the chief, find the chief."

The cops, my security, everybody said, "Stay in the office." There was an uncertainty. But I would never listen again. I would do what I thought I had to do and security just [would have] to cope with it.

When the wreckage of the riot was hauled away, it was estimated at twenty-five tons of debris, much of it thrown at the cops. Although no one was killed, the damage included sixty-five police officers and dozens of civilians injured, $400,000 worth of property destroyed, including fourteen burned police cars, and years of lawsuits.

In the aftermath of the riot, Feinstein's political future looked damaged, too.

QUENTIN KOPP HAD WASTED little time in making public his intention to run for mayor in 1979. On the Monday after the assassinations, when he cast one of only two votes on the board against Feinstein for mayor, Kopp told reporters that he would challenge her at the polls and attacked the behind-the-scenes maneuvering that had marked her ascension.

Kopp was furious because he believed he had a commitment from Feinstein to support him for mayor in 1979, made at the Jack's restaurant lunch that Barbagelata organized, in exchange for Kopp's support of Dianne for board president in 1978. Recollections of what was said at that meeting differ, but Kopp believed a date of April 15 was set for Dianne to announce her endorsement of him. That would turn out to be the day that Bert died. With Dianne preoccupied with his illness before, and depressed and grieving after, Kopp said, he did not press her on the matter.

Then, incredibly, Feinstein had become mayor by assassination, and Kopp was left to wonder what might have been if he had made a bid to be board president in 1978. Soon after taking office, the woman who had told reporters an hour before the assassinations that she would not run for mayor again, made clear that she would seek her own four-year term as the city's chief executive. With the blessing of Willie Brown and other Moscone allies who despised Kopp, she hired Don Bradley, the slain mayor's old manager, to run her campaign.

"Conditions obviously had changed," Dianne recalled of her decision to run in 1979. "I had no choice but to run. It was a terrible, terrible time and there was so much hatred and fear. If I was a lame duck going in, if I couldn't be a strong mayor, I couldn't bring the city together."

In the months following the killings, Feinstein's dignified and stately performance soared above the level of mundane politics, while Kopp's Lone Ranger critic act grated as petty bickering. But after the disastrous White Night riot, Kopp suddenly had a real issue to use against Feinstein. Although Gain was in charge of strategy and tactics during the disorder, and would be the main target of criticism in three major reports of the incident, Dianne bore buck-stops-here responsibility for supervision of the police department—and the brunt of the political fallout from the riot.

While the riot was still raging, Kopp went on a radio talk show to decry its handling. Before long, he stepped up the attacks. "In the eye of the storm, the mayor equivocates, assesses, consults, and postpones," he charged at a campaign fund-raiser a few weeks after the riot. "How can citizens feel confident when they see police cars burning . . . while the mayor sits in her office immobilized?"

Despite her years as a supporter of the department, Feinstein was also blasted in the newspaper of the Police Officers Association. "As far as the mayor is concerned," POA president Bob Barry wrote, "any nightmares that were created were created by her, and [those] that surround her."

The aftermath of the riot left Feinstein in a familiar political position: squeezed in the middle between two powerful ideological forces. Conservatives and the Police Officers Association were outraged at Gain's failure to contain the riot early; liberals and gays were incensed at the police brutality that occurred in the Castro and on the streets after the cops finally were ordered to disperse the mob. One side wanted Gain fired; the other wanted the mayor to stand firmly behind him and decry the "police riot."

She appointed a blue-ribbon commission to investigate the matter.

IN THE EARLY MONTHS of 1979, Feinstein in public kept urging the citizens of San Francisco to "rise from the ashes" like the mythical, endlessly reincarnating phoenix that symbolizes the city. But she was having trouble doing it for herself. Having been pounded with a series of quick-succession emotional blows, she felt genuine ambivalence and self-doubt about the way she had assumed office. She also had been sued for slander by a labor boss as a result of comments during a city workers' strike and, though she would finally prevail, the matter distracted her in 1979. And, despite her assertion of control and personal authority in the mayor's office, she remained surrounded by a staff that was loyal to George Moscone, and often felt trapped by conflicts between his vision and her own.

"What few people know, in that first year I don't think I really wanted to continue to be mayor," she recalled. "I was really undone by those assassinations, a lot more than anybody has ever seen."

In July she made her first major staff change, replacing a Moscone deputy mayor with Hadley Roff, her old acquaintance from Stanford who was working for Senator Ted Kennedy in Washington. When Roff, who had recently lost his first wife to cancer, flew out for an interview, he and Dianne sat on the deck at Lyon Street and talked about life and death and loss and he was taken with her "empathy and sensitivity." Then she and Blum took him on a long car tour of the city, during which the mayor reeled off an epic monologue of minutiae about federal housing programs, infrastructure improvements, and UDAG funds for public transportation. "Scrunched down in the back seat, it seemed endless," he smiled years later, recalling Feinstein's zest for policy detail.

A rumpled, friendly man with the instincts of a political pro and the body of a Hefty bag, Roff was the perfect counterpoint to Feinstein, and his office soon became a clearinghouse of political gossip and a favored place for staff to unburden themselves of their frustration at the mayor. "That's just Dianne," he would say many times over the next eight years.

Although Roff's arrival made Feinstein more personally and politically secure inside the mayor's office, she was still being handled by Moscone's team in the campaign being waged outside. A politician who excelled on television and in one-on-one or small-group discussion, Dianne at the time was more reserved and less comfortable with street-level campaigning. In 1979 she reverted to form as a cranky candidate who constantly questioned or resisted strategic and scheduling moves. "She never stopped complaining," recalled an associate of Don Bradley, her late campaign manager.

Louise Renne and Jack Molinari, her closest allies among the supervisors, and Jim Molinari, who became her driver and bodyguard, traveled with her constantly and all recalled the difficulty of getting her out on the streets. "She hated campaigning," one of them said. "She would always say, 'Why are we here?' and someone would say, 'If you don't, you'll be walking down the rotunda steps with Quentin Kopp on your arm.'"

Feinstein said that, "I didn't have a great sense of self-confidence at that point. I really didn't believe that anybody wanted me elected to the [mayor's] office."

Because former Moscone aide Corey Busch had experience dealing with Feinstein, Bradley implored him to take a leave of absence from his job and join the campaign. Busch agreed because, as a Moscone loyalist, he "was not interested in seeing George's murder have the effect of electing Quentin."

"You had to cajole her into doing events," Busch said, recalling that Feinstein frequently lamented that she would lose the race. At one point, Ted Kennedy was in town and drew a big crowd to the Hyatt Regency hotel for a political event. The campaign scheduled a "drop-by" for Dianne but, when Jim Molinari drove her there, she balked and sent him in to fetch Roff, who came out to the car.

"Why am I here? Who are these people?" she asked her top aide.

"They're Democrats," Roff patiently explained, "they're voters."

"Do they have name tags?" she replied.

Kopp, by contrast, was a happy warrior. His Grand Inquisitor style as a supervisor disappeared when he was on the stump. He reveled in the back-slapping, glad-handing style of San Francisco retail campaigning and mounted a vigorous challenge. Undismayed by his private poll, which showed him trailing Feinstein by thirty-five percentage points early in the year, Kopp hired an abrasive but smart young operative named Clint Reilly, who had built his reputation by staging upsets, to run his campaign.

While Dianne had to be talked out onto the streets, Quentin ran from dawn to predawn, seven days a week. Seeking to soften Kopp's hard-edged image, Reilly made TV ads of the candidate belly-laughing for twenty seconds after being asked to comment on his reputation as "the town grouch." "Well, my kids like me," Kopp told the camera. "At least I think they do."

They mapped a strategy for Kopp to overcome Feinstein's big early lead by studying her track record as a candidate. In 1971 Alioto had trounced her by painting her as the white-gloved matron, out of touch with ordinary people and not tough enough to be mayor. In 1975 Moscone and Barbagelata upset her by staking out clear ideological positions that made her "moderate" politics look weak and indecisive. Now Kopp tried to whipsaw Feinstein on both vulnerabilities.

Early on, he endorsed the liberals' latest ballot initiative calling for a limit on high-rise building. Taunting Dianne to take a position—she would finally endorse the initiative days before the election—he pleased those anti-Manhattanization forces that distrusted her on development issues. Completing the ideological squeeze, he attacked her over a looming city budget deficit, preaching strict fiscal conservatism while assailing her management skills, historically the biggest perceived weakness of women candidates for executive office. "Managing San Francisco in the 1980s will be one of the toughest jobs in America," Kopp's ads proclaimed, sending the subtle sexist message.

Despite her hesitancy as a campaigner, Feinstein's best moments came in performing her duties as mayor—in her own, unique way. Chastened by her mistakes at the riot, she began to show the hands-on style that would characterize the rest of her tenure. When a sniper held a hostage in a Market Street high rise, for example, she remained at the command post, near his line of fire, throughout the hours of the tense standoff.

In June she led a city delegation on a twelve-day trade mission to China, one of the first U.S. officials to do so. Even in China, though, she could not escape the shadow of White Night. While she was in Shanghai, the Police Officers Association in San Francisco staged a vote of confidence on Chief Gain. POA leaders trumpeted the overwhelming anti-Gain vote—1,081 to 22—in demanding that the mayor have the police commission fire the chief. "If Mayor Feinstein does not remove Gain, we must not endorse her," a leader of the politically powerful police union declared.

Feinstein, after canceling a pagoda tour and huddling in her hotel room with Blum and press secretary Wax, vowed support for Gain, although she urged him from across the Pacific to "get out and visit with his men at the stations." "I still support the chief," she told reporter David Dietz, traveling with her. "The employees of a company don't decide who becomes president and neither do the sergeants and lieutenants and captains decide who the general of the army will be."

But as she continued her Asian tour, the controversy simmered at home. Back home on July 5, just three weeks after expressing support for Gain, she demanded his resignation, saying that he was "not getting the kind of respect that is necessary from the rank and file and commanding officers of the force." In taking the action, Feinstein placated neither side in the bitter debate, however, since she asked Gain not to leave as chief until the following January 8, when the mayor elected in the fall would take office.

"It's senseless to presume that the police department will be able to be run effectively by a lame duck police chief," Kopp responded, leading a widespread chorus of criticism. "It shows the mayor can't make a decision." The mayor, at a press conference the next day, said she "knew the left would not be pleased, nor would the right be pleased. I knew it would not be a political situation where I would come out smelling like a rose."

With the campaign entering its closing weeks, Kopp now had momentum moving strongly in his direction, as he harped at Feinstein for trying to minimize the city's budget problem while allegedly preparing secret plans to deal with it. "All this is being done covertly," he charged her in a face-to-face debate. "I think it's time, Dianne, that you tell what these unidentified plans are that you've been preparing behind closed doors."

She countered with the refrain that "toughness doesn't come in a pin-striped suit," and by portraying him as an opportunist. "For those who would stand in these shoes—size eight, triple A—it's easy to be a Monday morning quarterback after something like a riot," she said, bristling at Kopp. "And yet where was he? Not in the office with five other supervisors helping me. He was on a radio talk show exploiting the situation."

The November primary campaign was hurtling to a tight finish, and it ended with a horrible scare. On the Saturday before the election, Feinstein was campaigning door to door in the Fillmore district when a man walked up to her on the sidewalk, pointed a silver pistol at her head, and pulled the trigger.

From the pistol's hammer, a small blue flame sizzled up; the gun was a cigarette lighter. Its owner clicked it off and walked away from the scene.

"Sure I was scared," Dianne said later. "There was no time to duck or react. It happened so quickly, I realized for the first time how helpless you are." It was 341 days after George Moscone's assassination.

12

ALMOST A BRIDESMAID

Network.

—Dianne Feinstein's Rules for Getting Ahead

SHORTLY AFTER 11:00 P.M. on primary election day, in November 1979, Feinstein entered the Emerald Ballroom of the Hilton hotel to address a crowd of supporters after yet another disappointing performance in a race for mayor. In her third campaign for the office, she had finally finished first in a race—but there was more disappointment than jubilation at her "victory celebration."

Despite big advantages of incumbency, fund-raising, and organization, Dianne had blown a thirty-five-point lead in the polls and failed to win the majority vote needed for outright election. She had barely edged Quentin Kopp and now faced a five-week runoff against her bitter rival, who had momentum on his side.

"Feinstein Stunned, Mayor Asks: Why?" the *Examiner* bannered the next day over a story describing finger-pointing and back-stabbing in her camp.

For the next five weeks, Feinstein and Kopp battered and pummeled each other, like two boxers in a fifteen-round fight, over ethics, development, the budget, and minority rights. In the end, the election came down to one key constituency: San Francisco's newly empowered homosexual community, which had cast a protest vote for a third, gay candidate in the primary. In a race that again drew national attention, Feinstein and Kopp would both aggressively woo the homosexuals who now held the balance of power in the city. When Dianne finally emerged victorious, it was largely because of gay voters.

In the middle of her term, however, many gays would turn on her with a vengeance. As mayor, Feinstein would veto "live-in lovers" legislation, so called because it would have allowed single people, primarily gays, to register their "domestic partnerships" in an effort to gain health insurance and other benefits enjoyed by spouses in traditional marriages. The veto enraged many in the gay community. Feeling betrayed by her promises of 1979, some now supported a petition drive to recall Dianne organized by a left-wing fringe group that opposed her bid to ban handguns in San Francisco.

The 1983 recall effort was a watershed, both personal and political, for Feinstein. Although she felt "humiliated" by the recall attempt, it turned out to be a huge blessing when she overwhelmed the effort and, in the process, built an independent political organization, boosted her shaky self-confidence, and scared away any serious challengers to her reelection. The recall episode also gave her a fresh burst of national publicity, and the next year she became the object of excited speculation that she might become the first woman to run on the national ticket of a major political party.

When the Democrats held their national convention in San Francisco in 1984, Feinstein was a star player. After a tense, behind-the-scenes drama, she missed this chance of making history. But she achieved national stature simply by being considered, without being identified with the Democrats' 1984 landslide defeat to Ronald Reagan.

Shortly after that campaign, she was asked on national television about her ultimate goal in politics. "To be the first female chief executive of the United States," she said.

FEINSTEIN EDGED KOPP 42 to 40 percent in the November election, short of the majority needed to win. The next morning she convened a meeting of several dozen key supporters in her office to plot a new strategy for the runoff. The group included her closest and most trusted advisers—Blum, Roff, Mo Bernstein, Gene Gartland, Henry Berman—along with some other faces, including a team of Sacramento-based political operatives allied with Willie Brown and Speaker Leo McCarthy.

From the meeting emerged an aggressive, hard-edged strategy. Feinstein would immediately challenge Kopp to a series of televised debates and start working the streets as hard as he did. The Sacramento operatives would prepare twenty-four attack mailers over the next five weeks.

"The reason we were all there for her was that she wasn't Quentin," consultant Richard Ross recalled. "Willie said, 'We're going to do a number on

Kopp.' " Brown today does not recall making the statement but acknowl-
edges his crucial role in crafting the runoff strategy, which required that
Moscone's liberal coalition, much of which had stayed home in November,
come out to vote for Feinstein in December. "She had to be sold to our
side" of liberal voters, Brown said.

Over the next five weeks, Feinstein and Kopp swapped constant attacks and
counterattacks through the mail, on the airwaves, and face-to-face. Each
charged the other with unethical campaigning, while Dianne railed at
Quentin as "divisive" and he sneered at her as "the appointed mayor." "Rather
than political adversaries," an out-of-town reporter wrote, "they act more like
a brother and sister who've been cooped up too long together."

At one point a pro-Feinstein coalition of black voters sent out a brochure
to minority voters recalling Kopp's opposition to busing that was headlined,
"The real Quentin Kopp; George Wallace returns." It appeared that the
harsh negative tactic might backfire—until Kopp mailed leaflets, featuring
photos of sorrowful old people, that charged Feinstein with raising the rents
on elderly tenants at her Carlton Hotel.

It would have been a potent attack against a self-styled candidate of compassion. But Blum, who had taken over management of the hotel, took one
look at the pictures and realized that they were not of Carlton tenants—but
of old people who lived in the Tenderloin. Given that Feinstein also had
canceled plans for a rent increase, the attack backfired on Kopp.

"Quentin was running a veiled sexist campaign and she had to prove she
was firm and tough and decisive," Roff recalled. "At that point, she was still
very insecure and kept saying, 'I don't know if I can do this,' " he added.
"But she proved she could thrust and parry. And she had an extra compo-
nent he couldn't touch—she was a person of recognized compassion who
had brought the city together."

Amid the nastiness and negativity, the election boiled down to who would
win the support of David Scott, a gay real estate man who had captured 10
percent in the primary, denying victory to either Feinstein or Kopp.

Kopp had never been popular in the gay community. A conservative Democrat, he was for years uncomfortable with the whole notion of gay rights.
As a supervisor he had once thundered, "Tolerance yes, glorification no," in
a gay-rights debate, a quote that homosexual leaders for years dredged up as
purported evidence of his opposition to their cause. But now he moderated

his views on gay rights, as he had on Manhattanization, and argued that, at the very least, he would be more honest and principled in his dealings with the community than would Feinstein.

Dianne had been a champion of gay rights but by the summer of 1979 she was in trouble with the community, then estimated to represent between 10 and 20 percent of the city's electorate. Many gays considered White Night a "police riot," and her decision in the wake of it to dump Charles Gain rankled. Gays considered the chief a friend who kept the police force in check. A recent, well-publicized incident of police harassment at a lesbian bar, coupled with Gain's impending departure, deepened the atmosphere of fear and mistrust. At the same time, advocacy groups reported an upsurge in violent street attacks on gays since the Moscone-Milk murders. Gay leaders accused Feinstein of indifference on the issue, along with failure to honor Moscone's vow to name a gay police commissioner.

As buttons reading "The Ayatollah Feinstein" and "Dump Dianne" appeared in the Castro district, a profile of the mayor in the *Ladies' Home Journal* rekindled resentment within the gay community. "The right of an individual to live as he or she chooses can become offensive," she said. "The gay community is going to have to face this. It's fine for us to live here respecting each other's lifestyles but that doesn't mean imposing them on others."

Despite her mild tone, the comments caused a furor in liberal gay neighborhoods. "Can you imagine Dianne telling blacks that certain aspects of their behavior were offensive?" complained one member of a gay delegation that met privately with her at City Hall. "No way." An editorial writer for the *Bay Area Reporter,* a weekly gay paper, put it more bluntly:

> Gay people don't trust her. She talks to us when it's convenient. She has prospered on the ashes of two men who did support the gay community totally.
>
> Since their deaths, we have suffered increased harassment and curtailment of our freedom. Unless the leader of the city is a strong advocate of safety for gay people, there will be and is harassment and violence at the street level from police and thugs.

With the Feinstein-Kopp race viewed by many as a Hobson's choice, some gays looked for an alternative. They found it in David Scott.

A real estate agent and Moscone supporter whom the late mayor had appointed to the powerful Board of Permit Appeals, Scott announced in June that he would run for mayor to give disgruntled gay voters a spokesman for their concerns. Feinstein, making good on her promise to commissioners issued just days after Moscone's death, promptly fired him. "You understand that it is not appropriate for a member of my administration to use his position in the administration to run against the administration," she said.

The firing became a cause célèbre and Scott's candidacy galvanized much of the gay community, despite the efforts of his major rivals. Kopp appeared before the Tavern Guild and promised an administration "free from intimidation, free from harassment." Feinstein raised the stakes by sending a telegram to President Carter, who had been quoted as saying he would not hire a homosexual for a high-ranking foreign policy job. "I am shocked," she wired the president. "You must be aware that sexual discrimination violates the United States Constitution. A person's right to work relates to his or her ability to do the job and not to sexual preference." A top Carter aide promptly replied that "the president wholeheartedly agrees with you" and called the news reports "wholly inaccurate." But Scott portrayed Feinstein and Kopp as "Tweedledum and Tweedledee" and won enough votes to make himself the key power broker for the runoff.

The political clout that was born with the election of Harvey Milk, that grew with the appointment of Harry Britt, and that was demonstrated with raw ferocity at the White Night riot was confirmed with the showing of Scott. CBS dispatched a crew to prepare a documentary on gay power in San Francisco. Cleve Jones, an ally of Milk's, told a producer that the riot represented a "right of passage," both for gays and "for the straight politicians of San Francisco, who thought for so long that by murmuring platitudes they would get our vote and our support and that we would stay in our bars."

The day after the election Dianne made a pilgrimage to Scott's home, paying homage to the man she had abruptly fired months before. Though she thought it would be a private meeting, she was ambushed by the CBS crew. "I am not here to bargain," she insisted, hurrying into Scott's house. That meeting was just the first of many pleadings she and Kopp made with gay leaders. "You couldn't go out and have a drink without seeing Dianne or Quentin," former Milk aide Dick Pabich recalled.

At one point Feinstein had dinner with leaders of the Harvey Milk Democratic Club, whose membership had soared after the assassinations, to seek their support, Pabich recalled. The liberal gays presented several demands, including appointment of gay commissioners and an apology for statements that had been deemed offensive. Not long afterward, at a showdown debate before the Milk Club, she offered one.

With a Mission district hall filled with cheering and jeering supporters of each, Feinstein and Kopp stood in the middle of the sweltering room and went toe-to-toe in the most crucial and competitive debate of the long campaign. "It was like a cockfight," Kopp's manager, Clint Reilly, recalled. "The place was mobbed, there were five hundred people in the room, packed to the rafters, and the two of them in the middle." Feinstein began:

> I don't come to you as a perfect person that knows all of the answers and that doesn't make mistakes. But I do come to you as somebody who has got a heart and a concern and a very deep interest and desire to represent this community.
>
> And maybe at times, I have been insensitive. It wasn't because of any calculated reason. If I said things that the community has found offensive or doesn't understand, I apologize for that.

The applause was thunderous. Reilly, pacing in the back, suddenly felt the election slip away. "When I heard that," he said, "I knew we were finished."

Not long afterward, Dianne phoned the White House to ask for President Carter's endorsement, to counter one that Governor Jerry Brown had given Kopp. The political aide who took her call recommended that the president endorse Feinstein because "she is regarded as being a close political ally of ours; she is in a close race but seems to be pulling ahead of Kopp [and because] we will need the help of Feinstein's more liberal supporters in the California primary."

Carter did publicly back Feinstein, but in the end the president loomed less important than Scott, who also gave her a last-minute endorsement, satisfied with Dianne's promises to the gay community. In the final, frantic days of the race, Scott was always at her side. She won the gay vote and she won the election.

On December 11, 1979, the forty-six-year-old Feinstein was elected mayor of San Francisco on her third try, by a margin of 54 to 46 percent. At last able to deliver a triumphant address at an election night party, she said: "I would particularly like to thank everyone that is standing behind me, those members of the board of supervisors. I would also like very much to thank Mr. David Scott for his support to my name."

Finally victorious after bitter defeats, Feinstein and Blum went to Kauai for a brief vacation, where she gave a bar-side interview over a vodka martini. "I feel a tremendous weight off my shoulders, because I now know people want me to be there," she said. "Up to this point, I didn't know that."

FEINSTEIN WAS SWORN IN January 8, 1980, the first woman elected to San Francisco's highest office. Before twenty-five hundred guests, she took the oath of office from Rose Bird on a red carpet that swept down the marble staircase of City Hall's rotunda. In her inaugural address, she vowed "to end, once and for all, the divisiveness that has taken such a heavy toll on this city in recent years" and peppered her remarks with nonideological, good-government references to "effective management" and "increased productivity."

"I have one immediate imperative," she also said, underscoring her favorite issue, "and that is to make this a safe city where violence will be countered by swift apprehension and where persons can live without fear."

She threw herself into her job with renewed energy and total commitment, a hands-on mayor who drove subordinates with unstinting demands but sent citizens a clear message that, agree or disagree with her, Dianne Feinstein was on duty and in charge in Room 200.

There was also some personal business to attend to. Ten days after the inaugural, Dianne and Dick took out a marriage license. They were accompanied by Hadley Roff and his fiancée, Susan Trommald, who had planned to wed the same day as the mayor.

"That will be $10, unless it's dutch, in which case it's $5 each," the city clerk told Blum.

"No Dutch," Dianne quickly interjected.

Two days later, Feinstein and Blum were married in a private, Jewish Reformed ceremony in her ornate City Hall office. "I am more nervous than I thought I would be," she said after her third wedding. "I don't feel like a mayor. I feel like a woman who has just been married." Four hundred invited guests—politicians and friends—greeted the couple in the rotunda, which was bedecked in pink flowers, before the reception was opened to the public and a crush of fifteen hundred people joined the receiving line.

Feinstein, who later gave her green silk wedding dress to the city archives, and Blum, who kept sneaking off to keep track of the Super Bowl played the same day, cut a seven-tiered, three-flavored wedding cake topped with roses. The party wound down after Her Honor threw her bouquet and garter from a second-floor balcony. People left the building carrying wheels of cheese and armfuls of pineapples that had decorated tables; some had to be stopped from carting off rented trees and plants.

The wedding celebration set a regal tone for Feinstein's mayoralty. The elaborate production was organized by Charlotte Swig, Dianne's longtime supporter, who would become an important behind-the-scenes player in Feinstein's administration, as the mayor set out to counter San Francisco's tarnished image with trade missions to foreign lands and with lavish receptions and events for international leaders.

AS DIANNE TRAVELED the globe to boost her city, its economy, and her own image, the street politics of San Francisco reared up and bit her again. In an only-in-San Francisco saga, two seemingly unrelated issues merged to deal what Feinstein would call the most "mortifying" blow of her up-and-down political career. It began with her weeping in the privacy of the mayor's office and ended with her publicly triumphant, one of the most recognized women politicians in America.

In 1982 Feinstein's anticrime crusade led her to sponsor a local gun-control ordinance. With great controversy, and over the strenuous objections of the National Rifle Association, a measure to ban ownership of handguns in San Francisco was narrowly passed by the supervisors in July.

The law provided a ninety-day grace period for pistol owners to turn in their weapons without incurring penalties—thirty days to six months in jail and a $500 fine—for handgun possession. With great fanfare, the mayor led the way, ceremoniously surrendering to police the .38 she had carried in her purse for a year and a half after the attempted bombing of her home, and calling on other citizens to do the same. "You can get rid of your handgun any way you want," she said. "Give it to someone outside San Francisco, sell it outside the city, throw it into the bay. We just want fewer guns in the city." A few months later, on a trip to Europe, she presented Pope John Paul II with a gunmetal-blue cross that had been sculpted by melting down fifteen of the handguns turned in to police.

Despite widespread attention, the gun law soon was thrown out by California courts, which ruled that state law preempted such legislation. Still it was popular in San Francisco, where sentiment for gun control ran high—except in a few pockets of armed resistance.

In the Haight-Ashbury a few dozen members of a sixties hangover group called the White Panthers ran a low-cost food cooperative and lived in a commune organized around the rights to bear arms, smoke dope, and listen to loud rock and roll. San Francisco's White Panthers were the sole surviving chapter of a once-flourishing radical group organized in the 1960s around an outlaw rock band from Detroit called MC-5, whose fans liked to chant "Up against the wall, motherfucker" at concerts.

The local group had been involved in a shoot-out with police in their Haight-Ashbury headquarters, and their jailhouse lawyering and confrontational style made them a minor feature act in the 1970s circus at City Hall. When Feinstein signed the gun-control law, they reacted with typical outrage and rhetoric, calling it a "ruthless, reckless fiat" that was "imbecilic, totalitarian, and misogynous." They threatened a campaign to force the mayor from office, and she charged them with trying to "harass and intimidate public officials by misuse of the recall process." After that, nobody at City Hall paid much attention.

Over the next six months, a group of twenty White Panthers patiently carried recall petitions to liberal neighborhoods, downplaying the gun issue while gathering the signatures of those discontented with the mayor on a host of other matters. Their effort would probably not have succeeded had it not been for another political battle that had brewed for months in the gay community, however.

Supervisor Harry Britt had tried since his appointment by Dianne to gain passage of a "live-in lovers" ordinance. The measure would allow unmarried couples, both gay and straight, to register their "domestic partnerships" with the city. These registrations could then be used as the equivalent of marriage certificates in attempts to gain certain insurance and other benefits enjoyed by married couples.

Even before the bill, Britt had been a disaster from Feinstein's perspective. After swearing loyalty as a condition of his appointment, he had deserted her on his first big vote, a proposed settlement of the explosive discrimination suit against the police department brought by minorities and women, which played a key role in the machinations behind Dan White's bid to be reappointed. Feinstein needed and expected Britt to be her sixth vote for her settlement. But he voted his liberal conscience, in favor of civil rights groups, and relations between him and the mayor had deteriorated after that.

After four years, Britt in late 1982 had finally succeeded in passing the domestic-partners bill, a key part of the gay-rights agenda, and had squeezed Feinstein between two important constituencies: gays, whom she had so assiduously courted in 1979, and conservative voters, who felt she already was kowtowing to homosexuals. The conservatives were joined by several prominent religious leaders in the city.

As much as any issue she confronted in nine years as mayor, the domestic-partners debate caused her great political anguish and turmoil. "At the time, it was the toughest," she said, recalling that Britt "did not discuss it with me until after it passed the board. He did not ask for any input and I think, for someone I had appointed, it would have been nice if he had come in and talked to me on such a difficult and controversial issue."

Feinstein tried to balance her personal concern that Britt's measure had sweeping, unknown social implications with the unanimous view of her advisers that a veto would damage her politically. "It was her most tortured decision from a moral, personal point of view," a senior staff member recalled. "She opposed the legislation but she felt it might be political suicide to veto it."

Characteristically, she convened meeting after meeting, demanding more information and seeking a compromise with Britt that it was too late to make. "She told me she was very sympathetic but she didn't want to blaze any trails," Britt recalled. "She said, 'Harry, I understand if it's a personal thing, but I'm mayor of all the people.' It really was a morality thing with her."

As the bill sat on her desk, she held many long meetings with her closest advisers—Blum, Roff, Bernstein, Henry Berman, Nothenberg, Tom Eastham, Jim Lazarus, and others. Unanimously, they recommended that she sign it, advisers recalled, placating the gay community while breaking new ground in civil rights. But Archbishop John Quinn publicly weighed into the debate with a statement saying that the measure "contradicts and imperils the deepest values of our common, public moral heritage and damages the fundamental well-being of society." His sentiments were echoed by the Episcopal Bishop of San Francisco, by Feinstein's own rabbi, and by the Board of Rabbis of Northern California.

In December, the mayor bucked her political advice and vetoed the measure. "On a personal level, this legislation causes me deep anguish," she said. "I would like to be able to sign legislation which recognizes the needs of single persons . . . but such legislation . . . must not divide our community."

The political reaction was swift and angry. At City Hall, a boisterous crowd quickly gathered, chanting "Dump Dianne" and portraying the legislation as a clear issue of dignity and human rights. "I've been in a relationship with a man longer than she's been married to her current husband," shouted the president of one gay Democratic club.

In Houston, where Feinstein had been invited to deliver the keynote address to the gay Human Rights Campaign Fund a few days later, her invitation was abruptly withdrawn. And out in the Castro, the White Panthers suddenly found people lining up to sign their recall petitions.

Jim Haas, the moderate gay attorney who had led Supervisor Feinstein's "think tank" in her days on the board, knew something was amiss when he "kept bumping into the White Panthers everywhere I went" after the veto. Possessed of a dry sense of humor, Haas is the author of an epigram, widely circulated in San Francisco, summing up Feinstein's love-hate relationship with the gay community: "Dianne Feinstein doesn't care who you sleep with, as long as you're in bed by eleven o'clock." Days before the deadline for recall petitions to be submitted, he asked friends in the mayor's office if they were monitoring the White Panthers' effort. They were not.

A few weeks after the veto, the White Panthers shocked City Hall by filing more than thirty-five thousand petitions, many more than needed to put a recall measure before voters. Feinstein was sickened and, in the privacy of her office, aides recalled, she wept. "It was like a knife going in," she said. "I felt a deep sense of humiliation that after fourteen years in public life, finally getting to be mayor in my own right—I don't think anybody has ever said I don't work hard, I work very hard—people wanted to throw me out of office. They were saying, 'You're a bum and we want you out.' And it hurt."

Said Roff: "She felt the recall was a repudiation of her personally. How could you walk down the street? How could you face people?"

Feinstein convened another big meeting in her office, with much the same cast of characters who attended after her near-loss to Kopp in 1979. "Dianne had lost so many times in City Hall elections that she feared running against herself," said Willie Brown, who again took a leading role.

There was one more key player on hand. Blum and Henry Berman were impressed with the way Clint Reilly had almost managed Kopp to a huge upset of Feinstein and run other campaigns. They had had a quiet lunch with him at the Lake Merced country club a few weeks before and asked him to come to work for the mayor's 1983 reelection campaign. Reilly then had met with the mayor and, over lunch, she had quizzed him hard about his ability to be "loyal" to her rather than Kopp, he said. Just weeks before, he had signed up to run her reelection bid but now found himself in the middle of an extraordinary recall.

He saw it as a rare opportunity. With Feinstein already facing reelection in November 1983, a crushing recall victory earlier in the year would clear the field of serious opposition. "If we defeat the recall overwhelmingly, we'll win the election six months early," he argued.

Dianne did not buy the silver-lining argument. She kept saying that she did not deserve this. "I've been a good mayor," she emotionally told reporters after the meeting. "There's been no scandal, no corruption, no incompetence, no malfeasance, no nepotism, no failing, if you will, to justify it. No one can say I have not served conscientiously. I can't work any harder."

But Reilly argued that it was a mistake to cast the recall as a referendum on her record. That would lend legitimacy to the effort; having made unpopular decisions on polarized issues like rent control and high rises, Dianne would have to defend herself against those unhappy with every tough decision. Instead, they should focus on the $400,000 cost of a special election, coming just seven months before the regular mayoral balloting; the unfairness of using a recall against an officeholder not remotely accused of malfeasance or corruption; and the message it would send about San Francisco to the nation.

In a memo written after conducting a poll, Reilly laid out the strategy:

> Voter sentiment runs heavily against the recall. There are more voters against the recall than there are voters who strongly favor your re-election. Our goal should be to maximize the anti-recall vote. In the process, we will create an illusion of strength which is greater than the strength you, in fact, have as an incumbent mayor standing for re-election. This perceived strength might well frighten away all potential opponents in November.

SHORTLY AFTER THE RECALL began, Dianne's emotions were roiled further when her mother died at age seventy-six. The story of Dianne's troubled childhood was still a well-kept secret, and she issued a written statement to the press before leaving on a planned trip to a meeting of the U.S. Conference of Mayors: "The death, while not unexpected, still is a terrible blow, and I am deeply saddened. The best therapy for me is to go on with the work scheduled in Washington."

Over the next three months, Feinstein combined her mayoral duties with heavy campaigning, and the anti-recall strategy worked. Her camp quickly marginalized the White Panthers, which wasn't hard to do. Although some tenant-rights, slow-growth, and gay groups, including the Harvey Milk Club, backed the recall, most disassociated themselves from the Panthers. Scraggly-haired, bearded members of the group helped her every time they made an appearance on TV. "We are people who support the Constitution," their spokesman said at one point. "Also we're communists. We're on the Marxist, Leninist, Maoist, Castroist side of most questions."

With no legal limits on contributions to a recall, Blum, performing a role that he would perfect in later campaigns, tapped the corporate and investment communities for donations of as much as $10,000, and Dianne soon had raised $500,000—a hundred times more than recall supporters.

Reilly hired twenty-five top political organizers, led by Fred Ross, Jr., the son of one of the founders of the United Farm Workers union. They recruited a volunteer army of more than two thousand people to oppose the recall. They used the then-new tactic of signing up absentee voters in advance, and assembled an overwhelming force of citywide precinct workers, a campaign ground operation of a kind Dianne had never had. Every Saturday, the volunteers would hold a huge rally at the campaign headquarters, where Dianne would speak; then they would head out to streets and shopping areas to sign up more supporters. The energy of the young volunteers transformed Feinstein the politician.

"That was really the first time that we went grass roots," she said. "For me, it was an overwhelmingly heartwarming experience that I will never forget. At the time of my greatest vulnerability and great hurt, not only was I not alone, but there were people who would spend all this time. It was such a bonding experience. It was the first time I really loved campaigning."

In April Dianne crushed the recall, winning more than 80 percent of the vote. As Reilly had predicted, the win scared off all serious opposition for the fall campaign and her overwhelming reelection was a foregone conclusion. "Anybody thinking of running is going to be creamed," she crowed.

For Feinstein, the recall was a personal and political rite of passage. The self-doubts that had haunted her, deepened by two bitter defeats and being dragged across the finish line in her only victory in 1979, were all but erased.

Now she was clearly the single most powerful political figure in San Francisco and widely recognized throughout California, according to the Mervin Field poll, although she did not hold statewide office. One of the most prominent women politicians in America, she was featured on a list of "America's ten most influential women" published in 1983, along with Supreme Court justice Sandra Day O'Connor, first lady Nancy Reagan, Gloria Steinem, Coretta Scott King, and Jacqueline Kennedy Onassis.

Soon after the 1983 election, Reilly prepared a twenty-two-page memo for Feinstein called "Your Future Career Options." In it, he noted the growing talk in Democratic circles about a woman being chosen as a vice-presidential candidate in the following year's presidential campaign. "Minimally, all Democratic presidential candidates will be forced to give public attention to a woman running mate," he wrote. "Whether the momentum will force more is not possible to accurately predict, but your strategy should include riding the wave of the momentum, however far it goes."

AT FIRST, DIANNE DID NOT want the Democratic convention in San Francisco. With the city strapped since the passage of Proposition 13, it was only recently that Feinstein had begun to turn the budget around. Focused on the nuts and bolts of governance, and some pet projects like raising corporate money to rehabilitate the famous cable car system, the last thing the mayor needed was a horde of thirty thousand Democrats and journalists descending on the city. But a trio of Democrats with local clout and national influence—Willie Brown, Democratic National Committeewoman Nancy Pelosi, and major contributor Walter Shorenstein—hatched a plan to sell Dianne on the idea. "She clearly did not want to do it," Brown recalled. "But we talked her into it."

"I wondered whether it made sense. The convention was going to cost money, lots of money, and I was still concerned about the residue of Jonestown and the assassinations. If there is going to be a demonstration in America, it's going to be in San Francisco," she said. "But the flip side of the concerns was that it would be the final healing experience for the city. It was an opportunity to put the past into the past once and for all."

Feinstein began the task of wooing and winning the Democrats with typical energy. She made several forays to Washington with delegations from the tourist industry, aggressively sold the city at lavish receptions, and offered favorable financial terms to the Democrats for the right to host the event at the recently opened Moscone Convention Center. Besides Brown, Pelosi, and Shorenstein, she had another major ally in the selling of San Francisco: the Democratic national chairman, Charles Manatt, a Los Angeles attorney, wanted the convention in his home state and backed San Francisco as a second choice with Los Angeles hosting the Summer Olympics. In the same month that she smashed the recall, Dianne triumphantly announced that the 1984 Democratic convention would be coming to San Francisco.

In his 1983 memo on her political options, Reilly told Feinstein that "The presence of the 1984 Democratic convention in San Francisco provides you with a rare opportunity . . . to firmly establish yourself as a national figure. Therefore, your strategy between now and the convention should be to solidify your position as the most prominent and qualified woman Democrat in the country," he wrote.

With characteristic attention to detail, the mayor set up a system to give her final authority over the most mundane details of convention planning. "I would like to have the sign-off on every logistical development, including parking . . . and where the concession booths are going to be," she announced at one early, weekly session with convention planners. "I feel like I'm going to get blamed if anything doesn't go right. I want to have the sign-off. I don't even want to discuss this. This is the way it's got to be."

By the time the convention opened the next summer, she would be doing much more than worrying about parking passes and where to put shopping bags full of gifts for arriving delegates. She would be making political history.

THE DAY IN SEPTEMBER 1983 that Walter Mondale, the front-runner for the Democratic presidential nomination, first said publicly that he would consider choosing a woman as a running mate, Feinstein was scheduled to address the Democratic Women's Leadership Conference in Washington. When she arrived she found delegates talking her up as a contender for the job and, after her speech, she was surrounded by women asking her about it excitedly.

The cautious politician in her, remembering the costly mistake of overreaching early in her career, at first downplayed her interest. "No, I am interested in being mayor," she said, adding that the vice presidency, "is not my interest; I do not intend to pursue it; I intend to continue to run San Francisco." A moment later, however, the politician who had broken barriers and been taught that nothing was beyond her reach, sounded quite intrigued by the notion: "I can tell you, I think the time is a lot sooner than I ever thought it would be. I would not say I would never be interested. Who knows what can happen in the future?"

Her shifting comments provided an early glimpse at the political roller coaster Feinstein would ride for the next ten months, as she tried to appear steadfastly uninterested in becoming the first woman nominated on a national ticket while steadily emerging as a leading candidate for the spot. Back at home, Feinstein sounded Shermanesque, not wishing to encourage the slightest speculation that she might loosen the grip on Room 200 that it had taken her so long to establish. "Let me say once and definitively, I'm not a candidate for any other office, post, commission, advisory committee, or cabinet office anywhere. I fully intend to spend the next four years here," she said, patting her desk.

Ten years later, she insists that she never took very seriously the notion of running for vice president because it would have distracted too much of her attention from being mayor. "People don't believe me, but I swear to God, I never think ahead politically. I found I can't do that, I can't make decisions while looking at the next rung on the ladder. When I'm finished with something, then I go ahead to the next thing."

Nevertheless, in January 1984 Feinstein returned to Washington to address the Women's Democratic Club. In previous Washington appearances, she had invariably focused narrowly on urban problems and remained almost stubbornly nonpartisan. Now, she launched a full-scale attack on the budget and foreign policies of the Reagan administration, "talking more and more like a national political figure than just another big city mayor," as one account put it. "She's running for vice president," a veteran national political reporter in the audience allowed. "The Democrats should take a good look at her."

Reilly kept urging her to be more aggressive in putting herself forward as a vice-presidential contender, but Feinstein only occasionally ventured out on a national appearance. In March she went to Chicago for the "Donahue" show, where she was cheered when she called for the death penalty for cop killers. Afterward, she shared a glass of wine with a reporter and discussed her future.

"If at the end of my term, all things being equal . . . I would like to go on, yes," she told *Chronicle* writer Evelyn Hsu. "In major national office. The presidency or the vice presidency." Asked if she "would settle for the U.S. Senate," Feinstein replied, "I've had the legislative side and the executive side and I much prefer the executive."

AFTER A BRUISING PRIMARY season, Mondale was marching inevitably to the nomination, and the drumbeat for a female running mate grew steadily more intense. Feminists seized his early comments to pressure him on the issue, and Ronald Reagan's popularity all but required Mondale to shake up the political calculus stacked against Democrats with a bold move. One way was to try to capitalize on the "gender gap" among the electorate. With women representing about 54 percent of voters, polls showed that they were the group among whom Reagan ran weakest. A *Washington Post* survey showed Reagan leading among men 60 to 37 percent while Mondale led among women 48 to 44 percent.

"Mondale kept saying, 'If I'm going down to a ten-point loss, I want to make some history,'" recalled Duane Garrett, Mondale's national cochairman. Garrett, the San Francisco attorney who got his start in politics doing opposition research on Dianne for George Moscone, had since become a supporter and adviser to Feinstein, and his presence in the Mondale camp did not hurt her chances in the vice-presidential sweepstakes. "We were looking for a way to turn the electorate on its head," he said. "We were looking for a bold way to change the stereotype of Mondale as a fifty-five-year-old white male button-down Norwegian."

In May NBC aired a news report on the strengths and weaknesses of various contenders for the job and featured Feinstein. In June she appeared on the cover of *Time* magazine, along with New York Representative Geraldine Ferraro, for a story called "Why Not a Woman?" The *Time* story, which surprised many San Franciscans who still thought of her as the Dianne who locked herself in the City Hall lavatory, was a measure both of how far women had come in politics and of how far they had to go. While noting that it had been only fourteen years since an associate of Hubert Humphrey's declared in public that women were unfit for high office because "every month they were subject to a 'raging hormonal imbalance,'" the story also sniffed that selection of a female running mate would carry "as much risk as logic" and dismissed both Feinstein and Ferraro as lightweights. "If Ferraro or Feinstein were a man, it is unlikely that either would be mentioned for the vice presidency," it said.

After the primaries ended in California in June, Mondale encamped at his suburban home in North Oaks, Minnesota, to begin a drawn-out process of interviewing potential running mates, including three women, two blacks, an Hispanic, and a white male, a kind of political Noah's ark that many analysts believed signaled a clear message of his ties to Democratic interest groups.

Feinstein insisted that while she was "flattered" by the attention, she did not take it seriously. But she was being taken very seriously. Besides Dianne's own relationship with Mondale, forged through her ties to Carter, Blum was a personal friend of the soon-to-be nominee, and had raised campaign money for him for ten years. "I knew Fritz before I knew Dianne," Blum said. "We were doing everything we could to help him win the nomination."

Clint Reilly now prepared another memo making the case, on a state-by-state, electoral-vote basis, of how she could help the ticket. "Dianne Feinstein would be a formidable asset to the Mondale presidential campaign," he wrote. "A Feinstein vice-presidential candidacy could help the Democratic ticket attract women, Jewish, urban, and black voters. In addition, Feinstein could help the Democrats win the key state of California." Besides traditional Democratic constituencies, Reilly argued, she would also attract swing voters because of what he called the "class factor." "Dianne Feinstein sits well with upper income, college-educated Democrats and Republicans. She appeals to both the [former Senator Gary] Hart Democrat and Independent, and to the Republican women troubled by President Reagan's policies on women's rights and foreign policy," said the private memo.

Despite such arguments inside her own circle, Dianne bet Blum $100 that Mondale would never call. She lost. On June 15 John Reilly, a top adviser to Mondale, called the mayor's office to speak to the mayor. In an inauspicious start, he was put on hold and then accidentally cut off. Not long afterward, Mondale called Feinstein and invited her to a vice-presidential interview. She couldn't make the date he suggested, she told him, because it conflicted with the grand celebration for the reopening of the cable cars. They settled on a meeting a few days after that event.

News of Mondale's invitation to her ran on the front page of the *New York Times* the next day. The woman who a few months before had said she was not interested in the job was now giddy with excitement. "I'm proud to be the first woman and first Jew considered" for vice president, she said in one interview. "All of a sudden when the call came, it was like one of these flashes and this recognition that there is a historical impact that I'm on that list," she said in another. "From now and forever on . . . women will be considered. It's crossing that threshold."

Attending a conference in Philadelphia that weekend, Feinstein was joined by Blum, who flew in carrying two copies of Mondale's biography. By now she was making a case for herself as a candidate, arguing that what she lacked in federal and foreign policy experience, she made up in determination and character. "I have staying power, I've had victory and defeat, I've been through that, the hard times, the good times," she said in one interview. "I think there is a record of accomplishments there that is fairly unique in the nation."

On Saturday, June 23, the day after her fifty-first birthday, Feinstein flew to Minnesota. Once again, she rose to a big occasion. After an informal luncheon, Feinstein and Mondale adjourned for a private two-and-a-half-hour meeting over iced tea and cookies. Blum meanwhile made some political history of his own, joining Joan Mondale on a museum tour, the first American male political spouse to socialize while his wife was occupied with presidential campaign business.

Among the topics she discussed with Mondale was whether Feinstein's ties to the gay community, so necessary in San Francisco politics, would turn into a major liability in a national campaign; she pointed to her veto of the domestic-partners bill as proof that she could stand up to special interests.

"I gave him my vision of what a vice president could be," she recalled, "being the oversight for domestic departments, setting the goals with cabinet secretaries and then following through."

Mondale and Feinstein emerged from the meeting beaming, he telling her she "got straight A's" and reporters that she was "a spectacular person." The national press corps, having dismissed her initially as a thrice-married Jewish woman from the kook capital of America, at first was openly skeptical. Dianne disarmed them. In her beige Ultrasuede suit, she handled their questions so deftly that the *Washington Post* headlined its story the next day, "Feinstein Stars at News Conference with Mondale." "Feinstein's appearance provided the most electric moment of a long week at Mondale's summer headquarters," it said, adding that she had "showed why the drive to put a woman on the Democratic ticket continues to gain momentum."

As she spoke to the press in the driveway of Mondale's house, press secretary Tom Eastham stood behind her and noticed that the mosquitoes that infested the property were landing on Dianne's legs in large numbers. While

Eastham and others shooed away mosquitoes, he watched in amazement as she did not move a muscle or even twitch. On the way back to the airport, her legs were covered with blood. But Dianne had never flinched.

AFTER MONDALE'S EXHAUSTIVE selection process, his choice narrowed to the two women featured on the cover of *Time:* Feinstein and Ferraro. While Feinstein had made a strong personal impression, Ferraro was favored both by Democratic activist women, with whom Feinstein was not close, and by party leaders in the Congress, including Speaker Tip O'Neill.

On June 30, Mondale addressed fifteen hundred members of the National Organization for Women who chanted, "Run with a woman, win with a woman," as he spoke. The next day they passed a resolution vowing to nominate a woman for vice president from the convention floor, if he did not select one on his own.

With the convention set to open in San Francisco on July 16, Mondale and his top advisers struggled with the final choice. On Sunday, July 8, Mondale dispatched top advisers to San Francisco to reinterview Feinstein. They spent a day and a half poring over tax returns and Blum's business and financial records, looking for potential embarrassments. "Then it was clear she was in the final finals," said Blum. "She was genuinely in shock."

As late as Tuesday, July 10, Mondale seemed to lean toward Feinstein. *People* magazine printed a standby cover with her picture on it in the expectation that she would be chosen. On Wednesday afternoon, a bottle of champagne was cracked open in the mayor's office for a mini-celebration after a false tip from Washington that Dianne was the pick.

But a few hours later, Mondale picked up the phone and called Ferraro, in San Francisco for platform hearings, and asked her to be his running mate. A short time later, he reached Feinstein, at home getting ready for a preconvention party, and said he had decided not to select her. "He said, 'I want to tell you that I think you're a star,'" Feinstein reported later. "He said, 'I want to tell you that you're on top of the media's list,' whatever that meant, 'but I've decided to go another way and I hope you will trust me.'"

Although it quickly leaked out that night, the news was formally announced on Thursday. When Dianne met the press that day, she said, "With Geraldine Ferraro go my hopes and all the hopes of the women of this nation." She added that Blum "took it harder than I did."

After Ferraro's selection, there was considerable speculation about why she finally had been picked over Feinstein. Garrett said it owed in part to some advisers' concerns that violent protests might "blow up" during the San Francisco convention. Mondale didn't "want to be married to Richard Daley," Garrett recalled one insider arguing, a reference to the violence that marred the 1968 convention in Chicago.

For years afterward there were rumors that it had been thought that Blum's financial dealings might embarrass the campaign. If true, this would be ironic, given the controversy that Ferraro's husband's business dealings later caused. But Mondale said in a 1990 interview that "in no sense was Dick or his business a factor. If anything, it was a positive factor." In the end, Mondale said, he felt that the feisty congresswoman from Archie Bunker's district better represented the immigrant values and middle-class message he wanted to convey than did the wealthy woman from San Francisco.

After the 1984 election, when Mondale and Ferraro went down to a forty-nine-state landslide, it was clear that Feinstein once again had won by losing. She had benefited from all the hoopla attendant upon the historic selection of a woman—but was not identified with the ignominy of the defeat. "It was," fund-raiser Henry Berman would say later, "one of the luckiest breaks she got."

Chapter 13

***

HANDS ON

She ran the city like a Roman empress.

—Political analyst Rollin Post

***

Eₐᵣₗᵧ ₒₙₑ ₑᵥₑₙᵢₙg shortly after she became mayor, Dianne Feinstein was headed to a campaign event at a child-care center when she spotted a fire in a public housing project on the way. From the car, she called in a first alarm to the fire department as she ordered driver Jim Molinari to the scene. As the car pulled up, the mayor told him to call in a second alarm, jumped out, and rushed off to start banging on doors and evacuating residents. When the first of the ninety men and twenty pieces of equipment needed to quell the blaze rolled up a few minutes later, Feinstein pitched in to start uncoiling hose and hauling it up to the burning building.

The episode summed up Feinstein's style during the nine years she was mayor—hands-on and intensely personal, sometimes to an extreme. Immersing herself in detail and working long days, she established herself as one of the most popular mayors in the city's history by paying passionate attention to day-to-day issues of providing government services.

As she rode around the city, Feinstein kept a notebook close at hand, writing "Mayor's Action Memos" to record the location of abandoned mattresses in empty lots or sickly plants in Golden Gate Park and then badgering bureaucrats about the problems. Every Saturday morning for years, she led neighborhood cleanup patrols, painting over graffiti with a roller while wearing coveralls and a blue bandana. One of her favorite pictures of herself was taken as she perched on her desk, wearing a custom-cut police uniform and holding an emergency call radio. She performed enough lifesaving, crime-fighting actions to earn it—giving mouth-to-mouth resuscitation to a stricken stranger in the seedy Tenderloin district, helping to thwart a robbery in progress, diving into a swimming pool to rescue a drowning boy.

"My fundamental view about running a city is that the so-called housekeeping chores are extraordinarily important. The day-to-day chores are in a way small things, but in another way the heartbeat of the city. If the streets are clean, the buses run on time, the crime rate is low, parks are flourishing, it provides a backdrop for all the things the private sector does."

The criticisms leveled most frequently at Feinstein were that she "micromanaged" or ran a "government-by-crisis" that reacted to problems rather than anticipating them. Some conservatives complained that she lacked the vision to address tough problems like reforming a byzantine civil service system dominated by City Hall unions. Many liberals assailed her pro-downtown business policies, which they blamed for spiraling housing costs, shrinking blue-collar employment opportunities, and snarling density in the neighborhoods.

Entering office after the assassination of George Moscone, Feinstein steered San Francisco politically to the center. "The city is best run from the center of the political spectrum, rather than from either extreme," she often said. The liberal, minority, and neighborhood coalition that had united to elect Moscone after eight years of opposing the big business–big labor policies of Joseph Alioto, was often disappointed and angry at Feinstein. On issues from redevelopment and rent control, to domestic partners and district elections, which were repealed by voters not long after the City Hall killings, Mayor Feinstein took a more corporate-oriented stance than had her predecessor.

Richard DeLeon, a San Francisco State University political scientist, wrote in *Left Coast City,* a study of grass-roots politics in San Francisco: "If the Feinstein administration is judged by the policy checklist of the progressive agenda, one would have to conclude it was a retrograde failure on nearly every point. On the other hand, Feinstein's centrist political instincts may have been well adapted to the requirements of governance during this period of turmoil."

Most voters seemed to agree with the latter proposition. As Feinstein prepared to leave office in 1987, a survey of registered voters found that two-thirds believed she had done a good or excellent job as mayor, while only 9 percent gave her poor marks. Forty-nine percent said that San Francisco was better off than when she took office, more than twice as many as said the city was in worse shape. Although many voters disagreed with her handling of specific issues, they gave her high marks for integrity, and her time in office was free of personal financial scandal.

"I was just amazed at her popularity level," said Mark Baldassare, who conducted an in-depth poll on Feinstein's years as mayor for the *Chronicle* shortly before she finished her final term in January 1988. "Any politician would be thrilled to have the public support she enjoys."

Feinstein's years as mayor were a period of great upheaval in San Francisco. The population grew from 670,000 to 750,000 and was transformed, as young white professionals displaced Irish and Italian families and ethnic minorities became the majority. Her terms spanned double-digit inflation, recession and economic expansion, the birth of the national taxpayers' revolt, and conservative Republican administrations in Washington and Sacramento that cut urban aid.

Still, City Hall's budget more than doubled, from $919 million to $1.92 billion, a growth rate one-third higher than inflation. By her final year in office, city government spent $2,500 a year for each man, woman, and child in San Francisco. In 1978 when she entered office, no one had heard of AIDS or homelessness; by the time she left nine years later, the city was spending nearly $30 million a year on the problems.

Entering office after the horrors of Jonestown and the City Hall assassinations, Feinstein worked hard to restore San Francisco's damaged reputation, across the nation and around the world. But it was more prosaic issues that most concerned her. "Some people said I micromanaged, that these things are too commonplace for the mayor to worry about. But that's a basic fallacy—that's what a mayor has to do," she said. "People can say what they want, but I ran that city with both strength and compassion. I ran it from the center and it wasn't easy and I did it."

THE MAYOR WAS RUNNING LATE for a meeting in her office with police chief Cornelius "Con" Murphy. When she bustled in, she complained that she had just heard several reports on the police radio of robberies in progress. "What are we going to do about this?" she demanded of the chief.

"Why don't you turn off your radio?" he answered with a smile. Murphy was a tall, distinguished-looking career cop handpicked for the job by Feinstein after she fired Charles Gain, and one of the few people in the mayor's administration who might get away with such a crack. Beneath

Murphy's good-humored remark, however, was an attitude, widespread but rarely expressed publicly within her administration, that the mayor's style could be a little too "hands-on." "At times, she was an unreasonable task mistress," said former deputy mayor Jim Lazarus. "The level of demand was unreasonable, but people accepted it because they knew she was hard on herself too. She was a stickler for image—she wanted desks clear and streets clean. If she was guilty of micromanagement, it didn't overwhelm her decision making."

Lazarus, the former deputy city attorney who had advised Supervisor Feinstein on the Dan White matter, took to walking his dog early in the morning to avoid wake-up calls from Mayor Feinstein. "Have you read this morning's *Chronicle?*" she would snap on the other end of the line, after seeing a story that reflected poorly on the office. "I suggest you look at page eight," she might add, before hanging up.

When the city's Candlestick Park was being renovated, Feinstein and Lazarus once inspected construction of the new luxury boxes. The mayor went into several to check the seats and sight lines, suggesting design changes if they did not meet her meticulous standards, then ordered Lazarus to repeat the process in the rest.

Although critics complained that Feinstein was too concerned with details, she was the first San Francisco mayor in nearly twenty years to come to office with substantial experience at City Hall. She understood not only the complexities of city government but also the deadening drag of the bureaucracy. That and her personal need to prove herself made her constantly demand more and more information and to be kept abreast of details. "She always did her homework," said Rudy Nothenberg, the former Moscone deputy mayor whom Feinstein appointed the city's chief administrative officer. "And her leadership proceeds from a set of strong values—compassion for people, the value of education, the value of effort, the value of discipline."

Feinstein's constant refrain to staff was that "I don't want to be blindsided," recalled former planning director Dean Macris. "She'd always say, 'If there's something I need to know, tell me so I'm not blindsided.'"

Once on a transcontinental flight, the mayor was leafing through an airplane magazine when she saw an ad for an executive organizer—a leather portfolio with two rows of laminated pockets inside to keep track of dozens of different tasks. She ripped the ad out and ordered the portfolio, which became the centerpiece of her Monday morning command-performance staff meetings. Inside, she kept a card for each department, and would cross-examine executives about tasks assigned the week before or questions that had arisen during the week.

"They were meetings as theater, more communicative and directive than collaborative problem solving," said Peter Henschel, a top Feinstein aide. "None of us felt we had a full delegated authority, but we had a very keen sense of accountability and communication with her." Aides who disappointed her were reprimanded in front of others. Some department heads who feared being "humiliated or belittled" came to the Monday morning meetings wondering, "What kind of mood will she be in today," recalled one close associate of the mayor.

"She was impossible to please. Her problem was perfectionism and neither she nor you could ever achieve [it]," said Cyr Copertini. "But we all respected her. You are who you work for and you never had to apologize for Dianne."

Jim Bloom, who worked on special projects for Feinstein in the final year of her term and her first year out of office, recalled that "In front of the staff, the thing with her was grades. She'd say, 'This is a grade Z report—fix it' or 'On a scale of one to ten, I'd give it a zero.' She either gives out zeros or tens."

Journalists who covered her were not immune from the mayor's temper. She would not hesitate to call reporters whose stories angered her or, sometimes, phone their editors first. When the *Chronicle's* Reggie Smith broke a story about the conclusions reached by a Feinstein task force on a new ballpark, which she was not ready to release, she summoned him to her office and sternly said that such "premature ejaculations" should not be in the newspaper. "I say what I think, for better or worse, and sometimes it's for worse," Feinstein said. "I don't have a lot of guile. I get things off my chest and don't harbor grievances or grudges."

As an administrator, the mayor's penchant for numerical grades was a "management by objective" system that she installed to keep track of precisely how city departments were performing and to hold their executives accountable.

In a prime example of Feinstein-speak, she boasted, in her sixth annual "State of the City" address, that the recreation and parks department "renovated 20 baseball diamonds and more than 200 acres of outfields this year, while planting 6,000 clumps of native and exotic bulbs in neighborhood parks." The public works department, she then pointed out, "repaired 20,000 potholes—not a record, but pretty good." The department "matched last year's all-time high of 105 lane miles of street resurfacing," she proudly added.

Nothenberg said that her close supervision and attention to detail were necessary because City Hall had long lacked strong management. "She has very high standards for herself and expects the same from others," he said. "The transition from legislator to administrator is never easy, but she mastered it. She discovered she had much greater reserves of strength than she thought."

If Feinstein was tough and demanding, she also was warm and caring, and she showed it in often-private acts of nurturing, support, and charity. When a policeman or firefighter was killed or seriously injured, she was often the first at the hospital to comfort the officer, or his family, and paid similar visits to victims of crime. She frequently sneaked away from the mayor's office to sit with friends or advisers who were dying of AIDS. When a reporter was stricken with cancer, she promised to "see you through this" and followed up for several years, checking in regularly by phone or with personal visits and making frequent calls to the woman's oncologist, who had also treated Bert.

Until she left office, almost no one in San Francisco knew that for several years she paid weekly visits to a classroom of poor kids in Hunters Point, to read or talk to them, because she kept it off her public schedule. She also all but adopted one of the boys at the school, inviting him into her home and paying his tuition for private school.

Jan Mirikitani, wife of the Reverend Cecil Williams, recalled that Mayor Feinstein was a familiar figure at Williams's Glide Memorial Church in the Tenderloin and that she took particular interest in the young mothers and poor women with alcohol or drug problems who came to the church for its innovative programs. "She'd stand and talk to the women—remembering their name and their particular situation. She gets involved with a particular situation and will follow through," Mirikitani said. "There is a class difference, but she doesn't take the position she knows it all. She never puts on airs. She listens and she's taking it in. People genuinely like her."

REFLECTING ON HER YEARS in office during an interview a few months before she left City Hall, Feinstein noted that, "A lot of people have said if I wasn't mayor, I'd like to be a chief of police. And that may not be far off." As mayor, her demand for statistical performance was greatest in the police department. The woman who began her career espousing liberal criminal justice reforms was a law-and-order mayor, and improving the police department was her top priority. The importance she placed on safe streets was symbolized by the fact that she required Chief Murphy to give the first report at the Monday morning meetings, updating her on the latest crime statistics, over time and by neighborhood.

During her tenure, more than three hundred cops were added to the force, which increased beat and street patrols as the department more than doubled its budget. Major crimes of murder, rape, aggravated assault, burglary, and motor vehicle theft dropped 27 percent, according to FBI statistics. She set a goal of reducing police response time to a crime in progress to two minutes, down from eight minutes when she entered office, and under her constant prodding, the department achieved it. Even in tight budget times she backed more spending for the department, including a computer-assisted dispatch system to assist radio cars and a state-of-the-art fingerprint computer.

In October 1984, Feinstein dispatched Con Murphy on the most sensitive of the countless missions she assigned to her police chief. Murphy flew to Los Angeles to meet with Dan White, who had been paroled after serving less than six years in state prison for his manslaughter convictions in the killings of Milk and Moscone. The chief met White in an airport coffee shop and handed him a letter from Feinstein urging the killer not to return to San Francisco.

"I didn't see any way for him to have any kind of life here. I really felt it jeopardized [White's wife] Mary Ann and their children. It jeopardized the equanimity of the city. This was one of those once-in-a-lifetime, huge emotional issues about which people felt very strongly, and time had not diminished the strength of feeling. I felt there was nothing good that was going to come of it," Feinstein recalled thinking when she heard that White might move back to San Francisco.

Feinstein's former protégé did not take her advice. In the fall of 1985 White was spotted in his old neighborhood, where people had once voted to make him their voice at City Hall. Although he kept a low profile, word that he was back in San Francisco soon reached the papers. On the morning of Monday, October 21, one month less than seven years after the assassinations, White played the final act in the tragedy that had shaken San Francisco and put Dianne in the mayor's office. He committed suicide at his home, using a garden hose to funnel carbon monoxide from the exhaust pipe of a 1970 Buick into the passenger compartment, where he sat listening to a cassette tape of Irish music.

That afternoon, the police chief formally announced White's death to a crowd of reporters that had gathered in front of the former supervisor's home. As he made his statement, Murphy looked extremely tired and drawn. By this time, after nearly five years as Feinstein's chief of police, he was just a few months from retirement. His last year was marked by a series of embarrassing scandals that rocked the police department despite its improved crime-fighting statistics.

They began in April 1984 with the disclosure that cops at a police academy graduation party had paid a prostitute to perform oral sex on a rookie who was blindfolded and handcuffed to a chair. During the Democratic convention, a few months later, TV cameras recorded policemen holding numbered placards to rate the attractiveness of women delegates. A few months later, plainclothes narcotics officers stormed a trendy fern bar and for ninety minutes searched and questioned sixty patrons. No charges were brought by the police. Unfortunately for them, the bar was full of lawyers, who filed a series of lawsuits against the city.

In early 1985, vice cops arrested porno queen Marilyn Chambers at the Mitchell brothers' theater, bane of former smut fighter Feinstein, for alleged prostitution charges that were never filed. A few days later, *Chronicle* columnist Warren Hinckle compared the cops to a "thundering herd of jackasses led by jackals" and soon thereafter was arrested in the paper's newsroom and taken to jail for unpaid tickets, including one for walking his dog without a license. Even the mayor, who disliked Hinckle, partly because he referred to her as "the widow Feinstein," called the police action "dumb."

Perhaps the most damaging incident to the department's image came in April 1985, when two officers carrying assault rifles invaded a fifth-grade classroom at an elementary school, loudly ordering the teacher and terrified students onto the playground. Only later did the police explain that it was an unannounced training exercise for a potential hostage situation.

The series of incidents politically embarrassed Feinstein, whose reputation as a hands-on manager was sullied. The law-and-order mayor saw her department made a laughingstock—"San Francisco's Keystone Cops" ran a *Newsweek* headline. After the story of the classroom invasion became public, Feinstein summoned Murphy back from vacation to discuss the problems in the department, and the two responded with a high-profile "reorganization plan," which included retraining and closer supervision of officers. Within a year, Murphy retired. At that point, Feinstein announced yet another reorganization, to be headed by a new chief, a public relations–minded commander named Frank Jordan. In 1991 Jordan himself would be elected mayor of San Francisco.

ALONG WITH CRIME, no issue occupied Feinstein more than San Francisco's budget, and no local aspect of her record would become more controversial and important when she entered statewide politics than her fiscal performance as mayor.

Feinstein came into office just six months after California voters overwhelmingly approved the Proposition 13 property-tax cut in June 1978. Like most politicians, Feinstein had vehemently opposed Proposition 13, arguing that it would devastate local government. As a tax policy, the popular initiative rolled back real estate assessments, which could be raised only marginally unless property was sold, and also strictly limited annual increases in the rate of property taxation. As a political matter, this meant that city officials could no longer pass a budget and then adjust the tax rate to pay for whatever they had passed. Now property-tax revenues for local government were limited.

Immediately after the initiative passed, politicians in Sacramento approved a "bailout" plan for money to be returned to local governments to cushion the shock of reduced property taxes. San Francisco in particular benefited from the bailout, both because it was entitled to more money as the only California jurisdiction that was both a city and a county and because assembly speaker Leo McCarthy, a San Franciscan, minded the interests of his city in devising the complex bill.

Still, city budgeting became an exercise in apportioning pain rather than handing out goodies, as politicians had grown accustomed to doing, and balancing the budget became more difficult. Unexpected costs, low revenue estimates, cuts in federal spending, drought or natural disasters routinely threw off carefully balanced budgets during the course of the fiscal year, and midyear corrections—accompanied by headlines about looming deficits, layoffs, and service cuts—became routine.

In San Francisco, the mayor proposes a budget to the supervisors, who can subtract from, but not add to, the mayor's plan. After it passes the board, the mayor cannot further amend the document; she can only sign or veto it. If corrections are needed during the course of the fiscal year, the same process is followed. California's constitution prohibits cities and counties from carrying over a deficit into a new fiscal year.

Coming to office familiar with the intricacies of the budget, Feinstein oversaw the process more closely than her predecessors. Eugene Friend, a businessman and major political contributor, had been an appointed member of the Recreation and Parks Commission under both Alioto and Moscone. He had grown used to the traditional, arms-length manner with which both mayors had treated his commission's business. Feinstein, by contrast, "would take that budget and go through it line by line," Friend said. "Dianne would say, 'Do you really need that $1,200 mower?' How the hell did I know whether we need the mower?"

Thrust into office by assassination, she immediately faced a $120 million projected deficit, largely because of Proposition 13. To ease the first crunch, she proposed, and the board or the voters approved, a series of tax and fee increases that she called a "fair share" plan. The mayor sponsored ballot measures to double taxes on business and impose surcharges on parking garages and the city's already high hotel tax. Public transit fares, parking meter rates, and parking fines also were doubled.

Proposition 13 backers, charging that some increases violated the initiative's strictures on new taxes, filed suit challenging elements of the plan. As the matter worked its way through state courts for several years, the disputed taxes were collected and placed in escrow. When the state supreme court upheld the legality of the plan, the money was released. So in 1982, the city suddenly enjoyed a surplus of $153 million. Along with the contested tax money, there were unanticipated higher revenues from power sales from San Francisco's Hetch Hetchy hydroelectric plant in the Yosemite valley.

Over the next few years, Feinstein devised budgets that addressed what she viewed as the city's most pressing human and capital needs: more than $30 million in new AIDS funding, $21 million for new and refurbished buses, $20 million for long-deferred road repairs, $14 million to increase the size of the police department, $14 million in medical care for the poor, and $10 million for housing programs, among other things. For a time, some business taxes also were reduced. But by 1985 the surplus was gone and the city faced yet another projected deficit.

Critics complained that Feinstein and the supervisors had squandered the surplus. With San Francisco public employees making substantially more than most of their counterparts in other cities in the region and the nation, critics also charged that the city hired too many new workers. According to Harvey Rose, the city's budget analyst, the number of permanent city jobs grew from 20,994 to 24,028 during the time that Feinstein was mayor.

In 1985, then-Supervisor Richard Hongisto warned that rapid depletion of the surplus was an ill-conceived policy and that San Francisco would face chronic shortfalls. Feinstein, riding high politically, dismissed Hongisto out of hand, and told reporters that he must be "smoking something funny" to level such a charge. "The mayor did not understand the phenomenon of raging and almost irreversible government growth. The only answer the Dianne Feinsteins of the world have is to spend more and tax more," said Hongisto, now out of office.

"What should I have done with the surplus?" said Feinstein, who is very sensitive to criticism of her budget record. "The surplus was there to be utilized on budget priorities for the city. That's the purpose of it. It was used to balance the budget. Twenty million dollars a year went to AIDS programs. We had homeless. There was nothing being spent on homeless programs—eventually it was $10 million a year. Some went on the Democratic convention. Some went on public works projects. That's what it was there for. It was there to use."

By September 1987, her final year in office, Feinstein faced a new, $77 million hole in her last budget. Three months into a new fiscal year, that projected shortfall was the amount of red ink fiscal experts estimated the city would encounter the following fiscal year, if no adjustments were made to cut expenditures or raise revenues. This was not unusual because ongoing budget projections often revealed such projected deficits.

"Almost every year there was a [budget] shortfall and every year you took care of the shortfall. You adjusted the budget. I would personally review department requests and I would hold all nonessential requests and that controlled the budget," Feinstein recalled. In 1987 the mayor responded to the problem with a $80 million proposal to save money by imposing a hiring freeze and delaying capital improvements, among other actions.

In the midst of a mayoral campaign to succeed her, she angrily denounced anonymous City Hall critics who complained to the newspapers that she was departing with a "Mother Hubbard budget"—leaving the cupboard bare for her successor. "If you want to suspend the charter and make me mayor next year, I'll prove this budget works and is balanced and that I could maintain it," she said, pounding the table during a *Chronicle* editorial board meeting that provided a rare public glimpse of her anger. "Now if you say to me, can I guarantee it the year after, the answer is no. I'm not Jesus Christ and I'm not Moses and I'm not Buddha and that's what ticking me off about the whole thing."

When her successor, Assemblyman Art Agnos, came into office in January 1988, it was the middle of the city's fiscal year. His budget experts produced a new report that estimated the shortfall for the following fiscal year at $172 million. This estimate factored in $40 million in potential liabilities from lawsuits filed against the city, $15 million in lost hydroelectric revenues because of a drought, $10 million from voter repeal of a utility tax, and $20 million in lower-than-expected revenues from other taxes.

Under Agnos, the city ended the fiscal year covered by Feinstein's final budget with a modest surplus of $16.2 million. But over the next two years, the economic complexities and nuances of San Francisco's budget would be lost amid a political cacophony of charges and countercharges about the "$172 million deficit," the clamor of which would follow Feinstein into a governor's race, where foes used it to assail her image as a skilled manager.

"There was no $172 million deficit. It was a projected shortfall [that had] everything but the kitchen sink in it," Feinstein would strenuously argue. "My last budget closed out with a $16 million surplus. And I've got this in writing."

WHILE FEINSTEIN'S BUDGET record as mayor would generate great controversy when she became a statewide candidate, there was considerably less debate about her handling of the worst health crisis that San Francisco faced, the scourge of AIDS. Soon after the late Randy Shilts began his pioneering reporting about the "gay cancer" in the *Chronicle* in the early 1980s, the city started building a public and private network of AIDS and AIDS-related services widely viewed as the best in the world. While urban leaders elsewhere ignored the epidemic or delayed financing AIDS education and treatment programs, Feinstein took a national leadership role, under prodding from the gay community, and approved steadily increased spending on AIDS—the annual appropriation had reached $20 million when she left office.

For months, she privately urged the city's director of public health to order a shutdown of gay bathhouses, sites of profligate and often anonymous gay sex. The director, who was supervised not by the mayor but by the chief administrative officer, said that such precipitous action might drive the still-emerging epidemic further underground; Feinstein argued that the baths were a menace to public health and eventually sent undercover policemen into the establishments to observe and report on unsafe sex practices. The bathhouses finally were ordered shut down.

In early 1983, Feinstein called on big-city mayors to help mobilize a task force to lobby the federal government for research money and to mount a national education campaign. Although the absolute number of AIDS cases at the time was still relatively small, she correctly cited the "almost geometric increase in the number of AIDS victims" in the first years of the epidemic as evidence that it was about to explode.

Often derided for her appointment of blue-ribbon commissions, she named an AIDS panel of top experts that produced ground-breaking information. "She would actually study the reports and come back with a list of questions and comments," said Dr. Sid Foster, her father's old friend who acted as a health adviser to the mayor. "Her attitude was, If I'm going to do something about this, I want to know more about it than anyone else."

Even some of her early critics in the gay community applauded Feinstein's performance on AIDS. Carole Migden was an ally of Harvey Milk's and a liberal gay political activist who had lent her name and influence to the recall of Feinstein in 1983. Migden, who was later elected a San Francisco supervisor, said when Feinstein left the mayor's office: "She's been extraordinarily sensitive to the AIDS issue throughout the epidemic. She does not understand what gay people are all about . . . but she has understood the issues of disease and death. And all other issues pale in comparison to this."

IN SAN FRANCISCO'S ENDLESS DEBATE over how and where the city should grow within its water-bound forty-nine-square-mile limits, a passionate tone was set early in the city's history. In 1847 a prominent surveyor named James O'Farrell was the target of a lynch mob responding to his publication of a new map of the city that included plans for a 120-foot-wide main boulevard called Market Street. With residents angry about the scope and cost of the plan, O'Farrell boarded a ferry for Sausalito and stayed out of sight until the furor over his survey abated. But the emotions over managing San Francisco's growth have never subsided for long.

Feinstein was first elected to office in 1969 as an opponent of intensive downtown development and, in her first run for mayor in 1971, had campaigned against Alioto's Manhattanization policies. But when she took over as mayor, Feinstein earned the enmity of the neighborhood, slow-growth movement as she oversaw the greatest downtown building boom in city history. More than 22 million square feet of office space were approved, according to city planning records, the equivalent of about forty-four Transamerica Pyramids, the city's most architecturally notable office tower.

"It's an economic issue," said Feinstein. "The number one responsibility of a mayor is the economic and social well-being of the people, and that means that cities have to remain places that can generate employment. San Francisco was never going to be an Italian fishing village. It was a corporate and service headquarters city. That remains its destiny."

To outsiders, the high-rise battle may seem puzzling. During two decades when urban centers across America changed from blue-collar to service economies, other cities lined up to attract developers to build, and corporations to fill, the same type of high rises that caused such consternation in San Francisco. "While other cities were providing incentives for such development, San Francisco was debating whether to stop it," said Dean Macris, the Chicago-born urban planner who served as Feinstein's planning director.

Although the banking, insurance, and financial corporations that drove the high-rise boom provided thousands of new jobs in San Francisco, the growth debate was more complex. For one thing, most of the new jobs created by the transformation of San Francisco went to suburban commuters, or to highly paid white-collar professionals better able to afford spiraling housing costs than were soon-to-be-displaced city residents. The daily influx into the three-square-mile downtown area of so many commuters, along with the demand for high-income housing, had ripple effects on neighborhoods that ranged from higher rents to fewer parking spaces. A study of property-tax records in the 1970s by the *San Francisco Bay Guardian,* a weekly newspaper and flagship of the neighborhood movement, fueled the debate by concluding that high-rise buildings cost the city more in services than they generated in revenues. An *Examiner* study of the high-rise boom, in 1986, estimated that while each Transamerica-sized high rise generated 3,100 jobs, it also created 3,000 auto trips a day, the need for 895 parking spaces, and the demand for 730 seats on the public transit system. In a small self-contained city where "quality of life" is sacrosanct, the increased density accompanying the high-rise boom caused great dissent.

As an elected official Feinstein had opposed most in the long series of citizen-sponsored ballot measures that sought to slow down or cap high-rise construction, although she endorsed one such measure during her heated mayoral campaign of 1979. Once she became mayor, Feinstein sided strongly with the pro-business forces in the development battle and opposed efforts to legislate limits through the ballot box. She also took more direct actions.

In 1981, two years after taking office, she replaced two Moscone appointees to the planning commission—one had consistently opposed high rises and the other was a foe of luxury condominium conversion projects—in favor of two more development-minded commissioners. "The time has simply come for me to put the stamp of my own priorities and concerns on the planning commission," she said at the time. Over the next six years, the commission approved virtually every major high-rise project before it, although projects were routinely subject to redesign or scaling down.

Feinstein's attempt at compromise on the high-rise development issue was called the Downtown Plan. Among many other features, the plan limited the size and bulk of high rises, imposed environmental restrictions on developers in matters of aesthetics, light, and shadow, and called for development fees for transit and housing programs. In its original form it received widespread praise, and was hailed as "the most carefully thought out system for intelligent, controlled growth that any large city had yet produced" by the architecture critic of the *New York Times.*

But the plan received far more mixed reviews in San Francisco. Several supervisors said that it did not go far enough. Sue Bierman, Dianne's old friend, whom Moscone had appointed a slow-growth member of the planning commission, complained that it did not have enough neighborhood input. Sue Hestor, a leader of the anti-high-rise forces, said the plan "created the illusion of dealing seriously with the problem [but] is not growth control at all."

In hearings before the supervisors, the plan was amended to include an annual ceiling of 950,000 square feet of office development and imposition of fees on developers for child-care programs, among other changes aimed at placating neighborhood critics. But the corporate development forces also won major changes, most notably the exemption from the annual growth limit of high-rise projects, totaling more than 3 million square feet of office space, that were in preliminary stages of planning. Not surprisingly, high-rise developers and associates were the largest single source of campaign contributions to local officeholders while the plan was being discussed. Led by those exempted from the plan, developers donated nearly $2 million to the

campaigns and causes of the mayor and the supervisors in a three-year period, an *Examiner* investigation showed.

Feinstein opposed the exemptions for the disputed projects. But when the
Downtown Plan legislation came to her desk with the waivers included, she
signed it anyway, calling it a visionary model for America. "There probably
never has been in the history of the city more sweeping legislation passed to
provide for significant control of growth," she said. But the plan did not stop
the bitter development debate.

"We have a planning process that is a permanent floating crap game. It's
just 'let's make a deal' time," Calvin Welch, a leader of the anti-high-rise
forces, declared at the time. The following year, 1986, Welch and his allies
finally passed a citizen ballot initiative to limit high-rise development.
Known as Proposition M, the measure put much tighter strictures on development than the Downtown Plan, limiting annual growth to only about
450,000 square feet. By then, however, San Francisco's office vacancy rate—
just 5 percent when Feinstein became mayor—had grown to nearly 20 percent and the market for downtown construction was curbed.

When Feinstein left office, the *Chronicle* poll showed that citizens believed
her greatest shortcoming had been the high-rise development issue. Frustrated by their inability to park, shop, or find affordable housing in the
neighborhoods, more than 50 percent said she had ignored neighborhood
problems at the expense of promoting downtown development.

A FEW DAYS AFTER George Moscone's assassination, Feinstein's first official
visitor was Chai Tse-min, China's first ambassador to the United States after
diplomatic normalization. He was visiting San Francisco to help determine
where to locate a Chinese consulate. When Dianne saw the appointment on
the calendar, made while Moscone was still mayor, she at first protested that
she could not handle a courtesy call from a foreign dignitary at a time like
this. But Copertini convinced her that it would be discourteous to cancel
the meeting. Feinstein met with the ambassador, impressed him, and set an
important tone for her administration.

Expanding the boundaries of the mayor's office to include an international dimension, Feinstein over the next nine years traveled more than
163,000 miles, the equivalent of six times around the globe, on more than a
dozen official foreign trips. She established "sister-city" relationships to improve trade relations and cultural exchanges with Shanghai, Osaka, Seoul,
Sydney, Taipei, and Manila, among others. In the process, she attracted wa-

terfront, high-technology, and other business to San Francisco and, at times, gently tried to nudge the policies of other nations. "Her tenure as mayor was an attempt to rebuild San Francisco's positive image. I saw her gaining exposure outside the city as an important way to rebuild it," said former press secretary Tom Eastham.

The trips abroad, which Feinstein paid for out of her campaign fund rather than with city money, were a combination of public relations, concrete accomplishment, and considerable adventure. Wherever she traveled, particularly in Asia, there was usually great interest in her as an elected woman leader, and she succeeded in nurturing a network of personal relationships with foreign leaders that she maintained after she left the mayor's office.

As a practical matter, the trips, though much criticized by political foes, did yield some economic and political benefits. China did establish its first American consulate in San Francisco, and its national airline began flights to the city's international airport. Taipei's major shipping line, one of the world's largest, made San Francisco its West Coast port of call. A year of secret negotiations, which began with a plea from a San Francisco woman whose family was behind the Iron Curtain, ended during a 1985 trip to the Soviet Union, when Feinstein won rights of emigration for thirty-six people to rejoin relatives in the United States. On the same trip, she also won agreement from the Russians on broad cultural exchanges and captured the personal attention of Mikhail Gorbachev, who delayed a formal state dinner to engage her in a lengthy one-on-one conversation.

But she also set off a major flap in the local Jewish community when she tried to establish a sister-city relationship with Leningrad, the city of her mother's birth. Under heavy pressure, she tabled the idea after it was sharply criticized by groups upset with Soviet discrimination against Jews.

There were more prosaic adventures. In Xi'an, China, in 1984, she slipped on a wet street and dislocated her elbow—which had been broken twice before, once in a fall in the White House driveway and once when she was rescuing her housekeeper's son from drowning. This time, Feinstein got a personal view of the state of Chinese medicine as she was treated at a public clinic where doctors took fifteen minutes to manipulate her elbow back into place after giving her only a local anesthetic.

On the same trip, she lectured *Chronicle* writer Evelyn Hsu, telling her that American reporters should be more like their Chinese counterparts: "They just write down what we say," she told Hsu.

On a sister-city voyage to Cork, Ireland, Feinstein stirred controversy before she left home by imposing a dress code on a two-hundred-member delegation, some of whose members canceled their trip as a result.

Gene Gartland, her old friend whom she had appointed executive director of the Port, recalled one trip to Asia that began with Feinstein setting forth a long list of dos and don'ts of protocol. "The one thing you don't do is hug people," the mayor informed Gartland, who was duly surprised upon their arrival in Shanghai when the Chinese mayor warmly embraced Dianne.

At a stop in South Korea on the same trip, the delegation was entertained at a banquet by a local singing group. After the dinner, Feinstein ordered those traveling with her to her hotel room, where she informed them that they must reciprocate the next night by singing "I Left My Heart in San Francisco." No one knew the words of the city's official song, however, so Feinstein called Cyr Copertini long distance to get the lyrics.

Her frequent foreign visits were part of what one top aide called "the constant carnival of international attention" during Feinstein's administration, which included opulent receptions for the pope, the queen of England, and Gorbachev. While Feinstein inevitably was the public star of these events, the behind-the-scenes heroine was Charlotte Swig, who worked full time as an unpaid chief of protocol to coordinate trips and celebrations. "Dianne's hospitality was hands-on," she said. "She has very good taste in that regard—how things look, feel, taste. She always wanted to know where each place card was."

Among the more notorious celebrations were those for the San Francisco 49ers' first Super Bowl victory in 1982, which turned into the worst riot since the Dan White verdict, and the fiftieth anniversary of the Golden Gate Bridge, when 500,000 people—more than ten times as many as expected—turned out to walk across the span, causing human gridlock and testing the bridge's strength in the process.

The most controversial reception for a foreign leader was that for the Philippine dictator Ferdinand Marcos in 1982, which was vehemently protested by San Francisco's large Filipino community. Feinstein's well-honed sense of propriety led her to welcome warmly and to heap praise on the dictator and his wife, Imelda. She presented the couple with a key to the city and told a carefully screened crowd that a reception the Marcoses had staged for her in their country "left a very deep sense of affection in all of our hearts." Although she privately presented Marcos with an Amnesty International report listing human-rights abuses in his country, in public she glossed over the violations, comparing the Philippines to Israel by saying, "We judge a country by its major deeds and the major deeds of [the Philippines] have been in friendship."

When Queen Elizabeth visited in 1983, Eastham recalled, Feinstein's welcoming remarks marked the only time the mayor ever actually delivered a speech as he had written it for her. "Normally, she would be on the phone early, seven o'clock, saying, 'This will not do,'" he said. "This time, she read the entire speech without changing a single word." When he asked her about it later, Feinstein replied, "I was too scared to change a word."

SHORTLY BEFORE FEINSTEIN left office as mayor, San Francisco attorney Bob McCarthy, who raised campaign money for her, came home from work to find his three sons playing a game, in which they had propped his one-year-old daughter up on pillows and surrounded her with his old briefcases.

"We're playing City Hall," one of the boys told him, informing him that the baby was the mayor. "Why is she the mayor?" McCarthy asked. "She's the only girl," the answer came.

The incident reflected the deep impact that Feinstein as mayor had upon the city and upon women in politics. Two decades after she stunned San Francisco with her upset 1969 win, the city not only had a woman mayor but also a majority of women on its board of supervisors and two female representatives in Congress. The kind of gender-based obstacles she had faced were fast disappearing, in part because of her resilience and performance in office.

Feinstein's last day as mayor was Friday, January 8, 1988. But the real effect of losing the job to which she had devoted herself for nine years hit her earlier in the week, when she convened her final Monday morning meeting. Staff members tried to soften the blow by wearing T-shirts that bore a caricature of Feinstein and the words, "I survived the mayor's staff meetings." Feinstein got one that read, "I thrived on the mayor's staff meetings."

Midway through the meeting, mayor-elect Art Agnos, a liberal assemblyman who had often feuded with Feinstein, walked in and was given a loud ovation. "Have you been doing this for ten years?" Agnos, who was often scornful of Feinstein's schoolmarm style, asked the group. "You look in remarkably good shape."

There was one more, eerie, interruption to the meeting. An official bumped a table, toppling a bronze bust of the late George Moscone, which broke off its pedestal. The bust of the man whose death had brought Dianne to office was quietly carried from the room.

"It's really hard to leave, I must say," Dianne said after the meeting. "I wish I didn't have to go through it," she added, blinking back tears.

14

YEAR OF THE WOMAN

*Women have begun to see that if I go through that doorway,
I take everybody through it.*

—*Dianne Feinstein, 1990*

IN NOVEMBER 1989 FORMER MAYOR Feinstein opened her voluminous files to Bill Carrick and Hank Morris, two political consultants who had recently signed on to her floundering campaign for governor of California. As Carrick sat in a study at her Presidio Terrace mansion, rummaging through material from her career in local politics, he heard his partner suddenly shout from another room, "Bill, come and look—this is it!"

For the next few minutes, the two watched a public television documentary about the City Hall killings that opened with news footage of Feinstein announcing the assassinations of George Moscone and Harvey Milk. Two months later, her campaign started airing a thirty-second TV spot that began with that moment of horror. The ad instantly catapulted Feinstein from nowhere to the front-runner's spot in the governor's race. "The grabber," as the ad was dubbed, marked the most dramatic turning point in the most high-profile political race in America that year.

After two rocky years out of office, Feinstein in 1990 reemerged as a national and even international figure, an intriguing personality who became the most visible symbol of what the media ballyhooed as "the year of the woman" in politics. In the end, Feinstein would fall just short of her goal of winning the governor's office but, as she had done throughout her political career, she would again win by losing. While Dianne would agonize personally over her 1990 defeat, politically she was strengthened, as she established herself as California's leading Democrat and set the stage for triumph two years later.

The campaign for governor was a race she almost didn't make. Uncertain of herself once out of office, she wanted in her heart to run but feared challenging a strong Republican incumbent and balked at taking the concrete steps needed for the daunting financial and organizational task of mounting a statewide campaign in California. While she hesitated, then suffered personal and political setbacks, her chief primary opponent built momentum and raised large amounts of campaign money. By the fall of 1989 she was written off, not only by many pundits but also by some of her closest advisers, who suggested she drop out to avoid embarrassment and secretly discussed terms of a dignified withdrawal with strategists for her Democratic rival.

But at her lowest moment, the politician who admired her physician father's "will of iron" just kept going. Assembling a campaign team, she made a long-delayed move to vote-rich southern California, finally stepping outside the warm cocoon of her hometown to learn the vast and complex political byways of a sprawling and diverse state. Benefiting from the dictum that "a political rally in California is three people gathered around a television set," Feinstein broke through dramatically with a modest TV ad buy, then demonstrated through months of a bitter and brawling campaign that she could stand up to intense statewide scrutiny.

"It was an abject bottoming out," she would recall of the dark days of her history-making race for governor. "But somehow, when they told me it was impossible, I became absolutely determined to do it."

ON JANUARY 5, 1989, Dianne was having lunch at Trader Vic's with friends when she got a phone call from Jim Bloom. A former mayoral aide who with several others had followed Feinstein into a self-described "government in exile," Bloom was calling from her office with some startling news: California's Republican governor, George Deukmejian, was about to announce that he would not seek a third term. "I better get right back," she said.

It had been a frustrating first year out of office. With no clear plan for her future, she made an unsuccessful attempt to write an autobiography, did some commentaries for TV, and traveled to the Far East. But her political future looked bleak. To Feinstein, the prospect of waging an uphill fight against the then-popular two-term Deukmejian seemed a risk not worth taking. Now, suddenly, California's political landscape had radically changed, and the road to the governor's office looked wide open.

From Trader Vic's, Dianne quickly headed back to 909 Montgomery Street, an elegant office building where Blum housed his investment business and where she kept a comfortable office furnished with Chinese antiques and art. By the time she arrived, the phone was ringing with calls from reporters and she quickly declared that she was in the race. As advisers drawn by the news began assembling in her office, the excitement and laughter contrasted with the somber mood that had prevailed in the Feinstein camp for the past year.

When assemblyman Art Agnos, an erstwhile enemy, was sworn in as her successor, it represented the last in a series of final-year setbacks for Feinstein. She had strongly backed Supervisor Jack Molinari, who had run on a promise to continue many of her policies, but he was overwhelmed by Agnos's powerful precinct organization, which represented the reemergence of the liberal Moscone coalition that had been disheartened, routed, or co-opted during the more conservative Feinstein era.

She also had stumbled on several major issues, including a comprehensive plan for homelessness; clearing the way for a new stadium for the San Francisco Giants, who were threatening to leave town; and completing arrangements to make the city the home port for the battleship *Missouri*. When she left office, the city faced a $77 million projected deficit; a few weeks later, Agnos reported that the figure had soared to $172 million. And after Feinstein tweaked him in a television commentary for not following through on her effort to bring the *Missouri's* battle group to San Francisco, he left little doubt about whom he blamed for the budget crisis. "We've been living on a false City Hall budgetary economy for the past two to three years," Agnos told reporters. "In an effort to be positive and constructive, I had refused to put the blame where it belonged—squarely on Mayor Feinstein's bad management." Ever sensitive to criticism, Feinstein simmered at the censure by her successor, but with no office or job to use as a platform, there was little she could do about responding.

In 1987, her final year as mayor, Feinstein had passed up a chance for federal office after Congresswoman Sala Burton, widow of the legendary Phil Burton, died in February 1987. Amid the scramble to succeed Burton, Feinstein would have been an overwhelming favorite in the April special election that followed. The mayor at first said she had no interest in the seat, then changed her mind and announced that she might run for Congress. The characteristically independent move startled the Democratic establishment, already lined up behind former state party chairwoman Nancy Pelosi.

Feinstein's public indecision set off a civic soap opera, played out by politicians hoping to replace her if she won the House of Representatives seat and resigned the balance of her term as mayor. Burton's death, along with Feinstein's already impending departure in 1988, and the recent election to the state legislature of Supervisor Quentin Kopp, represented movement by three of the city's most powerful politicians and created a huge vacuum of power. "It's not realignment, it's dealignment," chortled one political consultant amid a rush of candidates to fill it.

Feinstein, concerned about the unseemly struggle for succession, finally chose to finish her term rather than run for Congress. "I do not want to leave the office in a whirlwind of speculation about who succeeds me," she said with characteristic decorum. "There must be stability and continuity in this office." But the spectacle that had erupted was politically embarrassing, and she left office with the thought that she already could have missed her first, best chance to advance in politics.

Now, two years later, Deukmejian's unexpected decision was another of those abrupt changes that had long ago made Dianne fatalistic about her political future. "I had cleared my calendar to work on my book," she laughed, hours after Deukmejian's bombshell. "This makes for a whole new chapter."

THE 1990 CALIFORNIA GOVERNOR'S RACE was "the most important campaign in America," the late Lee Atwater, then head of the Republican National Committee, said at the time. Along with partisan control of the governor's office, which Republicans had held since the end of Jerry Brown's troubled second term, there was much more at stake in the state, driven by the sixth-largest economy in the world. Owing to California's rapid population growth in the previous decade, the state was in line for seven new congressional seats. The governor elected in 1990 would play a key role in reapportionment, the once-a-decade job of redrawing the lines for legislative and congressional seats.

Republicans had spent the past ten years bitterly complaining and fighting in court over the 1980 reapportionment plan. Drafted by Democrat Phil Burton on a cocktail napkin, it had turned the state's largest-in-the-nation congressional delegation from one almost evenly split between the parties to one dominated by Democrats. Any hopes that Republicans harbored of making a dent in the Democratic grip on the House and the state legislature depended on maintaining their control of the governor's office in Sacramento.

GOP leaders, agreeing that 1990 was too important for a fratricidal primary, helped clear the field for Senator Pete Wilson, who had been reelected to a second six-year term only a few months before. Among Democrats, the insiders' early favorite was Attorney General John Van de Kamp, the heir to a baking fortune and former Los Angeles district attorney who enjoyed the support of organized labor and other party interest groups.

Against these two "white guys in blue suits," as politicians put it, Feinstein was like a bold splash of color. Unfortunately for her, she also was the only candidate without an office, a campaign staff, or a base of financial support and the only one who had never run a statewide race. "I felt if she had a lot of money, with her mediagenic appeal and the gender gap that she would eventually win" the Democratic primary, recalled George Gorton, who managed Wilson's campaign. "But I had the same question we all had: Does she have the heart for this? Does she know what she is doing?"

Duane Garrett, chairman of Feinstein's campaign, was not too sure. "At that point, we could have lost the election if Van de Kamp had pushed us to say, 'Here is a map of California—show me where Barstow, Bakersfield, and Cucamonga are,'" he said. Before it even got started, the campaign was beset by major problems behind the scenes.

For one thing, Feinstein and Blum were involved in extended and bitter negotiations with consultant Clint Reilly over a contract to manage the race. Reilly also was increasingly frustrated that Feinstein kept ignoring his advice to start traveling around the state to build a network of support, which he had been futilely urging her to do since her second term as mayor.

At the same time, Feinstein was growing weak and pale as she suffered chronic bleeding from fibroid tumors. Trying to control the problem with medication, she kept putting off the major surgery that doctors recommended. "I was anemic and my energy level was very low," she recalled. Despite the problems, however, she began to make a few forays across the state after a California Poll in the spring showed her leading Van de Kamp among Democratic voters.

In April she delivered the keynote address at a Jefferson-Jackson dinner for the Democratic party in San Diego, a key swing area. But she bombed when she ignored the text that Hadley Roff had labored over and began to improvise, at one point describing in graphic detail how members of the Donner party committed cannibalism—for the benefit of an audience that was dining on rare roast beef.

In June she got a much better reception at a meeting of California newspaper editors in Sacramento, where she outlined a package of political reforms to lessen the influence of special-interest money on the legislature. But the fissures in the campaign were cracking open. On the day of the speech, her two top advisers had a bitter quarrel because Reilly wanted her to mention Willie Brown in her ethical indictment of Sacramento while Roff saw no reason to alienate a likely ally in the campaign. Feinstein did not mention Brown in her speech, and "things really started to deteriorate around then," another aide recalled.

By early summer, Reilly grew increasingly angry. In July the U.S. Supreme Court's decision in the *Webster* case upheld the right of a state to restrict abortion rights—and suddenly made abortion a volatile political issue again. Even before the decision, Reilly wanted Feinstein to jump-start her historic bid to become the first woman governor in California by sponsoring a ballot initiative on abortion rights. He pressed the strategy even more when Van de Kamp sponsored a series of three initiatives—on crime, the environment, and ethics—to use as his platform in the governor's race.

Feinstein found the idea of running statewide daunting enough, without the complications and expense of a separate initiative race. Her resistance to Reilly's plan grew after she contacted abortion-rights activists, who told her they would not welcome such an initiative. The tension between the candidate and her manager, two controlling personalities, was growing ever thicker when Dianne finally went into the hospital in July for a hysterectomy. On the same day, Roff underwent prostate surgery. As both recuperated for weeks, Van de Kamp dominated the political news of summer with his initiative program. The eight-point lead Dianne had held over Van de Kamp in the California Poll in spring turned into an eight-point deficit by midsummer. With no campaign structure yet in place, it began to look as if she would be a nonstarter in the governor's race.

Amid illness, delays, and growing disarray, Reilly's anger simmered and he demanded a $3 million commitment from Feinstein and Blum, along with complete control over campaign strategy. In mid-August, Feinstein recalled, the two of them had a heated meeting. "It was very much the control issue," she recalled. "I said, 'This isn't going to work, we ought to part.'"

The following Monday, August 21, was Feinstein's first day back in the office. Roff came in early and was greeted with a call from Gerry Braun, political reporter of the *San Diego Union,* asking for a comment on "Clint Reilly's statement." What statement is that? Roff wanted to know. Braun politely faxed Roff a copy.

The statement, which had been attached to a one-page resignation letter that Dianne had not yet seen, had been sent to every political reporter in the state. Charging that Feinstein was "unwilling to commit to a schedule, an organization, and a budget capable of electing her governor," Reilly said that "Dianne Feinstein has been unwilling to make a 100 percent commitment." She was blindsided. "We have a little problem," she informed Darry Sragow, a veteran Democratic consultant whom Reilly had hired to help begin organizing in southern California, when she reached him on his car phone that morning.

To reporters she was defiant. "This in no way deters my determination to continue my campaign for governor. In fact, it redoubles my commitment." At the time, though, it seemed like a potentially fatal blow for the Feinstein campaign. In a slow summer news season, newspapers played the story up. The next day Dianne met with Roff and the remainder of her small campaign staff. Sragow, scheduler Barry Wyatt, and Dee Dee Myers—who would later become President Bill Clinton's press secretary—had been hired by Reilly, but all stayed with Feinstein.

They devised a damage control strategy. The first step was to go to Sacramento, the heart of the state political establishment, where the most skeptical politicians and press corps could see her in public, see that she had the determination to make the race. Four days after Reilly's humiliating resignation letter, her press conference began when a reporter asked if she lacked "the fire in the belly" to run for governor. "I thought I had that removed," Feinstein answered extemporaneously. She was back in the race.

DESPITE THE BRAVE FRONT, Feinstein at that point had very few assets in her campaign. Van de Kamp had reaped a harvest of positive news coverage for his initiatives and jumped out to an eighteen-point lead in an October California Poll. He was lining up endorsements, fund-raisers, and a team of top-flight media consultants. About the only thing anyone seemed to know about Feinstein's campaign was that she had been fired by her manager. At one point, Feinstein tried to place a call to a southern California labor leader asking for support. His secretary did not recognize her name and, after having her spell it twice, asked Dianne what she was calling about. "My campaign for governor," she answered. "Governor of what?" the secretary replied.

Dianne finally made a move to southern California, leasing a condominium in Century City. Starting to make the rounds in an effort to gather support, she made an appointment with Los Angeles city councilman Bob Farrell. Farrell was out of the office when she arrived, but she was greeted by his aide, her old friend, Percy Pinkney. Years before in San Francisco, she had helped him raise money for his community-based programs working with youth gangs; now she asked him for help in her campaign. "She was wandering in the woods politically," Pinkney recalled.

He helped her put together one of the first building blocks of her campaign when he introduced her to dozens of local black officials and community activists at a meeting at Roscoe's Chicken and Waffle House. Soon after, he had an evening fund-raiser at his own house for her and was surprised when Feinstein arrived over an hour early for the seven o'clock affair. "She did not have a lot to do at that time," Pinkney said, recalling that Feinstein nervously paced the floor before the guests arrived. When they did, there were not enough chairs in his living room. "Everybody was standing around awkwardly and Dianne said, 'Let's just sit on the floor,' and sat down in her blue Ultrasuede suit. It just stunned the group."

A few weeks later, after Pinkney had guided her around a series of community, child-care, and drug-treatment centers in Los Angeles, she said to him, "I want to take some gang members to dinner—I want to meet some Crips and Bloods." With the help of a minister friend, Pinkney invited a half-dozen members of each gang to dinner with Dianne and Dick at a restaurant atop the glitzy Bonaventure Hotel. "There was an open and honest discussion of the violence," he said. "It was the first time I'd seen any white politician take that kind of attitude."

Although Feinstein had finally begun to learn her way around southern California, her campaign was still drifting. The bad news in the polls had virtually dried up fund-raising. There was no money coming in; there was no one to answer phones; calls were not being returned. Roff, a chief of staff with no staff, advised Feinstein to get out before she embarrassed herself.

To Duane Garrett it had a familiar look: after serving Walter Mondale, he had been the national chairman of Bruce Babbitt's failed presidential candidacy in 1988 and had some experience with lost causes. Without telling

Dianne, he called attorney Barbara Johnson, Van de Kamp's chairwoman, and privately told her there was a good chance that Feinstein would drop out soon. He wanted to know how that news would be handled by the Van de Kamp forces: Would there be a role for Feinstein in a general election campaign? Could they avoid humiliating her in the press? Johnson assured him that Van de Kamp would handle it with kid gloves.

Van de Kamp operatives spread the word that Feinstein was about to quit. Van de Kamp's campaign manager was Richard Ross, the Sacramento consultant who had worked for Feinstein in the 1979 mayor's race and the 1983 recall. "I remembered being struck by her wobbling under assault," Ross said. "So we pressed her and pressed her and pressed her. I always thought there was a real possibility she could be gotten out."

Amid the gloom in early November, Willie Brown, Garrett, Feinstein, and Blum met for dinner in a private room at Harris's, an elegant San Francisco steak house favored by political types. Garrett lubricated the evening with two bottles of vintage wine as Brown explained the state of California to Feinstein, assembly district by assembly district, and told her precisely how she could be elected governor of California.

Since 1980, Brown had been the Speaker of the state assembly, the second most powerful political office in California after the governor. As usual with him, there was more than one item on his agenda. He was furious with Van de Kamp both because the attorney general's reform initiative called for term limits on state lawmakers, which would force Brown from office, and because he had promised that as governor he would "drain the swamp in Sacramento" by stopping the kind of special-interest politics practiced by Willie Brown. Brown strongly advised Feinstein to stay in the race and suggested she interview Bill Carrick and Hank Morris to run her campaign.

A few days later the two strategists met with Dianne and Dick. Their lunch at Il Fornaio ended with a handshake agreement to run her campaign. Carrick is a bearded native of South Carolina with Coke-bottle glasses, a slow Southern drawl, and an habitual mumble. Morris is a native New Yorker, brash, outspoken, and seldom misunderstood. Together they formed an unlikely if brilliant partnership to pull off the biggest political upset of the year.

Conducting focus groups around the state convinced them that the race was wide open; real voters had few firm ideas about any of the candidates. "They didn't know whether Van de Kamp was the bakery or the frozen fish," said Carrick. When shown photos of male politicians, many voters would mix up Van de Kamp with Wilson, Leo McCarthy, or Controller Gray Davis. Nobody misidentified Dianne.

By Christmas, they had drafted a one-hundred-day plan for the governor's race and won a commitment that Blum would open his deep pockets for the campaign, a key issue in the falling-out with Reilly. The asset of personal wealth would make up for many of the blunders of 1989. By mid-January Carrick and Morris had the thirty-second spot that would soon be known as "the grabber" ready to go.

After the dramatic footage of Feinstein's assassination announcement, the ad featured quick cuts of photographs of her as mayor as the narrator said: "Forged from tragedy, her leadership brought San Francisco together. Tough and caring, she pushed for day care, cracked down on toxics, added police, and cut crime 20 percent. Named the nation's most effective mayor and always pro-choice, she's the only Democrat for governor for the death penalty. She's Dianne Feinstein."

On Monday night, January 22, four Van de Kamp strategists met with a pair of reporters covering the race at a San Francisco bistro near City Hall called Harry's American Bar and Grill. Through sources in Los Angeles, the Van de Kamp advisers had just learned about Feinstein's ad, which was going on the air that night. They also learned how much time she was buying: just over $500,000 worth, a pittance by California standards. "Half a million dollars," cackled one of the attorney general's operatives. "That's like pissing in the ocean."

FEINSTEIN FORMALLY DECLARED her candidacy on February 5, describing her campaign as a milestone for women and portraying herself as an independent political outsider and industrious problem-solver. "This is a big moment for me and a historic one for women," she said on a campaign swing that began in Los Angeles. "I am a nonincumbent in a race against two entrenched statewide politicians, a woman in a field of men."

While she recited a litany of expanded education, environmental, and social programs and proposed the creation of four new state agencies—without explaining how she would pay for any of it—Feinstein's vision of being governor was consistent with the themes she had used in every campaign since Stanford. As a moderate mediator, she would bring competing interests to reason together; she would be a nonideological chief executive "who convinces, cajoles, and yes, even knocks heads to get the job done." At times, her vision of the job sounded like governor as cheerleader: "Yes, we can solve the insurance crisis. Yes, we will provide health insurance. Yes, we will improve education," she promised. "Why? Because it can be done. If people care and come together, talk together, and decide to do it, it can happen."

Her announcement tour came in the final days of her early television advertising, and both attracted considerable media attention. But no one, least of all Van de Kamp, was prepared for the impact that the two tactics would have. On February 12, just one week after her announcement, Mervin Field's California Poll delivered stunning news: Feinstein had surged from an eighteen-point deficit to a four-point lead over Van de Kamp among Democrats and also was slightly ahead of Wilson among voters of all registration. "It's quite dramatic," Field said at the time. "When you have a shift of that magnitude, it shows considerable instability in voter preference. It also demonstrates again the power of television in California politics."

Seemingly in an instant Van de Kamp had lost his mantle of inevitability as the Democratic nominee. Suddenly Feinstein was the front-runner. Panicked, the attorney general's team went into intensive meetings, described by one participant as "brutal," that began a four-month disintegration of his campaign into warring camps. His team of high-priced consultants feuded endlessly about the initiative strategy and how to respond to the woman many of them had been lulled into thinking they could ignore. Richard Ross, who had conceived the idea of using the initiatives to portray a cautious and colorless career politician as "the candidate of real change," wanted the attorney general to emphasize their positive message about his platform. Others insisted that Van de Kamp had to go on the attack against Feinstein or she would run away with the race.

That argument won out. A few weeks after Feinstein's announcement tour, Van de Kamp staged his own. While he talked about the initiatives, his kickoff was most notable as a three-day exercise in Feinstein-bashing. With the help of some powerful allies, including Mayor Art Agnos and Congresswoman Barbara Boxer, Van de Kamp assailed Feinstein on everything from abortion to budgets, from the environment to Ferdinand Marcos. He charged that her record showed she lacked political convictions beyond personal ambition and opportunism. "We can't let her become the symbol of change in the race," Ross said on Van de Kamp's campaign plane. "We're using her record to show people she's just another politician."

The Van de Kamp attacks marked a major shift that shaped the remainder of the 1990 campaign. As the first serious woman candidate for governor in California, Feinstein had become not only the front-runner but the central issue of the race. Both primary and general-election campaigns in effect became referenda on Feinstein, as her record, character, and finances were exposed to intense scrutiny. She complained to a reporter at one point that

> There's always, I feel, this testing of me, this testing, testing, testing. The first anything in a situation is put through a whole host of litmus tests. And you have a feeling, once you get there, that your back is always against the wall and people are coming at you.

Van de Kamp's stump attacks were just a warmup for what came next: a media assault on Feinstein's record fueled by several million dollars' worth of TV ads. But when the attorney general went on the air with his first negative spot, Feinstein was ready. The campaign had managed to obtain a copy of the spot before it aired. Carrick showed it to *Los Angeles Times* reporter Keith Love, who wrote a long piece about the spot that appeared the day the ad began running. The article included a "truth box" that critically examined specific attacks made in the ad, using pro-Feinstein background information about the issues hastily assembled by Hadley Roff.

The strategy successfully blunted the attack. Other major newspapers, including the *San Francisco Chronicle* and the *Sacramento Bee,* instantly followed the *Times*'s lead in running truth boxes that examined in detail Van de Kamp's claims about Feinstein's performance on issues such as the budget and pollution—and found many of the claims misleading, overblown, or based on incomplete information. Within two years, newspapers and television stations across America from the *New York Times* to ABC news would run such "ad watch" features as a regular part of their political coverage. In the 1990 campaign, the innovation turned the tables on Van de Kamp—making the attacks themselves, rather than their target, the focus of much critical reporting.

For Feinstein, the toughest hit to defend against was the budget deficit. With the assistance of Agnos, whose fiscal controller blamed Feinstein in print for "leaving us holding the bag," Van de Kamp hammered away at the $172 million budget crisis the new mayor faced. While she responded in great detail, the charge was simple to make but complicated to answer. Feinstein was placed in a defensive posture, uncomfortable for any politician, of explaining complex financial issues in short sound bites. After the primary, Wilson would pick up the issue and she would be forced to keep defending herself through November.

Another Van de Kamp line of attack also set the tone for the rest of the campaign: his criticism of Blum for pouring personal funds into Feinstein's campaign while failing to disclose detailed information about his business. When Feinstein was mayor, Blum, under local campaign laws, was required to disclose information only about business that he did within the city of San Francisco, which was minimal. But as a state elected official, she would be forced to disclose far more about his business, and Van de Kamp early in the year began raising questions about Blum's financial dealings.

Blum for months resisted releasing detailed financial information about his $400 million Richard C. Blum and Associates investment firm. Although Dianne and Dick called the scrutiny of Blum's business "sexist," the fact that he put $3 million into Feinstein's primary campaign alone, in addition to raising hundreds of thousands more from his network of business associates, raised legitimate questions about whether she would face conflicts of interest as governor, overseeing dozens of regulatory agencies, while he had lucrative investments in industries from agriculture to television stations. In the end, after first Van de Kamp and then Wilson kept questioning what the couple "had to hide," Blum released a complete list of his clients in the fall, which led to a series of investigative articles examining details of various business deals he had done since his marriage to Feinstein, a period when his business grew substantially.

The *Chronicle*'s David Dietz conducted an in-depth examination of the couple's financial records and found that, in the first year of their marriage, Feinstein as mayor had failed to report seven investments by Blum on her 1980 statement of economic interest. One of them was stock in the Marriott Corporation, the hotel company that was bidding for part of a $3 billion city redevelopment contract at the time. Blum sold the stock two months after they were married and Feinstein had no legal jurisdiction over the contact. After the story appeared, Blum and Feinstein said the failure to report the investments had been inadvertent and quickly amended her disclosure statements. There was no other appearance of improper dealings.

But the release of their personal tax returns did contain some political embarrassments. The returns showed, for example, that Feinstein and Blum paid no income tax in 1985, reporting a net loss of $112,985 just months after buying their $1.65 million home at 30 Presidio Terrace, across the street from where Dianne grew up. In the years that followed, their joint income grew substantially, to $7.4 million in 1989, when Blum's firm generated $6.7 million for him, including a $900,000 salary. The returns showed that, in 1989, Dianne spent twenty-seven days on the island of Kauai, paid $30,151 in credit-card and other personal interest, while the couple claimed $134,870 in losses on two vacation homes, at Lake Tahoe and on Kauai, that they rented out part of the year. They also took tax deductions for a Mercedes and a BMW. While Feinstein in the governor's race had cast herself as the voice of the middle class, it was clear that she enjoyed a luxurious lifestyle far beyond the means of "Mr. and Mrs. Working California," as she was fond of saying.

As the candidates headed for their state party convention in the spring, Feinstein held her lead. Van de Kamp, whose liberal views matched those of most Democratic party activists, made a bid to regain momentum at the convention, but Dianne stole the show. In her address to the convention she highlighted her support for the death penalty—a position that was consistent with the views of a majority of Californians but unpopular with the liberal delegates. "Sadly, today in California only a few feel safe or believe they are protected by a halting and decrepit system of justice," she said, quickly adding: "Yes, I support the death penalty—it is an issue that cannot be fudged or hedged."

As soon as she uttered the words "death penalty," delegates began a chorus of boos and jeers that cascaded throughout the convention center in Los Angeles. TV news coverage of the convention played up the spectacle of Feinstein being booed by her own party—which played right into her hands. "Bless you, bless you," media adviser Hank Morris said, standing at the press table as the Democrats railed at his candidate. "They booed, exactly as they were supposed to." Soon Morris and Carrick had produced a new thirty-second spot out of the episode, which had been duly recorded by a video crew hired for the occasion, and aired it to demonstrate Feinstein's toughness and independence. "In terms of the audience outside the convention, it was basically a defining moment because Dianne amplified the independence that is the strength of her candidacy," Carrick said later.

Feinstein stumbled only once before the primary, and it was a mistake instructive about her "historic" campaign for governor. Answering a question about abortion at a press conference after a debate with Van de Kamp,

Feinstein said that as governor she might sign legislation to outlaw "sex-selection" abortions in California. Such abortions, in which a woman terminates her pregnancy because she does not want a child the sex of the fetus, are all but unheard of in the United States. But anti-abortion groups use the specter of them as a rallying point for their cause. Abortion-rights groups fiercely oppose legislation to ban sex-selection abortions, not because they approve of the practice but on grounds that it might erode the basic right of women to choose to have an abortion.

Seemingly unaware of the nuances of the abortion debate, Feinstein had misstepped. Her statement upset pro-choice groups, particularly because she had long argued that as a woman she automatically was more trustworthy in protecting abortion rights than any man, no matter how pro-choice. Under pressure from abortion activists, Dianne soon retracted her statement, but it underscored the problems she had wrapping herself in the mantle of the women's movement.

Although Feinstein was a pioneering female politician, she had never been a movement feminist, which was why many prominent women Democrats supported Van de Kamp in the primary. "John Van de Kamp is the best feminist in this race," Congresswoman Barbara Boxer, who was closely identified with the liberal feminist movement, proclaimed during the primary as she ticked off examples in Feinstein's record when she stood against the cause. In past campaigns Feinstein had treated and spoken of issues of gender as essentially irrelevant: she was as tough as any man, could meet the same standards as men, and would ask no special favors for being a woman. As a politician she had never put "women's issues" such as abortion rights and equal pay for equal work at the top of her agenda, and in fact had taken several actions and made public comments that angered feminist groups.

The 1990 campaign represented the beginning of a sea change in American politics, the first year that being a woman began to turn from a liability to a major asset in a political campaign. The change was fueled in large part by the *Webster* decision on abortion and also by growing resentment of the political establishment, which had excluded women and thus implicitly defined them as outsiders.

While Feinstein now cast her campaign as a "historic" event for women, some other female politicians saw it differently. "Some of us who lived it every day just never saw her," Bay Area Assemblywoman Delaine Eastin said of Feinstein in 1990. "Frankly, women's groups all over the state invited

Dianne to speak thousands of times, but she never seemed to be available. Other people were just as busy, but they took the time to go the extra mile, to send money, to raise money, or to walk precincts."

Dianne bristled at the charge that she was not a good enough feminist. "The point is, I've lived it," she said. "I've been alone with a small child. I've been passed over in the lines. I had to leave a job when I was pregnant because there was no maternity leave. I worked when there was no child care available." Despite the criticisms of her, in the final days of the primary, independent polls showed her beating Van de Kamp by a huge margin among women and comfortably ahead among men.

Still mindful of the 1975 campaign, when she had saved money for a runoff election that she ended up missing, Feinstein refused to sit on her lead. Just before the vote, she let loose a barrage of TV attacks on Van de Kamp. She assailed his mishandling of the notorious Hillside Strangler murder case as district attorney of Los Angeles with two thirty-second spots that included pictures of police carrying one of the strangler's victims in a body bag. The ads earned her censure on some editorial pages, but they were the final nail in the coffin of erstwhile front-runner Van de Kamp.

On June 5, 1990, Dianne Feinstein made history again. Defeating her rival 52 to 41 percent, she became the first woman to win the gubernatorial nomination of a major political party in California.

Feinstein's smashing win, along with that of Democrat Ann Richards in the Texas governor's race, was the most potent evidence of political advances by women, as a record number of female candidates succeeded in 1990, including seven others who won nominations for governor. As the U.S. media trumpeted "the year of the woman" in politics, Dianne's story made headlines around the world, where she was viewed as a potential national leader.

"America's 'Iron Lady' Sets Course for the Top," ran a headline in the *Times* of London the weekend after the primary. Noting Dianne's "double death" platform of capital punishment and abortion rights, the *Times* described her as "an imposing six feet tall with nerves of steel, limitless ambition and a pragmatic willingness to do whatever is necessary to win."

America may last week have spotted its political future and it is female. Dianne Feinstein, a former San Francisco mayor who came from nowhere to win the Democratic candidacy for the governorship of California, now stands a good chance of becoming the first woman to occupy the Oval Office . . .

Her willpower and tougher-than-the-guys persona is reminiscent of the early Margaret Thatcher. Feinstein's "ballbuster" image helped her close the gender gap which traditionally has afflicted female politicians in America.

Then she ran into Pete Wilson.

RUNNING AGAINST PETE WILSON, one Feinstein consultant said later, was like trying to walk while someone "throws marbles in front of you." While Feinstein was basking in a media glow of network news shows and national magazine profiles, the grim reality of her political situation began to sink in: by all conventional measures of campaigns, she was in trouble, despite an early poll giving her a slight lead over Wilson. Physically exhausted and with her campaign broke, Feinstein had been hit with several million dollars' worth of negative advertising in the past six months. Her GOP opponent meanwhile was rested, had $3 million in the bank, and had spent several million dollars in his uncontested primary running glowing TV commercials that burnished his already positive image. Wilson, whose combination of fiscal conservatism and liberal views on issues like abortion and the environment matched the profile of California voters, was running his fourth statewide campaign, with a seasoned strategic team. Feinstein, running her first state race, had an energetic but small staff that was overworked and overstressed. And even with Blum's deep pockets, she still faced the unnerving process of having to raise the equivalent of $3,000 an hour every day until the November election if she was to meet her goal of $10 million.

The day after the primary, Wilson previewed an ad recalling how, as a senator, he had helped San Francisco obtain federal funds for many projects for which Feinstein took credit—including the cable car renovation, Fisherman's Wharf improvements, and the home porting of the battleship *Missouri.* Feinstein and Wilson, two moderate, good-government political careerists, had long enjoyed an alliance of convenience that Wilson now tried to exploit by ending his ad with a copy of a gushing thank-you letter that Dianne as mayor had sent to Wilson with the handwritten inscription: "You're wonderful." When reporters asked her about the ad, she demonstrated the new, sexual politics of 1990. "I guess men like to be told they're wonderful," she cracked.

Wilson's attacks grew heavier in a hurry. While Dianne retreated for two weeks of rest, he took advantage of the congressional summer recess to move aggressively around the state, hammering her about San Francisco's budget problems and Blum's finances. On the air, Wilson introduced a new ad aimed at tarnishing her "year of the woman" appeal, accusing her of advocating quotas for women and minorities.

Campaigning in the liberal Democratic primary, Feinstein had repeatedly promised to "gender balance" appointments to state government between women and men, and to appoint women and minorities "in parity to their proportion of the population," an explicit promise that the *Los Angeles Times* and other media had characterized as "quotas." Using such news reports in his ad, Wilson hammered away at the quota issue. Feinstein complained that he was "distorting" her views, but he was simply using her own words against her.

The ad was a damaging one: Feinstein's internal polls showed her dropping fifteen percentage points in the days after it went on the air, and losing support among two key groups—Republican women and blue-collar male voters. So Feinstein did what any sane politician would: she changed the subject. She responded with her own attack ad, assailing Wilson for his massive contributions from savings and loan operators, who in the wake of the national savings and loan scandal were almost automatically considered corrupt.

But the Wilson camp was ready. Their extensive "opposition research" operation had made a special study of Blum's business dealings. Now, Wilson counterpunched Feinstein's savings and loan attack with another new ad showing that Blum's firm had obtained an interest in a failing Oregon savings and loan and accusing the candidate of benefiting personally from the thrift scandal. Dianne and Dick screamed foul, as reporters were inundated with reams of faxed material about SEC reports and FSLIC insurance rates that each camp wanted them to use in trying to sort out the complex claims and counterclaims for their TV ad "truth boxes."

Politically, the details of the ads were not as important as the fact that Wilson had forced Feinstein to expend scarce resources on a summer-long air war of attrition. Just as important, the exchange showed Feinstein as just another politician engaged in mudslinging. Ever sensitive to criticism, Dianne had risen to the bait. "It demeaned her candidacy," Wilson said later. "A lot of bloom came off the rose." Said Feinstein: "The poll numbers showed we had to respond. We were concerned if we just saved our money, waiting for September, we would be fifteen points behind and we would not be able to come back in fund-raising."

As Labor Day marked the traditional start of the campaign, both Wilson and Feinstein turned to more substantive matters. She put forth a detailed platform, highlighting proposals on early childhood education and the environment. But with the invasion of Kuwait by Iraq, and a recession gripping California, the quality-of-life issues that had dominated the primary began to fade. Californians anxious about the future looked to more basic concerns, and Wilson's more conservative themes of taxes and crime resonated in an atmosphere where he looked like a less risky choice.

But in her first campaign since 1983, Feinstein carried over the self-confidence on the stump that she gained from the recall experience. She seemed to connect with people as individuals, and women in particular roared in approval at her speeches. She was also aided by the presence of Katherine, who after a period of estrangement from her mother now joined her on the road, traveling with the campaign. "The governor's race was the biggest turnaround for her as far as being a campaigner," said Jim Molinari, who had watched Feinstein for years and now took a leave of absence to help with the campaign.

In September Feinstein carried her campaign to the Central Valley, a Wilson stronghold. In the days before her visit, she drove her staff to distraction with demands for information about agricultural issues—and for a western-style outfit suitable for the trip. At one point, she dispatched an aide to Presidio Terrace to search her closet for a pair of boots for her to wear.

"Did you know Dianne is going to wear blue lizard-skin boots to the Valley on Sunday?" adviser Hope Warschaw, concerned about the message such a fashion statement might send to conservative voters, asked Carrick.

"I thought," he drawled, deadpan, "they were an endangered species."

In October the two candidates met in their only televised debate, and Wilson dominated the news coverage by endorsing term limits for state lawmakers. For her part, Feinstein triggered a strange controversy by writing notes on her hand. Nervous before the debate, she scrawled three words—growth, education, and choice—on her palm in blue marker to remind herself of the themes she wanted to sound. But this technically violated a predebate agreement barring the candidates from bringing notes into the studio. The writing was visible to reporters watching on monitors during the debate. Afterward, when one of them asked her what was on her hand, Feinstein nervously tried to hide it. "I'm not going to show you," she said, putting her hand behind her back and walking away. Her strange reaction fueled the story for several days, as one Los Angeles TV station ran blowups of the writing and Wilson's campaign paid for a computer-enhanced picture. It was a silly issue, but it helped Wilson's attempt to portray Feinstein as too much of an unknown to be governor.

In the days leading up to the election, Feinstein finally gained momentum as she hounded Wilson about missing important votes in the Senate while he was in California campaigning. When he missed a key vote on an abortion bill, she stepped up the attacks and he finally returned to Washington. During their debate she had taunted him about his absenteeism, promising to suspend her own campaigning if he went back. When he did, she promptly reneged on the promise.

Running out of money, Feinstein got a last gasp from a Democrat-appointed federal judge in Sacramento who threw out Proposition 73, California's voter-approved limit on campaign contributions. In the primary, Van de Kamp had benefited from a preliminary ruling in the case when he was allowed to use money collected in excess of the limits but collected before Proposition 73 went into effect. Then, Feinstein had complained about the judge's decision against contribution limits. Now she jumped on it, quickly raising millions from labor and other Democratic groups keenly interested in reapportionment who had been hamstrung by the initiative's $1,000 limit on donations.

The big-check, special-interest money poured in at such a rate that her campaign could not keep up with it. In their low-overhead operation, Feinstein and Blum had left the accounting to a volunteer, a decision that would backfire two years later when she was charged with violations of campaign disclosure laws. At the time, however, all that mattered was that the last-minute infusion of money kept her competitive with Wilson in the all-important TV air wars.

"This campaign has been like an Indiana Jones movie," remarked Dee Dee Myers. "A snake bites Dianne on the leg, alligators are about to eat her up, then she gets a court ruling and a favorable poll. There's a certain energy that comes from getting out of a tight situation."

Election night was wrenching. There were early hours of false hope when some network exit polls showed her winning by a narrow margin. As the vote count came in, she trailed Wilson slightly. As Tuesday turned into Wednesday, final returns showed that, with more than six million votes, they had split the election-day ballots and he had beaten her by 240,000 in absentee balloting, a margin of victory that resulted from a huge GOP organizational effort assembled while Feinstein was bogged down in her primary battle against Van de Kamp.

Dianne went home at 3:00 A.M., not having conceded defeat. That would come a few hours later at a packed press conference at the Fairmont Hotel. Gerry Braun, the political reporter who had broken the news to the Feinstein campaign about Clint Reilly quitting, began by asking Dianne if she was interested in running for the Senate in 1992. "My life has been public service," Feinstein responded with a big smile. "It's what I want to do; it's what I want to continue to do, one way or another." Less than twenty-four hours after her defeat at the polls, the ovation from her supporters was thunderous.

15

DECADE OF THE WOMAN

Dianne's not one of the boys, but she's not
one of the girls, either.

—*Marcia Smolens, former campaign aide to Dianne Feinstein*

IN APRIL 1992, SEVENTEEN MONTHS after her loss to Pete Wilson, Dianne walked to the podium of the state Democratic convention in Los Angeles and received a loud ovation. "I'm Dianne Feinstein," she began her speech, "I am woman." The roar that greeted her opening statement was huge. Delegates, some of whom had booed Feinstein as a candidate for governor two years before, now cheered her as the party's best hope of capturing a U.S. Senate seat—and as the most visible emblem of what once again was being trumpeted as "the year of the woman in politics."

This time, the hyperbole seemed justified. Since her failed 1990 gubernatorial bid, many things had changed across America's political landscape. Gender had become a driving issue in campaigns around the country, as a series of court decisions eroding abortion rights kindled feminist political involvement by women at the same time that new organizations, notably a group called Emily's List, began raising large amounts of money for women candidates. The turning point came in October 1991 when the nation was transfixed by a real-life televised drama played out in a U.S. Senate committee room where law professor Anita Hill testified that Supreme Court nominee Clarence Thomas had subjected her to sexual harassment when she worked for him in Washington.

The Thomas-Hill hearings had a profound effect on the politics of 1992, galvanizing the outrage of women throughout the nation. "No matter what is said, there is a humiliation that a woman feels that a man doesn't feel at all about these things," said Feinstein, watching from California as the dramatic hearings unfolded before the Senate Judiciary Committee. "There is no question that if the Judiciary Committee had women on it, the whole issue [of Thomas's nomination] would not have moved until it was explored fully." Feinstein by then was gearing up her own campaign for the Senate. It was the first campaign in her career that would resonate with feminist themes, both in rhetoric and in substance. "Up until this election being a woman has not been an asset," she said, adding that in 1992 "Women have become symbols of change."

Feinstein cast her 1990 campaign for governor as a "historic" step for women. But consistent with the approach she had taken since her days in San Francisco politics, gender appeal was based largely on the notion that her personal advancement would serve as a symbolic marker to promote the political, social, and economic equality of all women. In 1992, by contrast, Feinstein connected her goal of attaining higher office with the language and policy agenda of "women's issues" in the economy, health care, and the workplace, including pay equity, women's health research, sexual harassment, and increased educational and career opportunities. "The women's agenda is becoming the American agenda," she declared in an interview early in the campaign. "Child care and family leave aren't social niceties, they're economic necessities. And there's been an enormous resurgence of women in all kinds of efforts to shatter the glass ceiling."

Building on the momentum and exposure she had gained in 1990, Feinstein in 1992 steamrolled a little-known Republican. Her victory was most memorable and significant, however, as part of a breakthrough year for women candidates. As record numbers of women were elected to state legislatures and the Congress, California voters sent not one, but two women to represent them in the Senate, the first state ever to do so in American history.

Representative Barbara Boxer was a movement feminist and a former political enemy of Feinstein's who had attacked her in 1990 for her record on women's issues. Putting aside past differences, however, the heavily favored Feinstein helped pull Boxer across the finish line in the closing weeks of her close race for the other Senate seat.

"Dianne came in as I started to sink in the polls, just at that period when I was in free fall," Boxer recalled more than a year later. "We were campaigning together in Los Angeles on a bus. She said at the time, Dick did too, 'Look, we're doing great. If we have people who want to donate to us, we're going to tell them, Help Barbara.' But more than donating the money it was her willingness to stand next to me, literally. It sent a very powerful message. The women were just so proud. It was a big message to the women across the country."

AFTER HER NARROW 1990 loss to Wilson, Feinstein retreated to the spacious house at Stinson Beach, north of San Francisco, that she and Blum had bought when they sold Pajaro Dunes several years before. As she had in 1975, Feinstein replayed details of the just-completed campaign, going over and over what could have been done differently to eke out a victory in the governor's race.

Almost unanimously, friends and advisers told her that she was, in many ways, lucky to have lost because she would bear no responsibility for a growing list of intractable problems that were changing the California dream into a nightmare. Soon after the election the state began an extended decline into deep recession, and Sacramento was overwhelmed with massive budget deficits. These, combined with an almost biblical series of disasters—fires, earthquakes, agricultural pests, and urban riots among them—inflicted serious political damage on Wilson almost from the day he took office.

Feinstein didn't see any silver lining. After coming so close to an unlikely, upset victory, her defeat tasted as bitter as any she had suffered in the past. "She was really moping around," said the Reverend Cecil Williams, who spent time with Feinstein after the defeat. "The loss was eating her up and she was talking about getting out of politics. Then she said, 'I can't give this up—it's become a part of me.'"

The day after the 1990 election, longtime Democratic senator Alan Cranston, enmeshed in the savings and loan scandal and afflicted with cancer, announced that he would not run again when his term ended in 1992. That meant that there would be two wide-open Senate races that year, an unprecedented situation. Cranston's retirement predictably drew crowded fields from both parties running for the open seat. Two months after Cranston's announcement, Wilson had appointed John Seymour, an obscure state legislator from Orange County, to Wilson's vacated seat in the U.S. Senate. Seymour was required by law also to face voters in 1992, merely for the right to complete the six-year term Wilson had won in 1988.

The governor's pick for the Senate was hardly a dominating politician likely to scare off competition. John Seymour was a short, rotund state senator whose foremost qualification was that he was personally loyal to Pete

Wilson and a political clone of the governor—a former Marine, conservative on fiscal issues, more liberal on social ones. The former mayor of Anaheim, home of Disneyland, Seymour made it a point always to wear a Mickey Mouse watch. Republican conservatives, unhappy about the abrupt switch in position he had made on abortion just before a failed campaign for lieutenant governor—becoming pro-choice after a longtime fierce opposition to abortion rights—thought that was appropriate.

Wilson's selection of Seymour was met with disbelief by politicians in both parties, who immediately perceived the new senator as seriously vulnerable. "He's a wounded white male who was beaten for lieutenant governor," said Republican congressman Bob Dornan in a typical comment from the GOP's right wing. "Believe me, it's going to be a mess." Bill Carrick, Feinstein's chief political strategist, tried to contain his glee with understatement: "I'm hard-pressed to see his strengths," he said.

Dianne and Dick were vacationing on Kauai when they heard of Wilson's selection, and it speeded up her political calculations. Although she had clearly signaled her desire to run for the Senate the day after she lost the governor's race, Feinstein had expected to have several months to think it through. Now, between Cranston's unexpected announcement and the surprise selection of Seymour, things were moving very quickly. New Senate candidates were popping up every day, trying to get their names into the early mix of speculation and gossip that is of slight interest to most voters but crucial to the network of political donors and cognoscenti whose opinions—and dollars—often shape a race. Typical was Barbara Boxer, a five-term House member representing part of San Francisco and Marin County, who declared her Senate candidacy shortly after Cranston's statement simply by calling *Chronicle* political writer Susan Yoachum and informing her that she planned to run.

Feinstein was convinced that, building on her 1990 performance, she could certainly win a statewide race if she could avoid the kind of bruising primary she had fought against Van de Kamp, as Wilson did in saving his money and energy in the governor's race for the general election. As a political matter, Cranston's open seat was a more attractive prize, since it had no incumbent and offered a full six-year term. The other seat would have an incumbent—and even though Seymour was now seen as weak, he still had two years before the election to build a reputation. It also offered only the last two years of Wilson's term. This meant that, even if she won in 1992,

Feinstein would have to turn around and run again in 1994 for a six-year term, which would be her third statewide race in six years.

As she huddled with Blum, Carrick, Morris, and Garrett, the decision of which seat to run for was largely shaped by her desire to avoid a primary. She also did not want to face either her ally Leo McCarthy, who had told her privately that he would seek Cranston's seat, or Boxer, also running in that race, because Dianne believed it "would be destructive" for two women to oppose each other. Both because it was perceived as the less desirable seat and because Dianne was seen as the most formidable Senate candidate, chances were good that she could clear the Democratic field by going for the Seymour seat.

On January 11, just one week after Seymour's appointment, a top adviser leaked word to the *Chronicle* that Feinstein would enter that race, a clear message to potential Democratic foes to stay out. "I feel that we Democrats tend to destroy each other, and that's a tragedy of our party," she said over lunch a few weeks later. "People were saying I was the six-hundred-pound gorilla in the Senate races, so I thought I'd pick the more difficult race in hopes I could discourage primary opposition." Within a month, Mervin Field's California Poll would show that most voters in the state had never heard of John Seymour. In a simulated early matchup, Feinstein at that point led him 46 to 41 percent. That was as close as Seymour ever got.

FOR A TIME IT SEEMED that Feinstein's bid to clear the primary field with her surprising early move would work. Most of the other Democratic contenders, including Boxer, McCarthy, and Los Angeles representative Mel Levine, soon made it clear that they were running for the six-year seat.

As Feinstein quietly began reassembling a statewide organization, she attended the 1991 Democratic state convention, where she reprised her performance at the 1990 party gathering, this time over the issue of the Persian Gulf war. Most other Democratic Senate hopefuls spent the weekend attacking President Bush's military actions in Kuwait. But Feinstein congratulated the president for his performance and publicly rebuked delegates, saying the party was "out of synch" with America for not displaying yellow ribbons and other symbols of patriotic support for the U.S. effort against Saddam Hussein.

"In 1990, it was part of a strategy," a top adviser said of her confrontation with her own party over the death penalty during the governor's race.

"Today, she was just being Dianne." While she was not booed as she was in 1990, Feinstein's criticism of Democrats, delivered at a women's breakfast, was met with stone silence. And before long, her bid to avoid a primary fight failed, as she drew a Democratic opponent who said he better represented the ideals of the party.

Gray Davis was a young and extremely ambitious politician, a prodigious fund-raiser who had been chief of staff to former governor Jerry Brown before winning election on his own, first to the legislature and then as state controller. In launching an uphill battle against Feinstein, he seemed to be recycling the strategy that John Van de Kamp had tried and that had failed against her in 1990. Portraying her as a closet Republican, he trumpeted his support from labor and other liberal interest groups—and cast himself as the best feminist in the race. "Dianne Feinstein is a Johnny-come-lately to women's issues," Davis proclaimed. "Now she's finally got the message and that's fine. But I've been there all along."

About 56 percent of Democratic primary voters in California are female, and Davis's gambit was an attempt to siphon off support from liberal, activist women, a group that had clashed in the past with Feinstein, who "never was, and never will be a banner carrier," as longtime aide Hadley Roff put it. Feinstein's political problems with the liberal feminist wing of the party dated back to her earliest days in local politics and grew through much of her tenure as mayor of San Francisco.

Marcia Smolens, a strategist in Feinstein's campaigns in the 1970s, was one of the founders of the National Women's Political Caucus and active in many feminist organizations. She had often represented Feinstein in appearances before women's groups in San Francisco and recalled the disdain that many of the women she met felt toward Dianne, as when the local chapter of the National Organization for Women endorsed George Moscone in the 1975 race for mayor. Said Smolens:

> Activist left women hated Dianne and I was continuously attacked for supporting her. I thought she was the best qualified, most articulate, most knowledgeable candidate, and that the National Women's Political Caucus agenda could be accomplished with her over time.
>
> But with feminists, as with other groups, Dianne was never what people wanted her to be. The woman's community wanted Dianne to take the torch and be the leader. But there were other things on her

plate. She did not see gender as an issue. She was not aware. She did not think she was held back because she was a woman.

Part of Feinstein's differences with some women's organizations derived from a philosophical difference about what defined feminism. To Feinstein it meant proving herself as an individual to be the equal of any man; to many feminists it also meant that female politicians bore special responsibilities to advance the careers of others like them and to steer public policy in the direction of an ideological "women's agenda."

"I've tried to live my beliefs as a feminist," she said a few months after she became mayor in 1979. "You have to do your apprenticeship. You get nothing because you are a woman. You just ask for the equal opportunity to be able to do the job." Those close to her said that Feinstein was hurt, and did not truly understand, the criticism she received from feminists over the years. Her sister Yvonne said that Dianne reacted to obstacles based on gender in the same way that their father treated barriers he encountered to his career because he was a Jew. "When doors were closed, both of their attitudes were, 'Like hell I can't do it,'" Yvonne said. "I don't think Dianne was ever aware of the drawbacks of being a woman."

Katherine said that as she was growing up, her mother never communicated to her the notion that she would face difficulties doing what she wanted to do because of sexism:

> I don't think she ever came home and said, "Gee, it's hard for a woman." I didn't realize there were any obstacles out there for women. I had no idea.
>
> There was no need for a feminist philosophy. My mother never stopped to think that she couldn't do something. She wanted to be part of the game. You didn't have to change the rules. Just be a strong and skilled individual, work hard, do your homework, and you can do it.

BEYOND PHILOSOPHY, the feminist critique of Feinstein in her years as a local official rested on specific issues and controversies in which she squared off against activists in the women's movement.

As a supervisor and mayor, Feinstein advanced the cause of equality for women simply by virtue of her longtime visibility and steadfast success. In the wake of Feinstein's many "first-woman" breakthroughs, others quickly advanced in politics and, by the 1980s, many of San Francisco's top elected offices were held by women.

An early supporter of the Equal Rights Amendment, Feinstein championed the issue of child care, as when the Downtown Plan required developers to pay fees that were set aside for child-care programs. She expanded the number and duties of women officers in the police department during her tenure. She also appointed women to prominent jobs—most notably Louise Renne, Treasurer Mary Callahan, and Supervisor Willie Kennedy—when she had the chance.

But Feinstein's inner circle of top advisers was exclusively male. And, overall, the nine years of her mayoralty did not result in significantly higher numbers of women appointed to posts in city government. In 1979, the year that she took over as mayor, 67.6 percent of mayoral appointments to boards and commissions were male and 32.4 percent were female; in 1988, the year that she left office, the numbers had barely changed—65 percent male, 35 percent female, according to city government directories. "She wasn't against women," said journalist Carol Pogash, who covered Feinstein extensively. "But you never got the sense that she was looking out for other women."

The paradoxes of Feinstein's politics marked her record with actions and statements, some symbolic, some substantive, in which fiscal conservatism conflicted with feminism, or when her notions of good government clashed with the agenda of the women's movement. In 1971, for example, the woman who later would proclaim that she was "always pro-choice" cast the deciding vote against a request by the Women's National Abortion Coalition for a routine street closing to stage an abortion-rights rally in front of City Hall. Voting with the conservative wing of the board, including archenemy John Barbagelata, she told reporters she was persuaded by a police captain who said the size of the Saturday rally would not justify the street closing. "I'm in favor of liberalized abortion laws, but I agree with the police," she said at the time. The vote marked "the first time in years that a valid request for the use of a street in front of City Hall for a rally was rejected," the *Chronicle* reported.

As mayor in 1983, she again snubbed abortion-rights advocates when she refused to sign an official resolution, supported by Planned Parenthood, NOW, and the California Abortion Rights Action League, proclaiming a

"Women's Reproductive Freedom Day" in San Francisco to mark the tenth anniversary of the Supreme Court's *Roe v. Wade* decision legalizing abortion. The symbolic proclamation, approved by the board of supervisors, was intended to "raise public awareness" of the abortion-rights issue, but Mayor Feinstein refused to endorse it, saying it would be "divisive." Years later, while running for statewide office, she would pointedly recant her action.

In March 1984 Mayor Feinstein praised the ruling of a federal judge who said that women who take maternity leaves are not entitled to return to their old jobs. In the case, United States District Court Judge Manuel Real overturned a California law that required employers to grant up to four months of unpaid maternity leave and then reinstate the women to the same or similar jobs upon their return. Asked to comment on the ruling at the time, she told the *New York Times:*

> What we women have been saying all along is we want to be treated equally. Now we have to put our money where our mouth is. What we were asking was to create a special group of workers that in essence is pregnant women and new mothers. I just don't happen to agree with that. I believe that women have the choice. If they make the choice for career and children, there is no question there are problems. But I don't think the work market has to accommodate itself to women having children.

At a time when she was being prominently mentioned as a possible Democratic vice-presidential candidate, Feinstein retracted the statement the day it appeared in print, saying that she had misunderstood a reporter's question. In her retraction she said she supported "reasonable maternity leaves" and the right of a woman to return to "a comparable job—but not necessarily the same job" after having a child.

Eight years later, Feinstein as a U.S. senator shifted her position in voting for the 1993 Family and Medical Leave Act, which among other things requires employers to grant up to twelve weeks of leave to workers to care for a newborn or newly adopted child. In remarks on the Senate floor, Dianne applauded the fact that "we have an opportunity, finally, to allow a mother to keep her job to give birth to a child."

On another economic issue, Mayor Feinstein feuded for several years with women's advocates and organizations over "comparable worth"—pay equity for female city employees. In the controversy, union leaders and liberal

supervisors led by Harry Britt promoted legislation to pay women and minorities, traditionally clustered in lower-paying jobs, at rates closer to those
of white males in jobs requiring similar skills. Beginning in 1985, Feinstein
vetoed pay-equity plans approved by the supervisors three different times,
including one program to award the targeted group a $5-a-day meal al-
lowance as extra compensation. While insisting that she endorsed the principle of comparable worth, the mayor criticized the legislation approved by
the supervisors as poorly drafted, as "phony" pay equity, and as too costly for
cash-strapped San Francisco. When the supervisors dealt Feinstein a rare
veto override on the $5-meal-allowance plan, she responded by submitting
the issue to the voters, who overwhelmingly approved her stand. A compromise between the mayor and the board was finally reached in 1986, but the
long fight left bitter scars. Sharon Johnson, a legislative aide to Harry Britt
who led the comparable-worth fight and later became executive director of
the city's Commission on the Status of Women, said when Feinstein ran for
governor, "She never understood what it's like to make $17,000 a year and
to have to provide clothing and health care for your children on that kind of
salary."

Confronted with specific criticisms of her mayoral record brought by
feminists, Feinstein replied that she put the interests of the whole city ahead
of specific groups. She also complained that women tended to be the harshest critics of women politicians, a refrain she sounded from her earliest campaigns. In 1990 Feinstein objected that her contribution to the women's
movement was distorted by feminists who pointed to individual actions
rather than examining her record as a whole. "We women can sometimes be
our own worst enemy because we tend to be so scrutinizing of others," she
said in a speech to a women's business association. "The question is, Will
women really vote for another woman, or put them through a litmus test to
find that one issue that gives them an opportunity to opt out?"

A few weeks later she delivered an address to the San Francisco chapter of
Queen's Bench, a professional organization for women working in the law. In
her speech, called "Women in the Nineties: What Will the Future Bring?"
she predicted that Americans would elect a woman to the presidency in the
1990s. The speech provided a distillation of her views on feminism:

> The future of women's rights to a great extent rests with women.
> Today, we are the majority of votes in most elections.

But our ability to control and direct a single agenda remains questionable. But there is one thing I do believe: women do open doors for other women. One woman's successful first achievement in any area opens the door forever for all those other women who will follow.

FOR FEINSTEIN, THERE WERE several major changes in the terrain of sexual politics in California by 1992. Her campaign for governor for the first time had made her a beneficiary of the passion and power of the national women's movement which, in her race against Pete Wilson, had united behind her. She not only gained politically but also was moved personally, and after the race made a conscientious effort to thank women and organizations who had helped her and to mend fences with those who had criticized her in the past.

"Dianne has really reached out to those of us who made that criticism and she now has a connectedness with women in politics and women in business," Delaine Eastin, a Democratic state lawmaker who in 1990 had accused Feinstein of opportunism, said in 1992. "The so-called women's issues are much more of a centerpiece of her campaign."

Barbara Boxer, who had called Feinstein's male opponent in the Democratic primary "the best feminist in the race," said that, "in my opinion, Dianne was changed dramatically [when] she was in the governor's race and she saw the women come flocking to her campaign, when she saw their hopes and dreams reflected in her and through her. It made her far more aware that the problems that women have faced really have been systematic. I think she began to see what she represented and the real problems that women have faced as a group, as opposed to individuals. I think that changed her and I think that made her into a feminist. I don't think she was before."

Presented with such comments, Feinstein herself, however, said that, "I'm not sure I've changed—the opportunity has changed a lot. As mayor, my hands were full just managing and administering and advocacy sort of took a back bench during that nine years. When you run statewide, and also when you run for a legislative seat, you're really running on broader public policy than when you run for mayor. Have I associated more with the women's movement since [the governor's race]? Yes, absolutely, no question. Because it's now part of what I'm doing."

The fusion of Feinstein's brand of feminism—electing more women to more and higher offices—and that of more liberal activists—advancing an agenda of women's issues—took place in 1992 largely because of the shockwaves of the Clarence Thomas–Anita Hill affair. "The whole episode gave new meaning to the term *gender gap*," Nancy Pelosi, the congresswoman from San Francisco and a Feinstein ally, said at the time. "The gap of understanding between men and women turned the Capitol into a Tower of Babel, with women and men apparently talking different languages." As "I Believe You, Anita" bumper stickers appeared across the nation, women's political organizations reported huge surges in membership and activity. None prospered more than Emily's List—the "Emily" in the name stands for "Early Money Is Like Yeast"—a group that formed in 1985 to provide start-up funds to Democratic women who both backed abortion rights and were seen as politically viable candidates. In 1992 Emily's List raised $6.2 million in sixty-three thousand separate contributions to fifty-five candidates, including substantial sums to Feinstein and Boxer. This total made it the largest single donor to House and Senate races, outdistancing the National Association of Realtors.

Across the nation, momentum and excitement grew behind a record number of women candidates for offices at every level. In California, where two women vied simultaneously for election to the U.S. Senate, the super-charged atmosphere of gender politics overwhelmed Gray Davis. "It's identical to Van de Kamp," sniffed Feinstein, when Davis began to criticize her on feminist issues. "I'm not concerned about it, because we went through this once before."

In 1990 John Van de Kamp succeeded in denying Feinstein key endorsements from leading women's organizations, and in embarrassing her with support from prominent female politicians, even though she trounced him at the polls among women voters. But in the 1992 Senate race, Davis's attempt to attract female voters to his campaign by attacking Feinstein's record on feminism was even less successful than Van de Kamp's.

As Feinstein campaigned on a platform that linked economic recovery to women's issues, and ran consistently ahead in polls, money, and organization, Davis got one big chance to make a run at her. On April 1, California's Fair Political Practices Commission, the state's political watchdog agency, filed a civil lawsuit charging Feinstein with multiple violations of campaign finance laws for misreporting $8.3 million worth of transactions in her $20 million campaign for governor in 1990. "The amount of money that went unreported in this case is unprecedented in the history of this agency," the FPPC's chairman said in announcing the suit. "By failing to report such a huge amount of money, Feinstein kept the voters from knowing the true sources and uses of her campaign funds."

The Feinstein camp admitted that "incredible and stupid accounting mistakes were made" in the governor's race campaign reports, particularly in misreporting $3 million in personal loans taken by Feinstein and Blum and in disclosure statements on the flurry of big checks that came into the campaign following the court ruling throwing out the state's contribution limit. Feinstein blamed the errors on a volunteer bookkeeper.

Davis jumped on the FPPC lawsuit, saying that it illustrated both poor management by Feinstein and her lack of understanding of ordinary people. It "speaks to Dianne's competence in handling money and her commitment to abide by laws she seems to think apply only to other people," he said.

"I think the race is over," Davis crowed in April. "There is no way the largest campaign violator in California history can receive the endorsement of voters." Then he went one step too far. Overreaching, he began comparing Feinstein to Leona Helmsley, the New York hotel queen who had been convicted on tax charges and was serving time in a federal prison. Several weeks after referring to Feinstein as "the Leona Helmsley of American politics" in public comments, Davis began airing a thirty-second spot comparing the civil charges against Feinstein with the criminal conviction of Helmsley. "Helmsley blames her servants for the felony; Feinstein blames her staff for the lawsuit," the spot's announcer said, over juxtaposed pictures of the two women. "Helmsley is in jail; Feinstein wants to be a senator."

The statewide political reaction to the ad was swift and angry. California news organizations, which had begun watchdogging TV ads during Feinstein's race for governor, hit Davis with a barrage of unbridled criticism. The *Sacramento Bee* labeled the spot "a new low" in negative advertising, while the *Chronicle* in a truth box called it a "gross distortion." In an on-the-air commentary, analyst Rollin Post of KRON-TV said the only thing that Feinstein and Helmsley had in common was that they were both rich and both Jewish.

Democratic women, whom Davis had set out to win away from Feinstein, were incensed. When he appeared on the podium at a "Democratic Unity" dinner with other statewide contenders at San Francisco's Fairmont Hotel just before the election, he was loudly booed.

After eight months of legal negotiations, the FPPC hit Feinstein with a $190,000 fine, the second-largest such penalty in California history, for the 1990 reporting violations. But the issue did nothing to damage her standing among voters. In the June primary, she beat Davis in a landslide.

The Year of the Woman was only half over.

WHILE FEINSTEIN'S PRIMARY VICTORY was expected, Barbara Boxer's was not. No candidate in America benefited more from the fallout of the Clarence Thomas hearings, and the energy that it created for women candidates, than Boxer, who began her race as the longest of long shots. Besides the fact that she was a liberal feminist crusader, little known outside her wealthy Marin County district, Boxer bore the added burden of trying to be elected at the same time as Feinstein. The chances of California voters sending to the U.S. Senate two Democratic Jewish mothers from the liberal San Francisco Bay Area were so long as to defy odds makers.

Anita Hill changed all the odds. When the affair began unfolding on Capitol Hill, Boxer was squarely in the middle of the action. With six women House colleagues, she marched on the Senate to demand that a vote on Thomas's confirmation be delayed until Hill's charges were fully investigated. When the women were denied entrance to the Senate, the moment was captured by news cameras—providing instant and vivid evidence for the argument they had come to make. "This really has riveted the nation's attention on the Senate, which is so out of touch as an institution," Boxer declared. "It's not whether the allegations are true or false, but the fact that the Senate, with ninety-eight men out of one hundred members didn't see this as a gut issue." From that moment on, her campaign caught fire.

Leo McCarthy, the veteran Democratic politician who had held a commanding lead in the primary for Cranston's seat, said the media coverage of the year of the woman—highlighted by the chance that California would elect two women senators—hit his campaign "like a hydrogen bomb."

It was almost like a holy mission. The "year of the woman" was
the single driving factor in the race. Every two years, we had heard
the same kind of buildup but the Clarence Thomas hearing magnified
it to five times as important. The women's fund-raising groups were
a decisive factor. And the geometric progress in the media coverage
absolutely killed us.

As national and state reporters raced after Feinstein and Boxer, San Francisco political observers were intrigued by how they would act toward each other after the primary. They had been political enemies, with Boxer a member of the liberal Burton wing of the local Democratic party, which had little use for Feinstein's "centrist" brand of politics. In 1982 John Burton had abruptly quit the House and Boxer, a former Burton aide and a Marin County supervisor, entered the special-election race to succeed him. In the decisive and bitter primary in the overwhelmingly Democratic district, Feinstein strongly backed her friend and ally Louise Renne. Boxer crushed Renne, dealing a blow to Mayor Feinstein's prestige, and was elected to the House five times.

A member of the hardball school of politics as practiced by the Burtons, Boxer in 1990 delivered some payback to Feinstein. She strongly endorsed Van de Kamp while assailing Feinstein's record on abortion, comparable worth, and other women's issues. As late as early 1992 there were rumors, floated by the Boxer camp, that she might challenge Feinstein for the Democratic nomination and the right to take on Seymour. In those days, during the Gulf War, this scenario was promptly dubbed "the mother of all political battles."

But they ran, and won, in separate races. The day after the June primary, Feinstein and Boxer not only embraced but campaigned together. In an emotional tour of the state, they were wildly cheered by large Democratic crowds. Even discounting their past political disputes, they were an unlikely pair—Feinstein, tall, moderate, and regal; Boxer, short, liberal, and feisty. Campaign reporters tagged them "Thelma and Louise."

WHILE FEINSTEIN HAD LONG KNOWN that her Republican opponent would be Seymour, Boxer was surprised when Bruce Herschensohn, a conservative Los Angeles television commentator, upset moderate GOP congressman Tom Campbell in her race. Because many of Herschensohn's right-wing policy positions were in sharp contrast to the views of most Californians—on abortion and environmental protection, for example—Boxer's camp quickly grew confident enough to send a message to Dianne that Barbara was prepared to help in any way she could against Seymour, who was perceived to be a tougher opponent.

But Seymour never had a chance.

Unlike in the governor's race, where she had gotten off to a stumbling start and then thrown together a campaign on the run, Feinstein systematically had been laying the groundwork for her Senate race for over a year. With her 1990 lists, she consolidated and expanded the fund-raising base she had built with continued help from Blum and his contacts in the financial world. Hank Morris and Bill Carrick again produced her media advertising. Carrick had been forced to seek medical attention for soaring blood pressure in the closing days of the governor's race, as he tried to do jobs ordinarily done by three people in statewide campaigns, and had since convinced Dianne to hire a new day-to-day manager.

His recommendation was Kam Kuwata, a well-respected former aide to Cranston. With the patience of a buddha, Kuwata had a personality that could handle Dianne's volatile moods, despite episodic moments of his own high blood pressure. Under his strategic plan, Feinstein with little notice in 1991 and early 1992 visited key, swing areas of the state where she only rarely campaigned in 1990, like San Bernardino and Riverside counties, moderate suburban areas where turnout was high and California's recent growth had been concentrated.

Although she attracted little notice from major media outlets, she got plenty of local publicity—and was able to use what had become one of her best assets, her much-improved style on the stump. Feinstein had begun her political career as a stiff and distant campaigner who came across better on television than in person and seemed more comfortable reciting statistics from a policy study than exposing her emotions to strangers in a hotel ballroom. But the traumas and triumphs of the past two decades had transformed her into an engaging campaigner who not only lit up a room with her stylish appearance but also made personal connections to voters.

"Living through the incredible things she did, she really worked through some stuff," said her friend Cecil Williams. "After she lost the governorship, I'd seen her really open up. She told me, 'I'm feeling different about myself.' She really feels she can make things happen that will create some kind of family or community for people."

THE DIFFERENCE BETWEEN the Feinstein and the Seymour campaigns was most clearly illustrated by the performance of each candidate at their national convention. At the Democratic affair in New York in mid-July, Feinstein made a high-profile speech, part of a prime-time package featuring herself, Boxer, and four other Democratic women Senate candidates designed to highlight the party's message of change. On the convention floor at

Madison Square Garden, Feinstein sat calmly in a delegate's chair next to Blum, until she rose to speak and was mobbed by supporters. "We're women and men standing together for change," she declared to deafening cheers. "The status quo must go."

A month later at the GOP convention in Houston, Seymour received a very different reception. Trying to borrow a page from Feinstein's political book, he defiantly declared his belief in abortion rights, as recent as it was, at a convention that passed an anti-abortion platform and was dominated by members of the religious right. But his speech, delivered in the middle of the afternoon, was scarcely noticed at all, and drew only a few boos over the din of delegates discussing where to go to dinner.

Although the nominal incumbent, Seymour was a big underdog to Feinstein. And, if it had not been clear before, his brief convention speech left little doubt that he would not overcome that status by campaigning on the issue of abortion rights. Over the next two and a half months, Seymour used the only strategy open to him—attack. He attacked Feinstein for the $8.3 million FPPC lawsuit. He attacked over Dick Blum's finances and possible conflicts of interest she might face in casting votes in the Senate. He attacked her on quotas, San Francisco's budget problems, flip-flops in her record, and her call for big defense cuts, which he said would cripple California's economy.

His harshest attacks came on the issue of crime. As Seymour campaign operatives pored through Feinstein's thirty-year-old record as a women's prison board member, they found, among the five thousand cases she had heard, that she had voted to release twenty-one murderers on parole, including some who had committed crimes of a most gruesome nature.

One was a woman named Violet John Berling, a Long Beach accordion teacher who was convicted in 1953 of the sadistic sexual torture-murder of a ten-year-old girl in her legal custody. When police found the little girl, strangled and strapped to a chair in Berling's home, the woman told them that the child thought she had occult powers and was in the habit of putting herself in a trance and inflicting injuries upon her body, then healing them.

Berling was convicted of second-degree murder, which carried a term of between five years and life imprisonment. When she came before the board for a parole hearing in 1964, having served just eleven years, Dianne and her colleagues voted to parole her under the indeterminate-sentence system, which was later changed to a fixed-term system.

In 1990 Dianne had campaigned on a platform of returning the state to the indeterminate-sentencing system, arguing that many violent criminals were not serving enough time under the determinate-sentencing rules. Although instituted as part of a get-tough-on-crime movement, the system in practice allowed felons to reduce their sentences for good behavior or participation in work programs. It also allowed the release of some notorious repeat felons, who might have been kept in prison longer under indeterminate-sentence terms. Feinstein had argued that indeterminate sentencing would make for longer prison terms.

But in 1992, Seymour used the Berling and other murder cases to charge Feinstein with "double-talk" on the issue. Although prison records showed that Berling was released from parole without further incident in 1974, Seymour insisted that, "When you look at the horrible nature of these crimes, there is no question that someone who is truly tough on crime would have voted to deny parole" in such cases.

Asked about the sentencing controversy, Feinstein said that "There are always going to be some mistakes made. But the human dimension of making decisions, of evaluating cases, is out of it now and I think that is a mistake. Now, is everybody always going to be right all of the time under the indeterminate system? No. And it's a damn hard job to have to cope with all of the variables that go into sentencing, and you can make terrible mistakes. But the determinate sentence has effectively eliminated any individual of responsibility. No one is responsible now—the system's responsible."

The political dispute over sentencing rules took on a terrifying reality in 1993, after the kidnapping and murder of thirteen-year-old Polly Klaas in Petaluma. The child's accused killer, Richard Allen Davis, might not have been released from prison under indeterminate sentencing, Feinstein argued, while officials under the determinate-sentence rules had no choice but to release the repeat offender. The Klaas killing set off a grass-roots movement in California for a "Three Strikes, You're Out" initiative, in which those convicted of three felonies would face life imprisonment without the possibility of parole.

But in 1992 Seymour's charges against Feinstein's parole board record made no more difference than any of the other attacks he raised. Beyond the discouraging independent California Polls, Seymour's own internal surveys showed him losing in every major media market in the state—except

Orange County, the birthplace of California Republican conservatism, where Feinstein was merely running neck and neck with him.

Seymour did not help matters with several of his own gaffes. At one point, he was asked his advice for middle-class families hurt by the recession: "Sometimes, you lose your job, maybe you've got to sell your boat to keep the family going," he replied. His biggest problem, however, was that shortly after Labor Day President Bush and the national Republican campaign simply abandoned California, ceding its fifty-four electoral votes to Bill Clinton and the Democrats. Seymour swam upstream against an electoral tide that would result in the Democrats winning California for the first time since Lyndon Johnson's 1964 landslide over Barry Goldwater, as Clinton made repeated visits to the state and Feinstein and Boxer drew huge crowds wherever they went.

Beyond feminist themes, Feinstein also put forth a detailed proposal for a $135 million program to improve schools, transportation, and technology. On the conservative side, she also emphasized her support for the death penalty, cracking down on crime, and tougher enforcement against illegal immigration from Mexico.

Characteristically, Feinstein fretted about her chances, urging advisers to start running TV ads in midsummer. But she was in her easiest race since the 1983 mayoral coronation that followed her smashing of the White Panthers' recall attempt.

By the fall, Boxer's once-huge lead over Herschensohn began to evaporate, as the Republican assailed her as a Capitol Hill insider who benefited from congressional perquisites such as the scandal-ridden House bank. Feeling more secure about her campaign by then, Feinstein began to make more and more appearances with her erstwhile enemy, urging voters to send two women and two Democrats to the U.S. Senate. "At the end, Dianne jumped in with both feet for Barbara," recalled John Burton, a Boxer ally who had never been a Feinstein fan. "It was the greening of Dianne Feinstein, as far as politics was concerned. It was the first time that she had been called upon to expend her own political capital that she came through."

In October Feinstein put a powerful punctuation mark on the year of the woman, when she appeared in an emotional thirty-second TV spot holding and cooing over her new granddaughter, Eileen. The child was born on September 18, 1992, to Katherine and her husband, developer Rick Mariano, and named after Gene Gartland's wife. "It was absolutely unbelievable, this little baby," Feinstein said after the birth. "I'd always hoped to be a grandmother."

ON NOVEMBER 3, 1992, Feinstein and Boxer became the first two women ever chosen to represent one state in the Senate. In the same election, Californians chose women in record numbers for other offices: seven for the House of Representatives, twenty-two for the state assembly, six for the state senate, and more than 25 percent of local elected offices, remarkable gains that "showed that California remains on the cutting edge of history," the *Washington Post*'s political reporter Lou Cannon wrote.

Because Feinstein's victory over Seymour was technically a special election for the last two years of Wilson's term, she was sworn in ahead of the rest of the freshman Senate class of 1992. On November 10 she became the first woman senator from California, as she took the oath of office from Senate president pro tem Robert Byrd.

To the cheers and applause of three hundred supporters gathered for the occasion, many of them from San Francisco, Feinstein was sworn in with her left hand resting on a Bible held by Dick Blum.

Upon taking office, Senator Feinstein at once began to demonstrate the work habits, independence, and political skills she had spent thirty years developing. In her first year in office, her staff was often in a state of ferment and beset by frequent turnover. But her first two years in office were also marked by an ambitious and largely successful legislative agenda, as Feinstein helped focus national attention on the problem of illegal immigration, passed a California desert protection bill, a major environmental initiative that had been stalled for years, and, most impressively, overcame intense lobbying by the National Rifle Association to forge a bipartisan coalition that approved a bill to outlaw manufacture of many assault weapons in America. In the process, she quickly defined herself as a major player on Capitol Hill.

But as she stood on the Senate floor in November 1992, her thoughts were more personal than political. She later recalled thinking at one point, "I wish my father could have seen this . . . my father would have been proud. My uncle would have been proud. Bert would have been proud." Then she paused and added, "My mother would have been proud."

BIBLIOGRAPHY

Boehm, Randolph H. and Heldman, Dan C. *Public Employees, Unions and the Erosion of Civic Trust: A Study of San Francisco in the 1970's.* Frederick, MD: University Publications of America, Inc., 1982.

Boxer, Senator Barbara with Boxer, Nicole. *Strangers in the Senate: Politics and the New Revolution of Women in America.* Washington, D.C.: Natural Press Books, 1994.

Clavell, James, *Shogun.* New York: Bantam Doubleday Dell Publishing Company, 1986.

DeLeon, Richard Edward. *Left Coast City.* Lawrence, KS: Univ. Press of Kansas, 1992.

Hartman, Chester. *The Transformation of San Francisco.* Totowa, NJ: Rowman & Allanheld, 1984.

Lubenow, Gerald C., ed. *California Votes, The 1990 Governor's Race: An Inside Look at the Candidates and Their Campaigns by the People Who Made Them.* Berkeley, CA: IGS Press, 1991.

Monroe, Keith. "How California's Abortion Law Isn't Working." *New York Times Magazine* (December 29, 1968, 32–42).

Moore, Sonia, ed., *The Stanislavski System: The Professional Training of an Actor.* New York: Penguin Books, 1984.

Pogash, Carol. "Mayor Dianne Feinstein's Twelve Rules for Getting Ahead." *Working Woman* (January 1986, 84–85).

Richards, Rand. *Historic San Francisco: A Concise History and Guide.* San Francisco: Heritage House Publishers, 1991.

Seixas, Judith S. and Youcha, Geraldine. *Children of Alcoholism: A Survivor's Manual.* New York: Harper & Row, 1986.

Shilts, Randy. *And the Band Played On.* New York: St. Martin's Press, 1988.

———. *The Mayor of Castro Street.* New York: St. Martin's Press, 1982.

Sophocles. *Antigone.* David Grene and Richmond Lattimore, eds. *Greek Tragedies,* vol. 1, 2d ed. Chicago: Univ. of Chicago Press, 1984.

Ware, Susan. *Modern American Women: A Documentary History.* Belmont, CA: Wadsworth Publishing Company, 1989.

Weiss, Mike. *Double Play: The San Francisco City Hall Killings.* Reading, MA: Addison-Wesley Publishing Company, 1984.

Wirt, Frederick M. *Power in the City: Decision Making in San Francisco.* Berkeley: Univ. of California Press, 1974.

INDEX

Abortion, 56–57, 261, 272; DF mayor
  and, 268–69; governor race and,
  244, 252–53; Senate race and, 264,
  269, 277; sex-selection, 253
Acting, DF, 21, 27, 48–49
Advisory Committee for Adult Deten-
  tion, 62–63
Agnos, Art, 230, 237, 241, 249, 250
AIDS, 221, 224, 228, 229, 230–31
Aiello, Frankie, 86, 166
Alanson, Ann, 49–50, 54; mayoral cam-
  paign, 104; supervisor campaigns, 65,
  69, 71, 76, 77, 120
Alexander, Mara, 48
Alioto, Joseph, 72, 126, 130, 193;
  mayor, 62–64, 86–87, 92–116 pas-
  sim, 126, 132–33, 161–62, 220, 228
Anspacher, Carolyn, 77–78
Apcar, Denise, 166
Atwater, Lee, 242
Autobiography, DF attempt, 5, 240

Baldassare, Mark, 221
Banks, Walter, 130
Banks, Yvonne: childhood, 9, 10,
  15–19, 22, 27; and DF feminist is-
  sues, 267; and DF mayoral campaign,
  113; father's death, 130; married/
  Seattle, 60
Barbagelata, John, 90–92, 123, 151;
  Board of Supervisors, 78–92 passim,

99, 101, 116–25 passim, 147–49,
  268; and labor, 91, 117, 124–25,
  133; mayoral race, 127, 130–31,
  133–35, 136, 139, 193; NWLF
  threatening, 145, 146; Proposition B,
  148
Barry, Bob, 191
Bay Area Air Pollution Control District
  board, 116
Bay Area Reporter, 200
Berling, Violet John, 277, 278
Berman, Henry, 29, 198, 206, 217
Berman, Jack, 37, 40–42, 43–47, 54;
  daughter, 47, 59, 89, 104; DF may-
  oral campaign, 104; suing DF, 89
Bernstein, Morris "Mighty Mo," 71–72;
  and domestic-partners issue, 206; and
  mayoral campaigns, 131, 198; and
  mayoral succession, 174, 178–79,
  180; and supervisor president, 152
Bickel, Lurline, 32, 34, 51
Bierman, Sue, 46, 49, 172, 233
Bird, Rose, 180, 203
Birth, DF, 13–14
Bloom, Jim, 223, 240
Blum, Dick, 158–59, 184, 215;
  Carlton Hotel, 184, 199; day of
  Moscone-Milk murders, 165, 171,
  172; domestic-partners issue, 206;
  financial information, 251–52, 256,
  273; and governor campaign, 243,